girl on the edge
a memoir

girl on the edge
a memoir

ruth carneson

face2face

First published in 2014 by Face2Face
an imprint of Cover2Cover books

www.cover2cover.co.za

© Ruth Carneson

ISBN: 978-0-9946516-2-4

Disclaimer
Some of the names of people in this book have been changed to protect
their identities and privacy.

Typesetting and book design: Peter Bosman
Cover photograph: supplied by Ruth Carneson
Cover design: Wiehan de Jager
Editing: Maire Fisher
Proofreading: Clarity Editorial

For my children, my goddaughter Martha,
and all children – especially those who live on the edge.

Contents

Once upon a time a child was born in a windy, troubled city.
She was blown across the world
and back again to an even windier island.
Her body was solid and definable,
her bones, heart and lungs were all contained within her skin.

But inside her body lived grief,
deep like an ocean.
And although this grief was contained within her finite body,
no time or space could contain
the immensity of it.

She stepped into her heart
and the world turned upside down
and there was nothing to hold on to.

So she left her body behind
and wandered into no-man's land ...

Me, aged nine, with Dad and a friend. Table Mountain, Cape Town

PART ONE

South Africa 1953–1967

I'm a brave, brave mouse

I was in a hurry to arrive on that hot January morning in the middle of summer. My mother said that if the traffic lights had changed to red on the way to the hospital I would have been born on the back seat of the taxi. At five o'clock, just as the sun was coming up, I arrived feet first and upside down, a breach baby.

My first clear memory in words and pictures is a dream of Johnny and myself. Johnny is driving Dad's car. I sit beside him in the passenger seat wearing my nappies, Johnny's head barely reaches the steering wheel as he drives the car to the edge of a cliff. We are two babies on our own looking down into an empty void, a gaping dangerous chasm.

Johnny and I share a bedroom. We have a record player that we wind up with a speaker shaped like a giant bellflower. We take it in turns to wind up the record player and then we watch the records spinning round and round on the turntable. We have to be careful not to scratch them with the sharp needle.

We march around the house singing songs from our favourite record. We are brave, brave mice and we are never, never scared. BOO! We jump out at each other from wherever we have been hiding. I love my brother, Johnny. We walk everywhere together holding hands. He is eighteen months older than me. When we fight, I measure my strength against him. When we climb trees, I like to climb higher. I have to run faster, I have to eat more than him.

Mum and Dad, Lynn, Johnny and I live in a house in Protea Road in Claremont. We have a three-legged dog called Brindy, and a cat. In the garden we have fruit trees, loquats and plums, and along the fence grape vines grow.

I sit at the dining room table drawing pictures. Giant fish and sea creatures are painted on the walls. Our bathroom wall is painted black like a giant chalkboard, so that we can draw on it.

I have a new colouring book and crayons. Johnny grabs my crayons and runs away with them shouting:

Run, run, as fast as you can.
You can't catch me, I'm the ginger bread man.

He runs around and around the table. Every time I get near him he runs in the opposite direction.

"I'm telling Mum." I run into the kitchen.

Mum is cooking tomato bredie. She stirs the pot before she puts the lid on and tightens the pressure cooker valve.

"Stop fighting, you two, go and play outside."

The pot hisses and steams, bubbles and boils. The smell of meat and potatoes makes me hungry. I stand in the kitchen doorway and watch as the pressure cooker explodes with a mighty hiss. The metal valve flies up and the stew hits the ceiling. Mum jumps out of the way as the food splashes to the floor. She laughs out loud before she cleans the food off the floor. After that I am always scared of pressure building up and exploding.

Johnny and I jump, jump, jump on our beds and try to touch the ceiling. I jump higher and higher and stretch my arms up to touch the ceiling. Mum shouts, "You will break the bed springs."

Quietly, quietly, I close the bedroom door and we jump more until Mum calls us for supper. Supper is at six o'clock and then it's bath time. Bed time is at eight.

Mum laughs a lot, I hear her wherever I am in the house, her laugh travels from one end of the house to the other.

When Mum goes out for the night, I sleep with her dress under my head so I can breathe in her smell. I can't get to sleep until I hear Mum's footsteps in the hall.

My nanny fetches me from nursery school at lunchtime and I sit and wait for Mum to come home.

"When will Mum be home?"

"She will be back in a minute," my nanny says.

"How long is a minute? Has it already been a minute? Is she coming now?"

"She is coming in five minutes," my nanny says.

"How many are five minutes? I can count five on my fingers. One two, three, four, five."

I cannot settle until Mum gets back.

※ ※ ※

In the evenings, when I hear Dad's car pulling up, I run to the driveway. Dad picks me up and throws me into the air.

At night Dad goes to meetings. Before he goes out he reads us a story. He is reading us a story about Peter Pan in Kensington Gardens. He reads us a different chapter every night. In the last chapter Peter Pan's Mum closes the bedroom window and Peter Pan can never go home again. That night I cry myself to sleep thinking about Peter Pan.

Dad smokes cigarettes, I like the cigarette smell of his fingers when he has been smoking. Dad is bald, we call him Mouldy Baldy. When we are naughty, he threatens to fetch his belt.

"I will beat the living daylights out of you," he shouts. But he never does. When Dad is cross he only shouts and swears, but one day Mum says something at breakfast time that makes him cross, very cross, and he picks up his plate of food and throws it at the wall. We watch the plate break in two and then the fried egg slides slowly down the wall as Dad storms out of the house.

At the weekend Dad says he will take us to the circus. The circus has come to town with lions and tigers and elephants. Dad says he will take us there. The circus is in a big tent that smells of sawdust and animals and Dad buys us popcorn and bright fizzy drinks. Enchanted, I watch as the trapeze artists and acrobats fly through the air. I leap, I jump, I twirl and grow in leaps and bounds. I am doing magic in my glittering leotards, doing somersaults in mid-air before hooking my legs over the swinging bar.

I swing upside down and then leap to the next bar in a death-defying feat high above the ground. The ground is far, far below with no safety net and below me are the jaws of hungry, roaring lions. The audience gasp and hold their breath before they get to their feet and applaud my incredible stunts. They love me the most out of all the other circus performers.

Every year *New Age*, Dad's paper, has a fund raising Bazaar in a big hall. Dad takes me to the Bazaar. The hall is busy, with lots of stalls. There is a stall selling old clothes, I don't like the stale smells of people's bodies on the clothes laid out on the trestle tables.

On another table are homemade cakes, chocolate cakes, ginger bread, coffee and walnut cakes. If you guess the weight of the cake with pink icing you can win a prize. I want to win the raffle for the beautiful doll in a frilly dress, I want some sweet candy floss that melts in my mouth and I want a sweet sticky toffee apple and I want coconut ice and fudge. Dad says I can choose one thing.

I hold on tightly to Dad's hand. He stops to talk to someone. I am bored so I let go of his hand and wander off. When I turn around Dad has disappeared, all I see are legs and I am scared I will never find him again. At last I see Dad's legs, I run up to him and I take hold of his hand. He looks down at me and when I see his face I realise it's the wrong Daddy. My heart sinks, how will I find my own Daddy? I start crying. I will never find my way home amongst the sea of legs crowding around me. When Dad finds me I hold onto his hand tightly until we get home again.

❋ ❋ ❋

At home I run to the bottom of our garden where we have made a hole in the fence. I climb through the hole and go and play next door. Jeremy lives next door with his big sister, Jill, and his baby sister, Hilary. His dad is a doctor.

Jeremy has a swing. I push myself higher and higher, so high that the swing flips over the top of the bar. I hang upside down with my legs hooking the top of the bar, swinging backwards and forwards high off the ground.

> *Here comes the bride, big fat and wide*
> *Break down the door way*
> *She can't get inside.*

Jeremy and I play at weddings, we dress up and pick flowers and throw the petals for confetti. For the wedding feast we have biscuits and bright orange cooldrinks and sweets. We hold hands. Then we play doctor-doctor. I lie down and Jeremy delivers a doll from between my legs.

Jeremy wears his father's waist-coat and I put on his mother's shoes and hat. We find cigarettes and matches and light up the cigarettes and smoke like grown-ups do.

Jeremy's sister's nappies are draped over the sides of the wooden play pen drying by the heater. The bars of the heater glow. Jeremy and I discover that if we poke toys through the bars of the heater, we can make sparks. We take it in turns to light up the toys. All of a sudden a toy catches fire and the nappies go up in flames. The grownups come running to put out the fire with buckets of water. I run home to hide.

Mum asks me what's the matter but I don't want to talk about what has happened.

Jeremy's big sister doesn't like us to bother her and doesn't let us inside her room. She is having a birthday party. At the party her friends tease me. I dare the big girls to hit me.

"Hit me harder," I say. "That's not hard enough, it doesn't hurt me."

I won't show them that they can hurt me, I won't cry in front of them and show them I'm a cry baby. When the big girls get bored of hitting me and no one can see me, then I run home and cry.

❋ ❋ ❋

We get in the car and go to the beach for the day, a long isolated beach with no other people on it. Johnny and I change into our bathing costumes while Mum unpacks our picnic. Dad puts up the umbrella. "Be careful of the sinking sand," Mum shouts but we miss the last part of her sentence as we run down to the water.

Slipping, sliding, sinking – "Help!" I shout to Johnny who comes running and holds out his hand for me to grasp and hold onto tightly. Johnny starts to sink too. The more I struggle, the more I sink. The sand shifts and sucks me in. Johnny is up to his waist.

"Mum, Dad," we scream over the sound of the waves and the wind.

Mum and Dad wave to us from under the umbrella.

"Mum, Dad," our panic stricken voices become more urgent. I am up to my shoulders.

Mum and Dad come running.

"We told you not to play here," Dad says.

"We told you it's not safe," Mum says, "but you never listen."

Mum is cross, but Dad laughs as he pulls us out of the sand.

2

Adenoids

When I am four I go into the Red Cross Children's Hospital to have my adenoids out. I am in a hospital for the first time. I lie on the hospital bed with metal cot sides to stop me falling out on to the floor. Even though it is daytime, I wear my pyjamas. Mum brings me toys and crayons and a colouring book so I can have something to do. I try very hard to colour inside the lines of the pictures.

After visiting hours, Mum leaves. "Don't go, don't go, Mummy, Mummy, I want my Mum," I sob. "Where's Mummy," I scream, trapped in my bed with the iron railings. "Mummmeeeeee." But Mum has gone, she has disappeared.

The doctor stands by the side of my bed and looks at me coldly, he is very, very cross. "If you don't stop this horrible noise right now I will spank you and really give you something to cry about," he tells me sternly.

The doctor in his white coat means business. I am frightened by his angry voice so I shut up, I close my mouth, I close my eyes and hide under my pillow. I am scared to make a sound in case the doctor hears me and comes back to spank me.

"Mummmeeeeee," I whisper quietly under my pillow, but Mummy doesn't come back even though I wait the whole night long. The time drags by forever.

In the bed opposite me is an older girl of six, the big girl sucks her thumb. I would also like to learn to suck my thumb, the big girl shows me how to, it is easy to do. Cry baby, cry baby, I won't be such a cry baby again. It feels comforting to put my thumb in my mouth.

In the morning the nurse puts me on a trolley and wheels me away to another room. In this room everyone wears masks over their mouths and noses and white plastic gloves and white caps on their heads. Only their eyes show above their masks. The room smells strange. The nurse cranks the trolley up and puts a mask over my nose and mouth and tells me to breathe deeply and I feel like I am fading away as the light in the room turns green and everything looks far away. I float away into another world. The people around me have become green shadows.

After the operation, the nurse brings me jelly and ice cream to eat and dresses me in clothes that don't belong to me. I wait in a room with other children until Mum comes to fetch me to take me home.

The doctor says I am better and I can go back to school. Mum walks me to school, Arden Garden Nursery School. At school I like to copy what the big boys do and fight with them. The teachers say I am too wild and noisy for the school.

At nursery school I want what the other children have. I take their things and pretend their things are mine. A girl comes to school with a beautiful baby doll, I want a baby doll more the anything else in the whole world. I steal her doll and pretend it is my doll and take a packet of biscuits and eat them all up with one of the boys in the toilet where no one can see us. Mum promises me a baby doll for my birthday if I am good. I will be five next birthday.

After we get back from school Mum asks me to carry Johnny's blazer inside from the car. I don't want to carry his blazer, it's not fair, I always have to carry his things, so I drop his blazer on the pavement and run inside.

Somebody walks by and takes the blazer from the pavement. Mum is very angry, she says she won't buy me a baby doll for my birthday. I lie on my bed and cry, my heart breaks and I sob until supper time for my lost baby doll.

3
High treason

On the night that the Special Branch raid our house Johnny and I have mumps, our faces are swollen up like little fat hamsters.

That night Mum kisses us goodnight and switches off the light. She leaves the door open and the hallway light on so it is not too dark. I have put all my dolls to bed and said my prayers for Jesus to keep us safe. We sleep soundly in our beds.

In the middle of the night the house is quiet and Brindy, our dog, lies curled up at the foot of Lynn's bed. I am dreaming of a loud banging sound, I am dreaming of a loud knock, knock on the door. I hear voices and the lights go on, bright lights and men in suits wearing hats are in the house ransacking and searching all the rooms. They are looking for secret documents. They turn the house upside down.

I lie very still in bed. The men come into our bedroom, Mum follows them in wearing her dressing gown. "The children are sick, they have mumps," she tells them.

I try not to move or to breathe, perhaps the men will not notice me. "If you catch mumps it can make you sterile," Mum tells the men. The men look worried and leave our room immediately.

They take Dad away with them. Mum comes back into our bedroom. "Dad will be back soon. Don't worry. Go back to sleep," she tells us.

I hear her in the passageway on the phone talking to Hymie, Dad's lawyer. "Sorry to wake you up at this time of night. Fred has been arrested."

Dad has been charged with High Treason along with 136 other people. They let Dad out on bail but he has to go to Jo'burg for the trial.

❋ ❋ ❋

Mum packs our suitcases and a big basket of food for us to take on the train. She packs in chicken and rolls and fruit. We are all going to Jo'burg to stay with Aunty Ida, Mum's youngest sister.

The train station is busy and noisy. Johnny and I run up and down the platform – we are very excited. Mum shouts at us not to go near the edge of the platform.

On the train the conductor shows us to our carriage. In the carriage are bunk beds. Johnny and I want to sleep on the top bunk. The guard blows his whistle and the train gathers speed. I close my eyes and am soothed by the clickety-clack of the wheels on the track and the gentle swaying of the carriage. The train travels all through the day and the night and into the next day. We pass houses painted in bright colours and flat, dusty, yellow brown fields with small hills that Mum says are called kopjies. In the night I look out of the window and all I see is a black sky. I listen to the clickety-clack, clickety-clack. At night the guard makes up the beds with starched white sheets and fluffy blankets.

We stop at small towns in the middle of nowhere and thin, dusty children wearing old clothes and broken shoes run alongside the train close to the windows waving and laughing, holding out their hungry hands. Mum gives them our clothes and bread and fruit and chicken. She gives the dusty children all the food we have packed for our journey.

That night we go to the restaurant car for our supper and eat a three-course meal served by waiters wearing smart uniforms with white cloths over their arms.

When we reach Jo'burg Aunty Ida's driver comes to fetch us from the station and takes us to her house. The house is at the bottom of a long driveway. Aunty Ida is married to Leo. They have four children, William, Zoe, Jasper and Roland. Leo is grumpy and has a long beard. Their house is huge with a swimming pool and a tennis court. Leo owns a factory. Everyone says I take after my Aunty Ida. She is the beauty of the family.

Aunty Bess lives near Aunty Ida, she is Leo's sister. Her house is even bigger and grander than Aunty Ida's and you can eat whatever you want there. Aunty Bess asks me if I would like a milkshake or a Coke to drink.

Mum doesn't let me drink fizzy drinks. "A Coke, please." The maid brings me a Coke on a silver tray. The table is laden with Aunty Bess's freshly baked cakes and scones and biscuits. I pile my plate high and Aunty Bess asks me if I want some ice cream. When I have finished eating my ice cream I sit under the big wooden table covered in a white embroidered cloth. Under the table is my secret hiding place. I sit quietly and look at the high-heeled shoes and smooth stockings my aunts are wearing.

Mum laughs loudly, she is enjoying herself. Aunty Bess is telling a joke. I listen carefully even when I don't understand the words, I listen to the way the words are said. Some words are whispered and some words are said in a tone of disgust. If they knew I was listening they would be more careful about what they said. They are talking about Aunty Molly, Granny's youngest sister, the one who was mad.

"She was meshugana, she was a morphine addict," Aunty Bess is saying.

"She wasn't right in the head, that's why they had to lock her up in the hospital," Aunty Ida says.

Then Mum says, "It was very sad that she died in the hospital when she was so young."

※ ※ ※

Every morning Dad has to go to court for the trial. At breakfast time I butter him a piece of toast. I make sure the butter is spread evenly from corner to corner and spread salty Marmite on top. I tell Dad he must eat it for his lunch. I worry that he will be hungry in court and that they won't feed him. Or even worse, that they will lock him up and he won't come back home ever again.

Dad tells us that when he is in the court room he has to sit in a special cage to keep the accused separate from each other – black people must not sit with white people and white people mustn't sit with black or coloured or Indian people.

The trial is adjourned so after a month we go back to Cape Town. Mum says that Leo has scratched our name out of his phone book. He is scared that the Special Branch will think he is a communist.

On the train we stop at the same dusty stations with hungry children barefoot running alongside the train begging for food.

Dad tells us that we are very lucky we have food to eat and a house to live in.

"Most children are not as privileged as you are," he says.

At the next station I give all my sweets to the barefoot children holding out their hands.

Uncle Alec, Mum's cousin, collects money from the family to send to Mum so she can buy groceries and pay the rent when Dad can't work because of the Treason Trial.

※ ※ ※

Woolfie Kodish has always been in our life. I can't remember a time when he wasn't there. I call him my other Daddy. During the Treason Trial when Dad is away, he comes to take us out for a drive. I sit on his lap. I have learnt a new word. "The Special Branch are Bastards," I say with relish.

Woolfie laughs. "Where did a five-year-old learn to say this?" he asks my mum and they both laugh.

The Treason Trial drags on for five years and carries the death penalty. In the end Dad is found not guilty along with the other defendants.

4
Kwela music

The sound of kwela music fills every room in the house and wakes us up. Dad must be playing his records. Mum and Dad are jiving in the living room before breakfast. Johnny and me are still in our pyjamas when we go into the living room and Lynn comes in looking sleepy, rubbing her eyes.

"Meet Spokes Mashiyane," Dad says proudly, "He is staying with us for the week."

Spokes Mashiyane plays the penny whistle while his friend plays the guitar. Spokes dances while he plays, moving his body down to the floor and up again, jiving and doing the twist. Johnny and I dance, turning around and around and up and down, twisting our bodies in time to the music.

Later that day we take our guests sightseeing. Spokes has never seen the sea before, not ever, in his whole life.

"Where does all this water come from?" he asks and we laugh at his surprise.

Mum and Dad have lots of friends who come to visit us and our house is always busy. Mum cooks big pots of food to feed everyone. Looksmart comes to visit with his friend Greenwood. They are comrades and sell Dad's paper, *New Age*.

Johnny and I jump all over Looksmart, we are so excited when he comes to visit us. He is tall and has a smiling face.

Greenwood has a beard, I sit on his lap and pull his beard. Looksmart and Greenwood sleep over for the night. If the police stop them in a Whites-Only area at night they could get arrested.

We wake them up early in the morning by jumping on Looksmart's bed. He pretends to be cross and tickles us until we beg him to stop and then he throws me up into the air.

Theo Green, Mum's friend, wears lace-up shoes and skirts and wears her hair short.

"She has green fingers," Dad jokes.

"No, she doesn't, she has pink fingers," I tell him.

Theo works at Kirstenbosch Botanical Gardens. Mum says she is a botanist.

Mum is sick, she lies in bed with a high temperature. Dad calls the doctor, he says Mum must stay in bed and rest. Theo comes to look after us and makes soup for Mum.

Johnny Morley Turner is our favourite visitor. Johnny Morley Turner has only one eye, his other eye is not real – he takes it out and shows us it is made of glass. He always brings us a bag of sweets, bull's-eyes or mint humbugs.

When I grow up I want to work in a sweet shop so I can eat as many sweets as I want to all day long. When I have money, I buy Stars, three for a penny, they stick in my teeth and my tongue turns a bright pink colour when I suck them.

Johnny Morley brings us a packet of fruit bonbons. I try to suck them for as long as possible until I get to the soft sweet centre. The red bonbons are strawberry and the yellow ones are lemon. There are green ones and black ones and orange ones. I save the wrappers with pictures of fruit on them and make a fruit shop with the wrappers laid out in neat rows.

Mum and Dad are invited to have dinner at Johnny Morley's house. They think he is poor, but when Dad tells us all about it he says a butler opened the door and showed them into the dining room to meet Johnny Morley's parents. Mum says the table was set with lots of knives and forks and crystal glasses. Johnny Morley lives in a shed at the back of his parent's huge house.

Mum wonders why we are so quiet whenever Gregoire comes to visit us. Johnny and I are scared of Gregoire. He is an artist and threatens to paint us if we don't behave ourselves. We have heard of a woman who painted her son from top to bottom in gold paint for a carnival and her son dropped down dead. His skin couldn't breathe and he suffocated to death.

We don't want Gregoire to kill us. We mustn't make a sound, so we keep out of his way. If he catches us and paints us we will surely die.

❈ ❈ ❈

In January I turn six and start at big school, Grove Primary, the same school as Johnny. On my first day at school the teacher blows a whistle and tells us to line up. The girls must make one line and the boys must make another line. I am very proud of myself in my new school blazer and white socks. Some of the other children are crying for their mummies, they want to go home. I watch them cry, I am not a baby like them.

We have taken the day off school and Mum and Dad dress us in our best clothes. Dad puts on a suit and tie. We are going to Cape Town station to meet Chief Luthuli. He is travelling through Cape Town and it is Dad's job to make sure he is safe. He is an important man, he is our leader, Dad tells us.

The station is crowded with people singing and shouting "Mayibuye iAfrica!" Dad tells me this means Africa! Come back. They raise their hands in a thumbs-up salute and I copy them, I also raise my thumb and shout "Mayibuye iAfrika". They have come to greet their leader, Chief Luthuli. We get to the front of the platform; people are pressing all around us. I hold on tight to Mum and Lynn. Dad lifts me up and passes me through the window of the train carriage. When we are inside the train Dad introduces me to Chief Luthuli. I feel shy as I shake hands with him.

✳ ✳ ✳

When I tell people my name they ask me "Are you Fred's daughter?" Usually people give me a big smile but some people frown at me and look away when I tell them my name.

We go with Mum on the bus to Town on Saturday and walk through the Parade and up to Barrack Street where Dad's office is. We climb the stairs to Dad's office. The office is busy with people coming in and out talking to Dad. Everyone makes a fuss of me.

Dad sits behind his big wooden desk. Behind his desk is a photo of the Treason Trail with all the one hundred and fifty six people on trial. Rows and rows of people. I like to look at the photo and see who I can recognise and find where Dad is in the photo.

On Dad's desk is a copy of this week's *New Age*. On the front cover is a photo of a man who has been badly beaten. Underneath the photo is the headline "Man Beaten to Death on Potato Farm."

"We have started the Potato Boycott," Dad tells Mum.

For the next six months we are not allowed to eat potatoes. Mum says it's because the farmers use convict labourers and treat them worse than animals. We can only eat sweet potatoes.

One day I forget about the boycott and buy a packet of chips, I know I am not supposed to eat them but I don't want to throw them away. As I put each chip in my mouth I crunch it slowly, enjoying the saltiness and the flavour. I want them to last a long time, but I finish them before I get home, before Mum and Dad can see me.

5
Dad goes into hiding

At home in our front garden I climb trees and pick sweet juicy loquats, orange with a big brown pip in the middle. Johnny digs an underground shelter, a dark tunnel in the ground. We sit in the darkness with our supplies of food and drink and light a candle. Mum worries that the shelter will collapse and we will be buried alive. She won't let us play in there but we sneak in when she isn't looking. I feel safe down under the ground where no one can find us.

When Mum goes back into the house we go back into our shelter. Johnny lights a candle and we sit and eat some Marie biscuits. Mum is calling us, she is very cross.

"You could suffocate to death," she shouts at us. "You never listen to me. When you grow up I hope you have children as naughty as you."

❊ ❊ ❊

The phone rings in the hallway and Mum picks it up. "Hello," she says and then she goes silent. She phones Dad. "I could hear gunshots. They are shooting people at Sharpville."

When Dad gets home his face is white and his hands are like fists. He doesn't shout like he usually does. But he is very angry. His voice is shaking. "How can they do this? Kill unarmed people in cold blood."

The phone rings again. Dad picks it up. He tells Mum, "They have surrounded the Townships. The police are breaking people's doors down and beating them up." Mum and Dad look worried. I ask Mum what is happening but she snaps at me so I keep out of her way.

Mum says the people in the Townships have no food to eat. The police are not letting anyone in or out of the Townships. People keep phoning to ask what they can do. Mum says, "We need food, plenty of it." A van pulls up outside the house and a lady I have never seen before gets out. She is called Crystal.

"I have collected some food for the people in Langa," she says.

Mum hugs her and says thank you.

Crystal looks at Mum and says, "If anything happens to you I will look after the children. My two children are the same age as yours."

Johnny Morley owns a shop and is allowed to drive in and out of the

Townships. The police don't stop him. He goes and drops off food that people have donated.

※ ※ ※

One afternoon I am playing in my bedroom with my dolls, dressing them up and telling them stories. There is a loud knock on the front door like a hammer going bang bang on the door to break it down, and four big men dressed in black suits and hats stand and wait. They are the Special Branch and they have come for Dad.

Mum walks down the long passageway and answers the door once she knows Dad is out of sight. This time Dad is too quick for them. He darts out the back door quick as a flash and through the hole in the fence, the fence that divides our yard from Jeremy's back yard. Dad slips in through their kitchen door and asks Sam, Jeremy's dad to hide him in the boot of his car and to drive him away.

"Drive where?" Sam wants to know while the Special Branch are busy searching our house. He refuses to put Dad in the boot. Dad sits on the front seat of Sam's car holding a newspaper in front of his face as Sam speeds away.

Sam is scared, he doesn't want to get involved and be arrested. He is worried that he will have to drive Dad all the way to Swaziland so Dad can hide there. But Dad asks him to drop him off on the other side of town.

The following day Lynn takes a suitcase next door and asks Sam to take it to Dad.

"What's in the suitcase?" Sam wants to know. He is worried, perhaps there are bombs or guns in the suitcase. Sam wants to be helpful, but he is scared he will be followed. He drops the case off at the address Lynn gives him. Dad opens the case and Sam sees it only has a change of underwear, a tooth brush and clean shirts in it.

Johnny and I wonder when Dad is going to come home. We notice that it has been a long time since we last saw him, it must be weeks. Mum doesn't say anything, she is pretending that nothing is wrong, that everything is still the same.

When Johnny and I are alone in our bedroom we whisper to one another.

"Where is Dad?" I ask Johnny.

"In Swaziland," Johnny says.

"I think he is hiding in the mountains," I whisper back to Johnny.

6

Granny's house

Mum packs our clothes in a suitcase. "We are going to Mount Pleasant to stay with Granny," she says. Mount Pleasant is the name of Granny's house.

I hear Mum speaking to Theo on the phone. "It's safer," I hear her say.

Theo comes to fetch Mum, Johnny and me and drives us to Granny's house in Oranjezicht. Lynn's not coming with us. She has gone to stay with the Tobacins, they have four sons, the eldest son drives a red sports car. They said Lynn could stay with them, they live in a big house near Lynn's school.

Mum locks the front door and puts the suitcase in the boot and we drive off with Theo.

Mount Pleasant is a big old house in Oranjezicht. The house has views of Table Mountain and the harbour. Steps lead up to the path where palm trees grow, their leaves sharp and dangerous. On the left is a small pond with a fountain. The garden has different levels and corners of wild flowers grow amongst the cultivated plants. The front door is made of heavy teak wood and has a brass door knob that gleams; at the windows are wooden shutters. The front door opens onto a hallway with black and white marble tiles. Delicious monster plants with large leaves grow in brass pots polished until they shine. The wide staircase with its wooden banisters is ideal for sliding down. Every day the stairs are carefully swept and the skirting boards are washed down.

At Granny's house Mum and Johnny and I share a room. Granny lets out rooms to lodgers. Jan Hoogendyke and his family rent rooms in the back of the house. Jan has a beard. He is an Afrikaner but he doesn't like the Government. He has broken his leg and walks on crutches, his leg is in plaster. Mum and Johnny and I share a room in the front of the house.

Early in the morning when it is still dark and cold outside I lie under the covers next to Mum and feel warm and sheltered. I suck my thumb and enjoy the closeness of Mum's body and her arms around me holding me safely.

But then loud knocking on the door shocks us out of our sleep. We have been waiting for this knock on the door since Dad left. Granny goes to the door in her dressing gown and I hear a man saying in a loud, gruff voice,

"We have come for Mrs. Carneson."

Mum quickly gets dressed and goes out of the room. A few minutes later she comes back into the room and puts clothes into a suitcase.

Mum lies down next to us on her bed.

"I love you very much," she tells Johnny and me. "You must be good children for Granny." She kisses us good-bye. We do not know when we will see Mum again.

The day feels strange and unusual, I feel unsettled, I don't know what will happen next.

Johnny and I just have each other now.

✳ ✳ ✳

Granny cracks an egg into a hot frying pan; it sizzles and spits. Jan comes into the kitchen slowly, walking on his crutches, hopping on one leg. Granny and Jan whisper to each other and look across the kitchen at Johnny and me. Jan ruffles my hair and reaches into his pocket and gives Johnny and me a shilling each.

The next day Theo comes to Granny's house and takes Johnny and me for a walk in Newlands forest, she says we are going for a picnic. We sit on a log in a clearing and eat cheese and sandwiches. A man walks towards us, I saw him earlier hiding behind a tree. He was further away but I could see that he was watching us.

"Hello," the man says. I run to him and hug him, it's Dad. He is in disguise, he has grown a beard and wears glasses and a different hat that hides his face. Dad has brought us a present, a picture of a rooster, and a chocolate, and a bottle of perfume. He says to give the perfume to Mum.

We don't want Dad to go, we hang on to his trousers. "You must be brave children, you mustn't cry," he tells us before he walks back up the mountain.

When we get back to Mount Pleasant, Granny puts my clothes in a duffel bag and puts them in Theo's car.

"We're going away for a few days," Theo tells me as we drive away in her car. I wave goodbye to Johnny. Johnny is going to stay with Uncle Anthony in Pietermaritzburg.

I don't know where we are going. Each night Theo and I sleep in a different house. I lie in the dark in a strange house on a mattress on the floor. Where am I? I am not sure where this house is. The family who live here are kind to me, but it is not the same as my home and my mum and dad, or even my granny. I must be on my best behaviour so that the people in the house will like me. What if I wet the bed? I will have to stay up all night and blow it dry. I am thirsty, the lady in the house brings me a glass of water and asks if I need anything. I lie in the dark, rigid, fighting sleep.

The next day we drive for a long time until we reach a farm. At the farm there are rabbits and chickens.

A big boy who lives on the farm hides Easter eggs for me in the rabbit's hutch. At home at Easter time we eat matzos and hot cross buns and Mum and Dad hide Easter eggs in the garden for us. In the farm yard I watch the chickens pecking at their food and go into the chicken run with the boy to collect eggs for breakfast.

"Go inside," he tells me later that day. "I want to chop the chicken's head off and it is not nice for a girl to watch."

"I am not scared," I tell him. "I am not a sissy." I want to watch him kill the chicken. I stay and watch as he brings the chopper down and chops off the chicken's head and see the blood squirt out. The headless chicken carries on running around the yard.

At home I like to watch Granny in the kitchen plucking the chicken for supper before she puts it in the pot to make soup with matzo knaidlach. My favourite is Granny's bean soup and blintzes. Granny's food always fills me up, but Dad says it gives him heartburn. She glares at him when he eats Rennies Antacid Pills at the table.

On the farm I wake up with a sore throat.

"I need to look at your throat," Theo says.

"Aaaah!" I stick out my tongue while Theo looks down my throat. She takes me to stay with her friend who is a nurse. The nurse takes my temperature and says I have tonsillitis. Afterwards she gives me a hot mug of Bovril to drink, so hot it can burn my tongue. I blow on it and watch as the steam rises from my cup. Theo buys me new striped flannel pyjamas to wear. We stay with the nurse for a few days and then it is time to move on.

When we are on our way again, driving in the car, Theo stops at the side of the road and a black car pulls up in front of us. Sonya, a friend of Mum and Dad's gets out of the car with a man I don't know. Sonya gives me a hug, I am happy to see her. Theo, the man and Sonya talk quietly under their breath, I can't hear what they are saying. Theo says I must not tell anyone who we have met or who I have seen. I know I must keep my mouth shut, if I say the wrong thing something terrible could happen to someone.

✳ ✳ ✳

Theo takes me back to Cape Town, to Granny's house. Crystal and her husband Natie come to fetch Johnny and me. We are going to live with them and their two children, Paul and Evelyn. They are the same age as us. Crystal and Natie are not afraid to help us. They promised Mum and Dad they would look after Johnny and me while Mum is in jail. Nobody knows how long that could be.

Johnny and I don't fight as much as we usually do, we need to stick together – we only have each other now. At dinner times I eat and eat, I am scared I will be hungry when I am not at my own house. At home Mum's food fills me up. I must prove I can eat more than anyone else. I can eat even more than Natie and he is very big. Even when my stomach is sore and stretches as far as it can go I must fit one last potato into my mouth.

Johnny and his friends are bigger than me but when we fight I have to win. I punch them harder, and kick harder, and pull their hair and scratch. They are scared to hit me because I am a girl. But during a fight Johnny punches me hard in the stomach and winds me. I lie on the couch in Crystal's living room trying to get my breath back. I cannot run to Mum for comfort, Mum is not there.

7
Republic

Mum has been in jail for three months, since before Easter, and we haven't seen Dad for a long time, since the day Theo took us to Newlands Forest. At Assembly the Headmaster is excited, he tells us that South Africa has become a Republic and we are no longer the Union of South Africa ruled by the Queen. He tells us we are a Democratic country with a President, we are now the Republic of South Africa. We line up in two rows, girls in one row and boys in another and the teacher gives each child a flag and a shiny gold chocolate Krugerrand to mark the occasion.

I know that to take the flag and the Krugerrand is wrong. It will be disloyal to Mum and Dad. But I am too shy to refuse to take them. The other children watch me, I take the flag, although I know Mum and Dad wouldn't like it. I feel ashamed and my heart pounds, but it is too dangerous for the teachers and the other children to see me refusing to take the flag. The other children will notice I am different and they could tell on me.

After school I go back to Crystal and Natie's house and make a fire in the back garden where no one can see me. I tear the flag to shreds and burn it. The Krugerrand won't burn, so I stamp on it and bury it deep in the ground. I hate the Krugerrand and I hate the Government and even more I hate myself for taking the shiny Kruger rand. I have nothing to celebrate.

The things Mum and Dad tell me at home are opposite to what the teachers tell me at school. At school they tell us black people can't be trusted, they are not intelligent, we need to look after them. They say it says so in the Bible.

One morning at Assembly, after we have said the Lord's Prayer, "Our Father which art in heaven, hallowed be thy name, forgive us our trespasses," the headmaster calls a boy from Standard 4 to come up onto the stage. He tells the boy to lie down over a chair. The headmaster lifts up his cane and brings it down with full force, the cane whistles through the air and lands on the boy's backside. "Six of the best," the headmaster says. "This will teach you in future to listen to what your parents tell you to do."

I don't know what the boy has done wrong but I feel every stroke of the cane as it lands on the boy's backside. The school hall is silent, nobody shuffles or whispers this morning in Assembly. I can only hear the sound of the cane. The boy stands up, but he doesn't cry. He drops his head down so we can't see his face.

I am in Sub B, in Miss Miller's class. I am seven and a half. I can walk to school on my own from Crystal and Natie's house. In class, I stand in line to do my reading. I need to go to the toilet to pee, but instead I hold on to my pee. I clench myself tighter and tighter and hold on. I am too shy to ask the teacher if I may leave the room. Miss Miller does not like to be interrupted, she will be cross. I hold on as long as I can, but the pee drips down my legs, it starts pouring down and leaves a big puddle on the floor. I hear the rain beating down on the roof. I look up at the ceiling hopefully, perhaps the other children will think the roof is leaking and the rain has left a puddle of water.

Miss Miller says I must go home and change. I feel wet and cold and I know I smell of pee. I run back down the road to Crystal and Natie's house and hide behind the door – perhaps I can change before anybody catches me and asks me why I am not at school.

✳ ✳ ✳

My big sister is the most beautiful sister in the whole wide world and the cleverest sister in the whole world. Lynn tries to be like a mother to us while Mum is in prison. She phones us every night.

I have heard a new poem and I try to remember all the words.

> *Nobody loves me*
> *everybody hates me,*
> *going down the garden*
> *to eat worms.*
> *Long thin slimy ones, slip down easily,*
> *see those little worms squirm.*
> *But big fat hairy ones stick in my throat*
> *til the juice runs down.*

I shout the lines of the poem over the phone. "That is disgusting!" Lynn says, and then we laugh together. Every night before bedtime I wait for Lynn's phone call.

8

Mum in prison

The maid clears up the lunch things before Crystal lays a plastic cloth on the table and puts crayons and paints in the middle of the table. Johnny and I sit at the table with Paul and Evelyn. Crystal gives me an empty wooden cigar box and a pile of large stamps of colourful birds and fish.

I recognise some of the birds. When I was at home with Mum she told me the names of the birds who came into our garden. Mum liked to watch the family of yellow buntings that came to nest in our back yard.

I cover my cigar box with birds and fish, careful not to leave any spaces on the box. When the outside is dry I open the box and line the inside with stamps. With scissors I cut out butterflies and hearts and draw patterns on them in red and blue and yellow and green. On the hearts I write "I love you Mummy." I lay them carefully in the box. My box is finished and I show it to Crystal. My box is beautiful, it is perfect.

Johnny makes a tile out of plaster-of-Paris for Mum. When it is dry he paints it and scratches patterns and a picture of a face and a fish on it.

Crystal dresses me in my best dress, a red dress with white polka dots and she ties matching ribbons in my hair. I put on my best pink panties with a frill on them. On my feet I wear shiny black patent-leather shoes with a gold buckle. We wait for Theo to fetch us, she drives us to Simondium where Bien Donné prison is. Bien Donné. Theo says it is a French name that's why it sounds so funny.

Lynn sits in the front with Theo and Johnny and I sit in the back of the car. We are visiting Mum on her birthday on the seventeenth of June. She has been in jail since March.

"When will we get there?" I keep asking Theo.

We drive for a long time. Johnny feels car sick and Theo has to stop the car for him.

※ ※ ※

The prison is a white building with green shutters at the windows surrounded by mountains and farms. The warder doesn't smile when he lets us in and shows us to the visiting room.

A wardress leads Mum into the room. I stand still and look at Mum, then

I look down at the floor.

"Ruthie," Mum says, and hugs me.

"I've brought you this," I say to Mum and give her the decorated cigar box.

Lynn has brought Mum a birthday cake and flowers. We light the candles on the cake and sing happy birthday and Mum cuts a slice of cake for all of us.

A man sits in the corner, watching us and taking notes of what we say. We must be careful to not say anything we shouldn't. The man puts his head in his hands, it looks like he is crying. Mum cuts a slice of birthday cake and offers it to him.

"Thank you," he says. "I have children the same age as yours," he tells Mum.

I sit on Mum's lap and she strokes my hair, she notices my ears have not been washed in a long time. She looks worried.

"Are they being looked after properly?" she asks Lynn.

Our visiting hour is over and the wardress comes to fetch Mum and take her back to her cell. Mum hugs us and kisses us. "You must be good children," she tells us before she disappears down a long corridor with the wardress.

When we get back to Cape Town I write Mum a letter.

Dear Mum,

I hope you will come back very soon. Mum I love you very much. I'm very happy.

I am being good. When will you come home?

All my love xxxx

I cover the letter in hearts and kisses and flowers and send it to Mum. In Bien Donné Mum stores my letters in the decorated cigar box.

Johnny and I sleep in the room next to Paul and Evelyn's bedroom. We sleep on bunk beds and I sleep on the top bunk. That night, after we come home from seeing Mum, I wet the bed again. I am dreaming, my bed is warm and cosy, I feel warmth slowly covering my whole bed but then it changes and my bed starts to feel cold and clammy. The damp wakes me up. I change my pyjamas and climb into bed with Johnny. I hope nobody finds out I have peed in my bed. I am too big to be wetting the bed, only babies wet the bed.

9
Mum and Dad come home

Our garden in Protea Road is overgrown and the birds have taken over. We stand at the front door waiting. We are all together again after six months. Lynn is back from the Tobacins.

Mum has lost the key to the front door. She can't remember what she did with it before she went to jail. Dad finds a window at the back of the house that he pries open and Johnny climbs through the window and opens the front door for us. The house is covered in dust and has a funny smell. Mum opens all the windows wide to air the house.

Dad makes us laugh, "I walked right past the bastards and the Special Branch still didn't recognise me." He shows us how he limped past them wearing his hat pulled down over his face and his funny glasses.

"We wrote notes to one another and put them in the bin and the wardresses never thought to look. That is how we communicated with our black comrades." Mum tells us funny stories about the different ways they outwitted the wardresses.

Dad laughs at Mum's stories. "Sarah it's good to be home," he says, and gives us all a big hug.

Mum and Dad have guests for supper. The grown-ups talk and laugh while I sit alone in my room. I refuse to eat the food Mum gives me. My supper is cold and I don't like the taste of the food as I eat alone. I start crying and Mum wants to know why, but I don't want to talk to her. Mum is like a stranger to me, she has been away for so long. That night as I lie in bed I watch colours and points of light swirling in the darkness, like small moths flying about the room.

❊ ❊ ❊

At the end of the summer holidays I turn eight and go into Standard One. Mrs Anderson, our new teacher, wants to know what church each child attends. Catholic or Dutch Reformed, Anglican or Baptist. The children say, "I am a Catholic or I am an Anglican or I am Dutch Reform," starting with the front row.

It is nearly my turn to speak and I am very nervous. What can I say? I don't go to church and I don't know the names of the different churches. When it comes to my turn I look down and say quietly, hoping no one will hear me, "I am an African," and when the words come out of my mouth I realise it is the wrong thing to say, this is not what is expected of me and will prove that I am different from everyone else.

After school the children tease me, "You are an African," they laugh at me, and chase me. "You are an African." I feel stupid, I have unwittingly called myself black and to be black is to be looked down upon.

On Monday mornings Mrs Anderson wants to know if we went to church on Sunday. I sit at my desk looking down at the floor pretending I didn't hear the question. At the weekend I find a Sunday School to attend and start reading Bible stories and picture books about Jesus. My family are still in bed asleep when I leave for Sunday School. Every Sunday morning I put on a beautiful pink dress with layers of frilly petticoats and a full skirt. At the back is a big pink bow that I carefully tie. I put ribbons in my hair and then I am ready for church. Usually Mum dresses me in shorts and T-shirts, clothes that Johnny has grown out of that I can run and jump and climb trees in.

At Sunday School we sing about Jesus and God and do actions to the words. The teacher gives me a little book and every week we get a different stamp to stick in our books. The stamp has a picture of Jesus on it from a bible story.

The Pastor visits Mum and Dad. He shakes their hands warmly.

"We haven't seen you in church recently," he says to Dad.

"Would you like a cup of tea?" Mum asks him and offers him homemade biscuits.

"I'm Jewish," she says. "My husband was Catholic but we are both atheists."

"It is up to Ruth if she wants to go to church," Dad says.

The Pastor quickly finishes his tea and leaves soon afterwards.

I try to convert Mum and Dad by telling them stories from the Bible, but it doesn't work. The story of God asking Abraham to cut his son's throat disturbs me. Doesn't God know it is wrong to murder a child?

❄ ❄ ❄

In January, two days before my eighth birthday, the phone rings and Dad picks it up. He is swearing, he is very angry. He screams, "The bastards, they have murdered Lumumba."

Mum comes to the phone, she looks upset.

"Who is Lumumba?" I ask.

"He was the President of the Congo," Dad tells me. "They have murdered a great man."

※ ※ ※

Johnny and I are not so close any more, the boys don't play with girls and the girls don't want to play with boys. Johnny pulls out his gun: "Stick up your hands, your money or your life."

I am scared of the big boys: just in case one of them bothers me I keep a spare piece of bubble gum stuck behind my ear to offer them.

The bubble gum sticks in my hair and at bath time Mum gets cross with me as she tries to wash my hair clean. She gives up and gets the scissors to cut it out of my hair. I take the scissors and trim the cat's whiskers and trim my dolls' hair with it.

I poke around in my belly button – that is where babies come from when a seed is planted in your belly button. A big boy wants to see down there inside my panties, he says if I show him he will give me money for an ice cream. I show him inside my panties, but then he wants to touch me there. I say no, and he says he won't give me any money for an ice cream. I run away, he can keep his money, he didn't keep to his side of the bargain.

※ ※ ※

On Friday nights I go to the neighbours for Shabbat. Jeremy's Mum, Freda, lights the Shabbat candles, she covers her head and says a prayer. Sam wears a yarmulke and says the blessings for the wine and the bread.

I am also Jewish. Mum says if your mother is Jewish that makes you also Jewish. She laughs, "You can always be sure you know who your mother is but not always your father."

On Fridays and Saturdays I go to Shul and learn about the Holy of Holies and the Ark and watch the Torah being taken out of the Ark. I learn to read in Hebrew. If you are Jewish you get more holidays at school and don't have to go to assembly to pray with the other children.

In the afternoons after school I have a long, hot walk home. June's mother waits for her outside the school gates in a car and they drive home past my house. For weeks I have been asking June's mother if she can give me a lift to my house, but her mother says I must first ask Mum's permission. "Mum says it's OK," I tell June's mum, and climb into the back seat of the car. We drive past my house to their house. I feel trapped, there has been a misunderstanding. I am not meant to be here. I want to go home, but I don't say anything.

All afternoon I am uneasy and cannot settle. Mum will be worrying about where I am and why I haven't come home from school. Mum won't know where I am. June wants me to play with her dolls, she wants us to make beds for them and put them to sleep. I don't want to play. I keep asking her mum when I can go home. June gets cross with me. "Stop fighting," her mum says. She pours us Oros and gives us a plate of Marie biscuits to eat. I don't want to drink the orange juice or eat the biscuits.

The time drags by. June's mum sits in the chair relaxed, smoking cigarettes, and only when it is late afternoon does she finally take me home. Mum opens the door. "Thanks for looking after Ruth," she says. "I hope she behaved herself."

Mum doesn't seem worried that I was gone all afternoon, maybe June's mum asked her if I could stay for the afternoon. She didn't understand I just wanted a lift home.

10

Rhyde Villa

When I am nine, we move to a new house in Rondebosch. The house is on the corner of Rosmead Avenue and Wetton Rd. Across the road is a cemetery. Rosmead Avenue and Wetton Road are busy roads – all day we hear the sound of traffic and the screech of breaks. Cars are always having accidents outside our house.

"They must put in traffic lights," Mum says. "It's a death trap."

"Well, they don't have far to get to the cemetery," Dad jokes.

Johnny and his friend, Eugene, tie invisible fishing line from the upstairs balcony on to the big oak tree across the road. They hide away and wait for motorists then they pull a red bucket on the fishing line up in the air and laugh as motorists look up in amazement at the bucket. Mum tells them to take it down before somebody gets killed in an accident.

Caroline and Max live next door. They are play whites, coloured children pretending they are white. The family keep to themselves. Caroline and Max's parents won't let other children come and play in their house. Mum says even though they are light enough to pass as white they are worried someone might see that they are not quite white enough and give the game away.

I want to go to the bioscope with my friend, Zinna, but Uncle Reg, her dad, won't let us. Uncle Reg patiently explains to us that because of Apartheid Zinna won't be allowed to go to the same cinema as me. We know she is not allowed in but we plead with him, we know she is light enough to pass as white. Uncle Reg looks sad and says it is unfair but that is the law and he doesn't want Zinna to pretend she is white.

※ ※ ※

Walter Sisulu comes to our house. He doesn't live in Cape Town so we don't often see him. He has a meeting with Dad. Johnny and I are in the backyard with Max from next door. We are fighting, Johnny is trying to grab the ball from me. Uncle Walter comes outside and asks us what the problem is. We all want to talk at once.

"It's not fair, I had the ball first," I say.

"But it's our turn now, she won't give us the ball," Johnny says.

Uncle Walter listens to each of us in turn, "This is a serious matter," he says, "but I am sure you can solve it. Why don't you share the ball and all play together?"

"That's a good idea," we say. Johnny kicks the ball to Max and Max kicks it to me.

✳ ✳ ✳

One afternoon after lunch, Mum and Dad have a sleep – it is hot and they leave the window wide open. Mum wakes up and sees a pigeon strutting up and down on the dressing table, pecking at its reflection in the mirror. The bird decides to stay, and follows us around the house, flying off through the window and coming back again. Now there are two birds in the house – the pigeon and my budgie Chichi.

Chichi struts up and down on her perch in the cage and stops in front of her mirror. She talks to her reflection and kisses the glass and fluffs out her feathers. I put my hand in the cage and Chichi climbs onto my finger. I take Chichi out of her cage and Chichi perches on my shoulder and nibbles my ear with her beak. Chichi flies round the room, in a flash of bright blue feathers before she flies back onto my shoulder. I teach her to talk, to imitate what I say: "Hello, hello, pretty bird."

Mum's friend comes to visit with her two-year-old son. Mum brings them to my room to show them the budgie. The baby laughs as he watches Chichi fly around the room. The baby is fascinated as Chichi walks towards him, he puts out his foot and stamps on Chichi. He stamps hard, Chichi makes a strange sound as blood drips out of her beak. I pick her up and hold her against my chest, but it is too late. Chichi's body grows limp and her heart has stopped beating. She feels so small in my hands. I can't stop crying.

Mum does not know what to do. She phones Dad to come home early, he brings me a new budgie, but I don't love my new budgie, it cannot replace Chichi.

✳ ✳ ✳

Lynn plays the main part in her school play. She plays the part of Ruth, in the Bible. "Wither thou goest, there goest I," Lynn says on stage to her mother-in-law. She bends down to glean the wheat and Boaz the wealthy landowner falls in love with her and at the end of the play they get married.

When it finishes people stand up and clap.

"Brilliant," Dad says.

Lynn wants to go to London to study Speech and Drama.

"Why do you need to go overseas to study?" Dad says. "You can stay here and get a job in a shop. I had to leave school at thirteen and go to work."

Mum gets very angry with Dad. "She is going to London and she is going to stay with Kay."

Dad doesn't have a choice, it is all arranged. Aunt Kay sends Lynn money for her fare.

I am nine when Lynn leaves to go overseas. When will I see Lynn again? I know I will never see the same sister again. When Lynn goes away she will become a different sister, she will get married and have a different name and a different hairdo.

Mum and Dad are bad tempered, they don't want to show they are sad that Lynn is leaving. They show a brave face, but their sadness creeps out of the cracks of their faces. I try to get some of their attention, but it is no use, I only end up annoying Mum and Dad more.

Lynn's suitcases are packed and waiting in the hallway to be carried to the car. It is time to drive to the docks to say goodbye. The ship is a huge passenger liner and it will take two weeks to get to Southampton and the White Cliffs of Dover. At the docks every one crowds around in their best clothes and Dad says it is a real holiday atmosphere. Lynn stands on the boat and waves to us and blows kisses. People cry as they throw streamers to each other, thin bright streams of paper join me to my sister. Balloons are let up into the air and there are more tears as they float up into the sky. But my family don't cry.

Two small tug boats come to steer the big ship out of the harbour into the sea. I carry on waving until my sister is no more than a speck on the horizon.

Mum and Dad argue

Mum and Dad have an argument. I don't like it when Mum and Dad argue, the shouting frightens me. I am afraid they are arguing about me and that I did something wrong. I listen outside the door. Mum mentions a man's name, she sounds angry. Mum calls him names. "He is a drunk, he is a good-for-nothing." Mum says if he comes to the house she is leaving. "You are as bad as him, you just end up getting drunk," Mum tells Dad and storms out of the house.

Dad's friend arrives. His friend has bad breath and I don't like it when he breathes over me. I go up to my room but I can hear them talking downstairs in the living room.

I feel lonely as I lie in bed in my pink and green bedroom. Usually Mum or Dad read me a story and tuck me up in bed, and switch off the light for me, but tonight they forget.

I am half asleep when there is a knock at my bedroom door. My bedroom is dark and all I see are shadows as a man opens the door and I smell the alcohol on his breath. He wants to kiss me. I can't let him so I push him away, but he comes to lie beside me. He touches me in places I should not be touched. I smell of smells that I should not smell of. Smells from between my legs, shameful smells, dirty smells, strong smells that will catch me out and tell on me, hidden dank smells.

All night I lie awake, afraid people will climb through the window in the middle of the night and kill my whole family, stab them to death in the most horrible way. This really happened to a family. I know because I read it in the paper. I lie awake and hear the mosquitoes whine.

The next morning, everything is the same as usual. Mum makes us porridge and tells us to get ready for school. I polish my shoes and tie up my pony tail in a green ribbon. I stare at myself in the mirror. I know something happened last night, but nobody says anything. Perhaps it did not happen? But I know it did. It was not my imagination. But everything stays the same as usual and "It" vanishes like a puff of smoke.

"Hurry up. You will be late for school," Mum shouts at me as I stare into space.

Every night I cry, I hide my head under the pillow so no one can hear me sob. I cry for my budgie who has died, trampled underfoot, and my sister who is far away in England, and a man has come and done things to me he shouldn't have, and nobody knows.

Mum tries to comfort me and brings me a glass of water, she tries to put her arms me and asks me what is wrong.

"Nothing," I tell her. "Nothing."

I don't know what's wrong, I hate Mum. I have a secret to keep, I do not know how to describe it even to myself. I do not know the words for what has happened.

※ ※ ※

Mum and Dad take Johnny and me to see Macbeth at Maynardville open air theatre. We go at night and sit under the moon and stars in Wynberg Park. In the play Ophelia goes mad, and I laugh during the serious part while the audience is deathly silent. I laugh at Ophelia's madness. Then I feel embarrassed, I don't understand, I think Ophelia is playing the fool. She looks so pretty lying drowned in a pool of water surrounded by flowers.

Johnny and I pretend to be the witches. "A drum, a drum, Macbeth doth come," we chant as I stir my cauldron. Johnnie puts in toads and spiders, snakes and puppy dogs' tails. We shout louder and louder, "A drum! A drum! Macbeth doth come."

12

Mount Pleasant

We move out of the house we are renting in Rondebosch, the landlord does not want to renew the lease and nobody will employ Dad because he is a Communist. The newspaper Dad was manager of has had to close down, Dad has been banned and isn't allowed to run the newspaper any more.

Mum and Dad have to obey special rules called Banning Orders. They are not allowed to be in a room with more than one other person at a time or attend social gatherings and they are not allowed to talk to anyone who is on the banned and named list.

The Minister of Justice sends Mum and Dad a letter saying that because of Special Circumstances even though they are both Named and Banned people, they are allowed to talk to one another, he signs it: John Balthazar Vorster.

Mum and Dad laugh when they get the letter.

It has become too dangerous for other people to be seen talking to us. People would rather cross to the other side of the street than be seen greeting us. Our friends disappear, they leave the country or are arrested. We have become almost completely isolated.

❈ ❈ ❈

We move back to Granny's house, Mount Pleasant. Mum and Dad run it as a boarding house. They are up early in the morning, cooking breakfasts, porridge, bacon and eggs, stewed fruit, toast and marmalade, tea and coffee.

In the centre of the dining room is a large oval table where we eat three-course breakfasts and three-course suppers. Granny cooks heavy, rich food, blintzes and bean soup. She gives us bread to eat spread with chicken fat. Dad says Granny's cooking gives him indigestion.

In the afternoons after school we sit in the large kitchen with a scullery and a walk-in pantry that is kept locked. Inside the pantry are jars of sugar and salt and sacks of flour and rice and jars of olives, big like plums, which Dad pickles himself. We sit around the large wooden table in the kitchen with steaming mugs of tea, eating thick slices of bread, covered in peanut butter and honey, listening to Granny's stories about Russia where she grew up, about the pogroms and the Cossacks.

Dad starts selling paintings on commission, reproductions of Gauguin and van Gogh and work by local artists. The bright colourful paintings that Dad doesn't manage to sell end up on our walls.

※ ※ ※

Under Mount Pleasant is a dark, damp cellar that runs the length of the house. Johnny and I dare each other to walk to the end, expecting to find hidden treasures, but instead we get covered in coal dust and spider webs. We find an old mattress and some blankets. The gardener is living in the cellar, Mum and Dad don't know he is. He is homeless and doesn't have a pass allowing him to stay in the area. If he is caught he could go to jail. Johnny and I don't tell anyone he is there.

An old fridge stands in the garden and Dad uses it for making smoked fish. Johnny and I play hide-and-seek in the garden and Dad warns us not to hide in the fridge because we would suffocate to death if the door closed and no one knew we were inside it.

Outside my bedroom is a passage lined with bookshelves from floor to ceiling, filled with books. Uncle Eli sends us crates of books from Swaziland and I spend hours looking through the books and the pictures. When I open the books I go travelling into another world.

Granny is fierce, all my friends are scared of her. Granny disapproves of Dad, he smokes and drinks and swears.

I share a room with Granny and at night she grinds her teeth. She suffers from painful gallstones and wakes up in the night moaning with pain, sick as a dog. One night it is so bad that I get out of bed and go and fetch Mum who calls the doctor.

Mum is strict, like a sergeant major, supper is at six and bedtime at eight. She only lets me buy sensible shoes. I would rather go shopping with Dad; he lets me buy shiny shoes with pointed toes and drink Pepsi floats and bright green cream soda floats.

※ ※ ※

It is too far to travel to Grove Primary in the mornings so I change schools after the summer holidays. I turn ten and Mum gives me a birthday party and says I can invite the girls from my class. Mum makes me a beautiful cake with a maypole made out of a barley-sugar stick with ribbons tied to it and little dolls dancing around the maypole. There is a doll for each girl to take home with them. We have hot dogs on rolls with tomato sauce. Mum has ordered an ice cream cake especially for my party and offers the girls a piece after we have eaten our hot dogs and chips.

A lot of the girls in my class are Jewish and only eat Kosher food. One by one the girls politely refuse the ice cream cake. They look shocked: "We are not allowed to eat ice cream after eating hot dogs, it's not kosher." I feel ashamed, I want to run away and hide.

At my new school, Goodhope Seminary School for Girls, the other girls won't play with me or talk to me. They talk in whispers, and I feel invisible. I run home and go straight to bed and sleep and sleep. I want to wipe out the days. In the mornings I pretend to be sick, so I can stay at home. I suck on my arms and make love bites like welts on my arms and tell Mum I have a rash. Mum thinks I have an allergy and I have to wear a Medic Alert bracelet. At night I can't sleep, I listen to the radio while everyone else sleeps in the dark silent house.

I do not pay attention in class. The teacher asks me questions that I cannot answer – I have not heard what the question is. My mind is elsewhere as I look out of the window. I imagine I have blue eyes and live in a mansion, my bedroom has wallpaper with pink rose buds, the room is pink and lacy and I smell of perfume. There is a man who gives me everything I want, who adores me and thinks I am the most beautiful girl in the whole world. I have never seen this man, but I know he is very rich.

The girls all cluster in groups talking animatedly, but when I approach there is silence.

My loneliness feels like a disgusting disease. I stand by myself, I sit by myself, I feel wrong. I am wrong. There is something wrong with me. Why else will no one talk to me? They whisper that my parents are communists and kaffir lovers.

I hate myself. I can hear the voices of other people in my head as they comment on every clumsy move I make. I look at myself from the outside in through cold, angry eyes. I don't like what I see, I have been caught out for every small action, the way I eat, the way I dress, the way I talk. I sit apart, people can smell my loneliness. I feel ashamed; I would not sit alone if people liked me.

I wish I wasn't here. I do not know how to get through the day. I play the fool, the children laugh and I become more and more outrageous in class. I become the clown of the class, I am popular. When the teacher isn't watching the other girls egg me on. My marks plummet, I go from top of the class to bottom. I fail dismally.

Mum and Dad are disappointed in me. I try to hide my report card from them. When Dad finds it he shouts at me. "This isn't good enough. You can do better than this. You should be ashamed of yourself."

Dad drives me to school. In the car he lectures me. "You must concentrate in class. You must pay attention and stop day dreaming."

He flicks the ash of his cigarette out of the window and the wind blows it back into my eyes. I am silent. Mum and Dad don't understand me. They don't see me. All they care about are my stupid marks at school. They don't love me, they only love me if I get good marks at school.

At the end of my last term at primary school, the head mistress says she has had enough of my bad behaviour and I am expelled. I must pack my bags and leave the school.

13
Secret gardens and bombs

I have a favourite place under the hedge, it is completely hidden, and no one can find me there. Mum can call and call but I need not answer. I am in a world of my own and do not like to be interrupted. Hidden, I read and daydream. What I read about in the stories is real and the people are real. But the world around me is a shadow.

I read my favourite books over and over again. I have a book about a bad-tempered orphan girl, Mary, who is sent to live in a huge old house up on the moors with more than a hundred rooms in it. Up on the moors it is bleak and icy cold and the wind howls down the endless corridors. One day, when the girl is digging in the garden, she finds a key and a bird takes her to a door, which is hidden behind a bush. The door opens onto a walled garden. It is wild and overgrown. Beautiful perfumed roses and honeysuckle grow everywhere and in the spring time the garden is transformed by daffodils and snowdrops.

Late at night, the girl hears the sound of sobbing and wailing. Night after night she hears the sobbing. "Hush," the servants tell her, "it is only the sound of the wind." One night she tiptoes in her long white night dress and follows the sound of the sobbing. At the end of the corridor she opens a door into a room and lying on an enormous four poster bed is a pale, thin boy with huge eyes. He cannot walk, he is weak and crippled and very spoilt. His father avoids him. The boy is Mary's cousin.

The garden is Mary's secret place. She wheels the pale sick boy into the garden in his wheel chair. Slowly the boy learns to walk again in the garden and grows stronger. His father sees the boy walking and at last is proud of him and every one lives happily ever after.

＊ ＊ ＊

On Guy Fawkes Night, people let off fireworks, sparklers light up the dark with magic stars and sparks of light, Catherine Wheels with different colours of fire spiral round and round. There are Big Bangs and Jumping Jacks that chase after you and rockets flying into space exploding into a million stars. Johnny finds a broken rocket lying on the road; he brings it home and mends it. The stick has come off so he ties a new one on. We are ready to launch the rocket in the back garden. Johnny puts the rocket in a milk bottle like he has seen the grownups do and I stand back as he lights the fuse. The rocket makes a fizzing sound as the fuse catches alight and then a big bang, but instead of going straight up in the air the rocket travels sideways, straight in the direction of my stomach. I step aside just in time before the rocket crashes into the wall with full force. I get a fright, I know that if I got hurt Mum would be very angry, we are not allowed to play with fireworks or matches.

A couple of days later, Johnny and I are at home. I am in my room reading and Johnny is in the front room. I hear a loud bang and the dog begins to bark. Johnny runs into my room.

"Somebody has fired a bullet through the window," he shouts, but I don't believe him. Johnny likes to make up stories to scare me.

"It is just a firework," I say.

"Come and look, the bullet just missed my head," Johnny insists.

I don't want to stop reading, but I put down my book and follow him into the front room and see that he is telling the truth; I see the window glass shattered and the bullet lodged in the wall.

The Special Branch have launched a campaign of terror this weekend. Sadie, a friend, phones Mum, and tells her someone has fired bullets into her baby's room.

We go with Mum and Dad to Esme and Denis Goldberg's house where a policeman sits outside guarding their house. The front of the house has been blown away by a bomb. Dad jokes with the policeman, he says it is a bit late for the policeman to be sitting there. The grownups are laughing because the children, David and Hilary, slept right through the bomb blast and did not hear a thing. I join in with the laughter. The worse things are the funnier it seems and the louder we all laugh.

※ ※ ※

"Ruth and Johnny need a holiday," Granny tells Mum and Dad.

The day we leave I have my best dress on. The skirt is full and balloons out when I twirl round and round. I wear my best panties and white socks. Our bags are packed in the car and Mum and Dad drive us to the docks. Granny is taking Johnny and me on holiday to Mozambique by boat.

The boat sets sail and Mum and Dad wave to us until we cannot see them any more. The steward shows us to our Luxury cabins, a large suite with wooden panels and large soft armchairs. On board the boat, there is a Third Class, a Second Class and a First Class, but we are even better than

First Class, we are travelling Luxury Class.

Children are not allowed to eat in the adult dining room and Granny goes with Johnny and me to the children's dining room. It is noisy and smells of old food and cabbage. Granny does not trust the hygiene, she insists that we will eat with her in our own dining room in our suite. We have our own steward and stewardess. Granny spoils us, every day after lunch we have ice cream. There are different flavours to choose from – chocolate, vanilla, strawberry and lemon. Johnny and I spend our days swimming in the pool up on the deck.

In our cabin, we listen to Granny's stories. "They confiscated our land and our bakery because we were Jewish. They said my father was using the blood of Gentile children to bake matzo." Johnny and I don't know whether to believe Granny's stories. Perhaps she is making them up.

"When the Cossacks rode through our village I rolled marbles under the hooves of the soldiers' horses. They were the Czar's soldiers come to cause trouble for us. The soldiers took my father and threw him into prison," Granny tells us.

We have just eaten a four course lunch and the stewardess comes into our cabin with our ice cream, three different flavours. I choose the chocolate and Granny dishes herself vanilla.

"When I was sixteen we travelled steerage class on the boat to England. There we worked in a factory in Leeds, a clothing factory," Granny tells us.

The ship docks in Lorenzo Marquez and we go on land, exploring. There are pictures on the road made out of fragments, mosaics. In the public gardens there is a zoo where an elephant eats my hat.

The people in Mozambique look even poorer than the people in South Africa, they are hungrier and leaner. Here brown and white children are allowed to swim in the same swimming pool, not like at home.

14

Mushrooms for the Minister of Justice

On Sunday mornings in the winter time, when the weather is cooler, Dad takes Johnny and me up the mountain. I wear shorts and sturdy boots. Mum stays at home to get some peace and quiet for the day. We set off early before the sun gets too hot and we stop for breakfast along the way. Dad makes a fire and balances the billy can over the flames for the coffee, then takes out the frying pan for the eggs, sausages and beans.

Johnny and I find green sticks to poke through the bread and hold the bread over the flames to toast. When our breakfast is finished we set off up the mountain track. The sun climbs higher in the sky and the day becomes warmer and the track gets steeper. It is hard work. "When can we stop and rest?" I ask Dad. I am hot and thirsty.

"Just around the corner, then we will stop," he tells me.

After what seems like a very long corner we get to a place on the mountain where ice-cold, clear water cascades down the rocks. Dad cups his large hands under the water and holds them out for me to drink. The water tastes full of the flavour of fresh mountain smells. I copy Dad. I cup my hands under the water and the spray from the water cools me as I drink.

On the mountain slopes, hidden amongst the trees, is our favourite place. Growing from tall branches of the trees are thick vines, twisted like ropes hanging down. I hold on tight to the vine and swing from one tree to another, flying through the air. Then it is Johnny's turn to swing through the trees and fly through the air.

We walk up to the top of the mountain and look all around us at the sky and the mountains and the city below them. In the late afternoon we begin the long descent down the rocky mountain slope. By the time we reach the bottom my legs are shaking and scratched from the thorny bushes and my muscles are aching.

When we get home, Mum has a hot supper waiting for us and she runs a warm bath for me to soak in. My tummy is full and my body feels tired as I lie between clean sheets. Mum tucks me in and kisses me good night before she switches off the light and I drift into a deep peaceful sleep.

✳ ✳ ✳

I am eleven when I get my periods and start counting my pubic hairs. I have my own room now and a new friend. Meg and her Mum and two brothers come and stay with us in Mount Pleasant. Meg is the same age as me and Nancy, Meg's mum, is pregnant. Their dad has been locked up in a mental hospital.

"He is meshuganah," Granny says to Mum when Meg's mum is out of earshot. "He shot their mother's lover. How could he do a thing like that?"

Mum shrugs her shoulders. "They locked him up and now the children don't have a father. It's very sad," she says to Granny.

Mum says Meg's brothers are wild when she sees them climbing up the balcony railings and sliding down the bannisters. Granny shouts at them, but they don't listen.

After a few months they move into their own flat in Tamboerskloof and Meg's mum has a baby girl. I go and visit Meg. Meg lives at the top of a very steep hill. It takes me fifteen minutes to walk to Meg. I walk barefoot. The soles of my feet are tough, I can walk over broken glass and not cut my feet.

I go everywhere I can barefoot. Dad doesn't like it, he says I could stand on something sharp and injure myself. It is unhygienic and I look like a tramp, a poor white. "You can't go out until you put shoes on," Dad shouts at me. He won't let me go to Meg's house. I storm out the door banging it behind me and walk up the long steep hill to Meg.

Dad comes to fetch me. "Get in the car and come home," Dad orders me and drives me home. "Put your shoes on and then you can go."

I won't put my shoes on, but I walk back anyway. Dad comes to fetch me again. All afternoon there is a war of wills between us as I walk back to Meg and then Dad fetches me again. I am determined to win the fight. In the end I wear Dad out and stay at Meg's house barefoot.

Camilla and Meg are my best friends. Camilla's mum, Caroline, is Mum and Dad's friend. They are from England. Caroline is divorced, she is the niece of Macmillan, the British Prime Minister and First Earl of Stockton. Caroline jokes, "I have blue blood," and she laughs at the top of her voice. They rent an upstairs flat nearby in the Gardens. Students rent the flat downstairs and are always having parties.

Camilla and I sit in Meg's bedroom playing a game of cards. We are listening to music on the radio when the song is interrupted. The announcer says in a shocked and horrified voice: "We interrupt this program to bring you a special bulletin from ABC Radio, America: Three shots were fired at President John F Kennedy's motorcade today in downtown Dallas, Texas."

Meg writes a letter to Jackie Kennedy to say how sorry she is to hear the news of her husband's death. A few weeks later she shows us a card from America with a black border thanking her for her condolences.

Caroline invites Mum and Dad for supper and cooks her speciality, a delicious spinach lasagne. Mum and Dad and Caroline laugh and joke as they sit around the table eating lasagne and drinking wine. Dad says he likes to pick wild mushrooms. Caroline laughs and says, "Why don't you cook a special dish of mushrooms for the Minister of Justice?"

There are microphones in the wall and the conversation is recorded and played back to the Minister of Justice as evidence of a Communist plot to overthrow the Government and poison him.

Johnny and I are at home sleeping while Mum and Dad are at Caroline's eating dinner.

In the morning Theo wakes us up and tells us Mum and Dad were arrested last night and they won't be coming home. They were not supposed to have supper with Caroline, they were breaking their Banning Orders. The Special Branch were watching Caroline's house and even the maid and all her friends, who were busy having a prayer meeting in the backyard, were rounded up and arrested.

Mum and Dad are released on bail the following day. Their trial will be in a few months' time. They could get sent to prison for two years for breaking their Banning Orders.

※ ※ ※

Lynn writes letters to us from London on blue aerogram paper. Every day I run down the garden steps to check the letter box. Lynn writes to tell us that she fell off a horse and banged her head and had to go to hospital. Mum writes back to her and says she must be careful. Lynn says she has a boyfriend who drives a sports car and they are engaged to get married. I love getting letters in the post; I love it so much that I write letters to myself and post them. Every day I get a letter from myself.

Early in the morning, the roads are quiet as I ride Lynn's old bicycle up and down the street before it is time to go to school. It is too big for me and I must stand up to reach the pedals. I feel free and powerful as I gather speed freewheeling down the hill. The world belongs to me at this time of the morning.

※ ※ ※

We go to the Goodwood Show. Dad is friends with the man who runs the fun fair. He is a funny looking man but Johnny and I like him because he gives us free tickets for all the rides. We can go on as many rides as we like, the merry-go-round and the Ferris Wheel, the Octopus and the Wheel of Death.

I get my fortune told by a man in a caravan who reads my future by looking at the bumps on my head. He tells me my lucky colour is blue and asks me if I am Fred's daughter.

Everywhere I go people ask me if I am Fred's daughter. Everyone knows my Dad.

There are coconut shies where you can win prizes – teddy bears and gold fish. We buy hot dogs and fizzy drinks and candy floss that melts in your mouth.

Camilla is with me. We ride on the Octopus; the Octopus has giant tentacles with little seats attached to the end of each tentacle. The seats go around and around at great speed while the tentacles come crashing down to the ground before soaring up into the sky. Round and round they go while the seats dip and spin before they plunge to the ground. We scream with terror. Camilla is so scared she wets herself, but she insists that we climb straight back on again for our next ride of dizzy terror.

The Wall of Death spins around and around, faster than you can think and all of a sudden the ground beneath my feet disappears far, far below me. If I fell I would plunge to my death with every bone shattered and blood everywhere but somehow by sheer luck the speed of the wall holds me to the sides and I don't go hurtling down through space.

❄ ❄ ❄

On New Year's Eve, Mum and Dad wake Johnny and me up before midnight. We are still in our pyjamas when we drive into town. In District Six people line the streets waiting for the Coons to come. Front doors stand open. Inside tables are laden with food, plates are piled high with samosas and cakes.

"Help yourself, help yourself."

An old man sits proudly on his chair as he shows us his newspaper cuttings and photographs, he has a letter from the queen congratulating him for turning a hundred years old. He boasts about his many grandchildren and great-grandchildren.

The Coons are on the way and excitement grows in the crowded street as we wait.

"Here they come, here they come." The Coons come dancing down the midnight street.

A Coon dressed as a Red Indian, with a feathered headdress and boot polish on his hand, slaps my cheek, leaving a large black palm print on my face. That is for luck, I will be very lucky they say.

But this time maybe not so lucky. This is the last New Year Mum and Dad and Johnny and I will spend together, before every one is dispersed in different directions and the houses in District Six are bulldozed to the ground and the people scattered.

15
Disintegration

Lynn has been away for three years. She left when I was nine and now I am twelve going on thirteen. I will be turning thirteen next month. She is coming home for a visit. We can't wait to hear her news about overseas and all the things she has done. What will she bring for us? Has she changed? We are so excited, we talk about nothing else as we count the days and plan all the places we will take Lynn to and all the things we will do when she gets here. Mum and Dad are so proud of her, she is the first person in the family to study for a degree.

School holidays start next week and Johnny and I are looking forward to spending days on the beach with Lynn, swimming and eating ice cream, making sandcastles and entering bubblegum-blowing competitions.

※ ※ ※

It is a hot summer's day and the sky is blue, the sun is shining. Johnny and I are in the front garden when we see a car pull up outside the front gate. We jump up with fright and my heart sinks as I see the Special Branch in their hats and dark suits walk up the stairs to the front door and bang on the door. Their visit is not unexpected. Dad says that the net has been closing in. "They are hunting us down, one by one," he says. Every day there has been news of a new arrest of someone we know, and we hear about our friends who have been tortured. Mum doesn't want me to read the newspapers.

When Johnny sees the men from the Special Branch he jumps out of the back window and runs to warn Dad who is in the garage. But Johnny is too late. The Special Branch have already found Dad and there is no time to escape. They take Dad away and bundle him into the car while we watch helplessly.

※ ※ ※

At school I sit under a tree on my own and sing a song to comfort myself. I wish I could turn the clock back and my family could all be together again. The news is out, on the front page of all the newspapers. The girls at school have read all about Dad's arrest. My feelings are all mixed up, feelings of sadness and relief. We are no longer waiting with our nerves on edge for Dad to be arrested – the worst has happened.

Dad is being held under the 180-Day Detention Act. My dad can be kept in prison without trial for 180 days because of the new law John Vorster, the Minister of Justice, has brought in. Dad will surely be tortured. My dad is a hero. He risks possible death. My dad will protect his comrades to the bitter end and not waver from what he believes is right. I need to protect Mum and Dad and to take on their pain, but I don't know how to. I am not a hero like my dad and my mum. I am not as brave. The world is a threatening place.

I scuff my shoes in the school playground and unearth a stone, a fossil. It has a perfect imprint of a leaf on it, I put it in my pocket for safe keeping. Mum always tells me not to ruin my school shoes, but Mum is at home, she is not here to see me. This is a private space. My world breaks apart and there is no place to hide, no place of safety.

❄ ❄ ❄

A week after Dad is arrested Theo drives us to the airport to fetch Lynn. We wait impatiently at the barrier for her to arrive. Lynn has cut her hair short and looks different. She hugs us tightly. She looks worried, "How is Dad?" she asks Mum. Lynn and Mum talk quietly together so that we can't hear what they are saying.

All night long Lynn and I talk to each other in bed; we have a lot of catching up to do. In the morning we can't remember what we have said to each other. But there are microphones in the skirting board recording all our conversations. We must be more careful what we say to each other.

Lynn stays with us for the Christmas holidays before she has to go back to London. Christmas and New Year are not the same without Dad. Mum looks distracted and worried all the time and doesn't hear me when I talk to her.

Dad is held without trial in solitary confinement. They are keeping him awake and making him stand for days and nights on end while they interrogate him.

"This fascist government is murderous," Mum blurts out when she reads the headlines in the paper. Looksmart has been murdered; tortured to death.

❄ ❄ ❄

I escape into reading my old fairy tale books. I read about a boy who runs off with the Ice Queen. His best friend is a girl called Gerda, they love each other very much but one day a splinter of glass goes into the boy's eye, it is a splinter from an evil magic mirror. After that nothing is the same and everything around him looks ugly and hateful. He finds fault with Gerda about everything, he doesn't want to be her friend any more. The Ice Queen comes riding by on her sledge dressed in furs and picks him up and takes him to her palace. In the palace he grows colder and colder until his heart freezes into a block of ice. His little friend, Gerda, who loves him dearly, goes in search of him. When she sees him sitting frozen in the Ice Queen's palace she cries hot salt tears. The tears melt his frozen heart and wash away the glass splinter from his eye. He sees the beauty all around him and Gerda and he are together again and live happily ever after. When I read about Hans and the Snow Queen I know what it is like to have a frozen heart and a splinter of glass in my eye that makes the world look evil.

Upstairs outside my bedroom is a wide balcony. In the corner is a table where I sit and draw. The afternoon is hot and I sit upstairs with my huge box of chalk pastels. Inside the box are many shades of greens, of blues, of browns, of purples, pinks, oranges and reds. Dad bought the pastels from an art shop that was closing down before he was arrested, they were a bargain. I spend hours and hours drawing.

In front of me is a view of Robben Island and the bay and the docks, the Island where many political prisoners, many of our friends, are held for life, doing hard labour in the quarries, breaking stones.

At the back of the house is a view of the mountain. When the wind blows the clouds fall thick and white over the mountain. I suck lemons dipped in sugar and draw pictures of wild-eyed girls, suns and sunflowers. When the nights are hot I take my mattress onto the veranda to sleep. Sometimes I stay up all night drawing pictures.

❋ ❋ ❋

In January, I turn thirteen and go to a new school. I start at Westerford High School. In the mornings I get the bus to Cape Town station and then a train to Newlands. When I come home from school I go straight to bed, I like crawling back under my blankets. I lie curled up, like a little baby, sucking my thumb. I sleep and sleep but then wake up in the night, trembling and fearful. I lie awake in the dark, watchful, just in case something happens.

At school I can't concentrate, I am tired because I have been awake all night watching and waiting. I put my head down on my desk and drift off to sleep until the sound of the teacher's angry voice wakes me up to ask me a question.

I am alone with Mum now. Our family has disintegrated. Lynn is teaching in London and Dad is in prison. Johnny has left to go overseas. I don't remember Johnny leaving, I don't remember which day it was or which week, but he is gone. A family from Amnesty International have adopted him. Mum said he would have been conscripted into the South African army if he didn't leave before he turned sixteen. The Quakers have given him a scholarship to go to Leighton Park, a British Public School.

When Mum goes out at night I wait up for her to come home, not sure if she will come home at all. I write a long poem about Dad in prison, I will not see him for many years. I think about Lynn and Johnny who have gone away. I wonder if anything is real any more, if Lynn and Johnny and Dad really exist or are just figments of my imagination. I feel cut off and distant.

❄ ❄ ❄

I go with Mum to visit Dad at Pollsmoor Prison in our big old Plymouth Deluxe. I am not allowed inside the prison. Children under sixteen are not allowed inside, and I am thirteen, so I wait outside the barbed wire fence, hoping to catch a glimpse of Dad as he is led back to his cell.

A soldier with a gun patrols along the fence with an Alsatian dog. I see Dad as he is escorted back to his cell. I wave and wave until he is out of sight, he waves back to me.

It is the last time I see him for six years.

Dad is alone in his cell, he spends more than a year in solitary confinement in the condemned cells. He hears the men singing through the night and praying as they wait to be hanged the next morning.

Dad goes to trial at the Supreme Court. He is charged with Sabotage and of being a member of the Communist Party and being in possession of banned books. I read in the paper how Dad collapsed and needed to be put in an oxygen tent when the Special Branch took him up in the air and hung him upside down from the helicopter. Dad is found guilty of being a Communist and having banned books. The Sabotage charge doesn't stick. Everywhere I look I see the newspaper headlines:

CARNESON AQUITTED OF SABOTAGE
SENTENCED TO SIX YEARS

I write letters to Dad when it is allowed, I count the words. I am only allowed to write 300 words per letter every six months. I must be careful what I write or it will be censored.

16
Learning to smoke

I am thirteen when I discover smoking. I smoke in the toilet and lean out the window so the smoke will blow away. As I smoke I think about life and death. What is life all about? It's meaningless: Go to school, come home, go to sleep, get up, go to school. Round and round it goes. The emptiness of my life makes me cry.

I wear dark glasses so nobody can see in, I even wear my glasses in the dark.

I hide my cigarettes inside the piano where the strings are, but Mum finds them and tells me smoking leads to drinking and drinking leads to drugs. Then it's downhill all the way and I am sliding all the way down the slippery slope.

Now that I have started my periods, Mum says I must be careful of boys that they don't touch me in certain places and I mustn't be alone with them. They won't respect me if my virginity is broken, no decent man will want to touch me. At school the other girls say if you use tampons they can break your virginity. I won't use tampons, just in case.

* * *

Boys only want "one thing". "Good" girls don't let them touch them below the neck or above the knees, girls who are "nice" to boys let them feel their breasts. Sometimes, I have heard, "nice girls" even go "all the way" with boys.

I wear tight jeans with a wide patent-leather shiny red belt and a tight sleeveless top.

"Jail bait," the stranger calls me as he offers me a lift as I walk down the street. "Where are you going?" I climb into his car "How old are you?"

"Thirteen."

"You look eighteen."

He drops me off outside my house. I can see the Special Branch parked outside our house taking notes. Duncan is my first boyfriend, he is in my brother's class at school. His dad is a Baptist minister from Scotland and his mum is from Holland. She walks barefoot in the house and the lady who cleans their house sits and eats at the same table with them at meal times.

Duncan and I hold hands and kiss and listen to music together. But then I break up with him to the sounds of Bob Dylan singing about being alone, like a rolling stone.

Smoking makes me feel dizzy, but I like the sensation of feeling out of control. I stay out of school and go for a drive with Philip, a long haired hippy from England; he wears purple and pink shirts and plays the guitar and sings. We sit and look at the sea as Philip rolls a cigarette made out of dagga. He shows me how to breathe in deeply and hold the smoke inside my lungs. I feel strange, I can't stop eating, I want to eat everything in sight, but when I try to eat a sandwich the cheese sticks in my throat and makes me feel sick.

"Hi," Max says, and smiles at me when I meet him walking down the road. "I live around the corner," he tells me. He lives with his parents and is a drama student at university. "Can I come and visit you?" he wants to know. He offers me a cigarette and I tell him where I live. He has cold fish eyes and he is 18.

The next day, Max knocks on the door and introduces himself to my Mum. He says he wants me to act in a play he is directing – "Blood Wedding" by the Spanish playwright, Lorca. Mum says I can. I go to rehearsals four nights a week and I play the part of an old woman.

Clive plays the part of the husband in the play. He is tall and has a beard. He is also a student. We walk through the courtyard. The stones hurt my bare feet and Clive picks me up and carries me across the courtyard to the theatre.

Ruth, Ruth, tell me the truth
Are you a virgin?
And do you catch sturgeon?

I laugh and he puts me down. Clive lives in Newlands near my school.

I play truant from school and go to Clive's house. The dishes are piled up high in the sink and the floors are unswept and the ash trays are overflowing. I love the squalor in his house. He has books of poetry by Sylvia Plath and Allen Ginsburg. I read Sylvia Plath's poems and cry. I learn her poems off by heart and recite her poem "Daddy" in English class. Clive shares a house with his friend David. David sleeps on a brass bed which is always unmade. He plays strange discordant music by Stravinsky and Mahler which I listen to for the first time.

At night, I hear a knock on my bedroom window and see Max standing outside. He puts his finger to his lips and climbs through my bedroom window so Mum won't see him. He has brought a bottle of brandy and a packet of cigarettes for me. We drink the brandy and kiss. I have a piano in my bedroom and I store my cigarettes and brandy inside the top of the piano so Mum won't find them.

Mum calls me "a joiner". I joined Sunday School, I joined the Shul, and I joined the Girl Guides. We went camping and learnt how to tie knots and make fires and sing "She'll be coming round the mountain when she comes". But I have outgrown the Girl Guides and join Habonim, a youth group. The big attraction for me is the boys. We meet every Sunday night and go away to camps. I meet lots of boys, Sidney and Michael and Gary, they are good boys from nice homes. They live in Sea Point.

At night, I wait till Mum has gone to bed and climb out of the window and catch the bus into Town and then another bus to Sea Point to Michael's house. At this time of night it is quiet and I am the only person on the bus. Michael's Mum and Dad have gone to bed by the time I get to his house.

Michael and I kiss for a short while.

"I am hungry. What is there to eat and drink?" I ask him.

Michael raids the fridge and comes back with some chocolate cake and a can of his Dad's beer. We cuddle up in bed and fall asleep. His mother comes in and catches us together in his bed. His mother thinks the worst of me, she thinks we have had sex but she does not know how chaste I am. She doesn't approve of me. At dawn I hitchhike home to be in time to get back into bed before Mum comes into my room to wake me up for school.

On Saturday afternoon, I go and visit Michael. We walk around Sea Point looking for something to do. We are bored.

"I know a flat we could break into," I say.

I ring the bell to make sure nobody is in. The flat belongs to a man I know; he tried to kiss my friend and feel her breasts. He is a dirty old man. My body is small enough to crawl through the opening where the dust bins are kept. Once inside I open the door for Michael to come inside and we rifle through the flat. We are looking for cigarettes and alcohol. I don't take any personal items, just the cigarettes and booze, I am careful not to make a mess.

We walk down to the beach where I tip the bottle of neat vodka down my throat and feel it as it goes straight to my stomach and my head. I find myself talking loudly, reciting poetry and performing. I am a wild child, things are getting out of control. Some bikers pull up and I laugh with them and offer them vodka. Michael pulls me to my feet and we stagger back to his house. Michael's mother takes me home. She says she is worried about me, she knows it can't be easy for me with my Dad not at home. When I get home I tell Mum I have a headache and go straight to bed.

✳ ✳ ✳

Dressed in my new blue jeans and shiny red patent-leather belt and my tight fitting sleeveless top I am ready to party. Mum is chaperoning me to see that I don't get into trouble. We are on our way to a party in Sea Point. It is New Year's Eve and it has been three years since Mum and Dad, Johnny and I went to watch the Coons in District Six together. This year Johnny is far away in England and Dad has been sent to a Maximum Security Prison in Pretoria.

Mum's friend, Ethel, is driving us to the party. I see a car driving slowly behind us.

"We are being followed," I say.

"Don't be paranoid," Ethel tells me, but Ethel doesn't believe that the Special Branch are everywhere, and we need to be careful. I know we are being watched. We arrive at the New Year's Eve party and Mum sits and drinks tea and eats cake with the adults, although she knows she shouldn't, it is illegal, she is breaking her banning orders drinking tea with more than two other people in the room. I am with the young people outside by the fire and the music.

The music is loud and we don't hear the banging on the door before the Special Branch burst into the house. Eight burly six-foot-tall men, dressed in dark suits, have come to arrest my five-foot-tall mother.

"Mrs Carneson we have been watching you all night, you are under arrest." Two burly men walk on either side of my Mum, two in front and two behind.

Mum laughs. "I feel like Mata Hari," she says as they escort her to the car. "Six of you? Why so many?"

"We need to protect ourselves," the Special Branch man tells Mum.

Then they are shouting at me.

"You too, come with us."

I run and hide and lock myself in the toilet, but they corner me and bundle me into the car with Mum and drive us to the police station.

A Special Branch man grabs hold of my arm, "This woman can come with me," he says.

"Leave her alone, she is only a child," Mum commands him as they lead her away and the man lets go of me. Mum is escorted to her cell and I am left alone in the police station.

I hear the clock strike twelve.

"Happy New Year," I say to myself.

Ethel comes to fetch me and take me home. She offers me a cigarette to calm my nerves.

Mum is out on bail, but she isn't allowed to speak to most of her friends, the ones who are named and banned. Her other friends are too scared to speak to us. Mum is only allowed to move within a two-mile radius of the house and my school falls outside of this area.

I am always in trouble at school. Most weeks the headmaster phones my mum: "We are having problems with your daughter, you need to come in and see me again."

Mum has to go to the Magistrate to get permission to visit my school or she will be arrested.

※ ※ ※

Mum gives up setting any boundaries for me, she knows I won't keep to them. Mum has her own problems, she lies in bed shaking like a leaf – she is bleeding heavily, menstruating. The blood flows out of her, soaking her bed. In the mornings when she wakes up, Mum takes stock of who has been arrested, who has disappeared, who has survived torture or has broken and talked. A roll call of friends who have died or who have fled. Not many friends are left.

People are scared to come to the house. They are warned to stay away or else the Special Branch ask if they will spy on us. People cross to the other side of the road, rather than be seen talking to Mum or me. These are dangerous times.

I am used to people in my life disappearing, No one can get close to me. I hide behind my smile, I am loud and funny and outrageous and take everything to extremes, challenging the world around me and challenging authority.

17

A worm for the Prime Minister

The Prime Minister has been assassinated. People are celebrating in the townships, but at school the mood is sombre. The teachers are talking in hushed, shocked tones, walking up and down and in and out of the classrooms. I want to jump up and down for joy when I hear the news, but I will be out of place here, so I go to the girls' toilets to look at my reflection in the mirror. I smile at myself, it is safe to share the good news with myself.

A madman has killed the prime minister, he said there was a giant worm in his stomach that told him to do it. They say it was not a plot to overthrow the government.

It is not good news for long. An even worse prime minister is put in Verwoerd's place. The laws are becoming more repressive by the day.

I become more anxious. I find myself trembling all the time and wanting to hide. It feels like the buildings are crowding in on me. People walk too fast. I am disorientated and confused.

I can't remember if I must walk up the road or down the road. I can't remember if my school is on the left hand side of the road or the right hand side.

"You are late again, you must report to the office," I am told when I get to school. Most afternoons I have to stay in for detention. "I must not come late for school. I must not come late for school, I must not come late for school." I must write lines, over and over again.

One hundred times, two hundred times, three hundred times, four hundred times, five hundred times.

My arm aches and my hand aches.

After school, my friends and I experiment with makeup. I put on lipstick and eye shadow and mascara on my lashes. I draw a dark black line around my eyes with eyeliner. I tease my hair with a comb until it stands up on top of my head. I wear my skirt as short as possible – it barely covers my bottom. I wear the shiny, white patent-leather boots that I saved up for and tight-fitting T-shirts that show off my new breasts. When I get home Mum calls me a slut and a floozy and tells me to wash my makeup off.

✳ ✳ ✳

At night, I dream that a woman, perhaps it is my mother, invites me into a warm and cosy room. But if I enter into the warm room I will turn into a whore. It is very dangerous, I must run and hide. I am looking for a safe space to hide in. I find myself in a very cold place. The places I want to hide in become colder and colder, icy cold. At last I find a safe place. It is narrow and hard and freezing cold, but if I hide there I will escape becoming a whore.

Rumour has it that Dirty Old Men go to Café Bioscopes during the day on the lookout for naughty school girls bunking off school. They sidle up to you and put their hands up your skirt and offer to buy you an ice cream. Rumour has it that these places are flea-ridden and frequented by the lonely and the shiftless and the dirty minded.

The bioscopes are called the Ritzy, the Regal and the Gem and show double features of John Wayne and *Annie Get your Gun*. You can sit in a Café Bio all day and all night for the price of one ticket. Your ticket entitles you to a drink of coffee or tea or a brightly coloured cool drink served to you in your seat by an usherette. In front of the seat is a small wooden shelf for your drink.

I bunk off school and sit all day watching movies, laughing and crying in the dark. I go and see the *Seven Faces of Doctor Lao*. The film stops and starts, the picture is scratchy and the reel breaks mid-way through the movie. I see the *Seven Faces of Doctor Lao* four times in a row until the images are etched into my brain.

One Saturday afternoon, I go to see the film again with Patrick Smith, a boy from school. He is sweet sixteen, older than me, and smokes and has a bad reputation. We sit holding hands.

Doctor Lao is a wise old Doctor who runs a circus with a freak show that mirrors the people of the town and causes them to see who they are and change their wicked, foolish ways. At the circus is the face of Medusa with hair made of hissing snakes who can stop you in your tracks and freeze you into a statue. There is the god Pan and a serpent who smokes a cigar. The god Pan, half man, half goat plays his mischievous pipes and seduces the beautiful school teacher. With his good looks he leads her a merry dance. The school teacher undoes her top button of her clean starched white shirt with lace and ruffles while he plays hide and seek with her. The next thing she does is take out the pins from the tight bun on top of her head and shake her long hair free. Pan plays his pipes and she starts dancing, slowly at first then faster and faster. She moves her body from side to side, swaying rhythmically.

Patrick takes my fingers one by one and slowly sucks each fingertip sending shivers of pleasure down my spine.

The god Pan kisses the school teacher before he gallops away into the sunset leaving her sweating and dishevelled.

✳ ✳ ✳

I must not allow myself to get close to anyone because I do not know who I can trust, it is dangerous to talk to anyone. They might be an informer or could crack under torture. Any information could be dangerous. I am followed and watched wherever I go.

The tension stored in my body takes its toll and my senses start to distort. I look at the world through the wrong end of a telescope. The world appears very far away and I hear the person sitting next to me as if from a great distance. When I lie down my body grows from tiny to huge to miniscule. I keep changing shape.

I wait for the knock on the door, wound up, listening. I can never let go of my vigilance. I want to protect Mum but I am powerless and I can do nothing to stop Mum getting arrested.

✳ ✳ ✳

Beth lives in the flat downstairs from Caroline. She is older than me, she is a student and she shares a flat with other students. She can do what she likes. She can drink and smoke and have boyfriends to stay the night. She is very pretty. We sit in a café and Beth orders two coffees and offers me a cigarette. I feel sophisticated sitting there with Beth. I can talk to her, she understands how I am feeling. At school the other children don't understand, I feel as if I live on a different planet from them. They are not interested in reading poetry or discussing ideas and the meaning of life and death.

I take a puff of my cigarette. Beth understands when I ask "What is the point of living?"

We go out to see Fellini movies together that are full of strange images that I can relate to. Mum thinks I am safe with Beth.

Caroline is arrested under the 180-day laws and held in solitary confinement and Camilla is sent to boarding school. Macmillan, her uncle, the British Prime Minister, has a discreet word with the South African government and Caroline is released soon afterwards. Caroline and Camilla go back to London, they are not allowed to stay in South Africa.

Mum is also good at finding loyal friends who will help her. In spite of our isolation and the fear people feel, Joan becomes Mum's friend. She comes to look after me and the house during the times when Mum is arrested for breaking her Banning Orders. Joan is down to earth and practical. Whenever Joan arrives Tinky, our dog, jumps up and down and runs around in circles, wags her tail, yaps and wets herself with excitement.

Joan drives Mum to the police station where she has to report three times a week. She also drives Mum to go and visit Dad in prison. When Mum is arrested she goes to fetch Mum from the police station and takes Mum to court for her trial.

One Friday night, I stand on the veranda looking at the lights of the city. Joan joins me outside. "I was with your mother in court today," Joan tells me. "It looks like she will get a suspended sentence."

Joan lights a cigarette. "I saw Beth in court today," she says. "She was giving evidence against a woman in the next courtroom. She is probably an informer."

I don't want to believe Joan. But she says, "It is better if you do not see Beth. She mustn't come to the house any more. It's not safe."

The next afternoon I walk down the street and feel myself crumbling. Something breaks inside me and I know I can no longer hold my life together. The four corners of my heart collapse. The street is the same, the weather is the same, but I am not the same any more, my will to live is gone.

Beth is an informer. Beth has given evidence in court. She was my friend, I loved her, I trusted her and could talk to her. But Beth is dangerous and not to be trusted now. I don't have any friends any more, it is too dangerous for anyone to become my friend: they might be arrested, or banned. It is too dangerous for me to make friends with anyone. They might be listening to every word I say, waiting for a chance to go back to the Special Branch and tell them everything. Beth might have informed on Caroline. She is dangerous. She could be a snake in the grass.

※ ※ ※

I wear a uniform to school, a grey skirt, maroon blazer, tie, long grey socks, black shoes, blue shirt. In summer we wear a gingham dress, regulation-length short white socks and an old-fashioned hat. Even on the hottest day it is compulsory to wear a blazer.

At school, I am called into the office again. My name is called over the intercom system. What have I done wrong now? The headmaster's voice drones on and on and I switch off. He is telling me I have been seen smoking and wearing my skirt too short. I must understand black men will lust after my body if I dress like that:

"They are not like us, they have no self-control," he tells me.

Something snaps inside my head and I start screaming. Why can't he just shut up? On his desk are books, notepads, a telephone and other office paraphernalia. I pick the books up and hurl them in the direction of the headmaster. Inside of my fury I lose consciousness of what I am doing as I scream, telling him to fuck off and leave me alone.

I run out of the office and across the playground. My fury gives me superhuman strength and I vault over the wall to escape the teachers running after me:

"You bastards," I scream, running down the road.

At Clive's house, I sit on the doorstep sobbing. After a while I calm down, but now I can't stop crying. When I get home Mum tells me the headmaster phoned and I must go and apologise to him for my bad behaviour. But I am not sorry. He should leave me alone and not go on at me all the time, he provoked me. I will apologise to him because it is Mum's disappointment I am scared of, I cannot backchat my mother.

At school, I become silent and withdraw into myself. I fall asleep at my desk from boredom. The teacher calls me to the front of the class and tells me I must stand in the corner by the window until I can behave myself. The window is dusty and the teacher's voice drones on. To occupy myself I wet my finger and start writing in the dust on the window pane.

Hendrick Vervoed Memorial Window
Vorster is a fascist
Make love, not war
Taylor is a hypocrite

Vorster sent my Dad to jail. Taylor is our headmaster. The bell rings and we all file out to the playground for break. The bell rings again and it is time to go back inside. At the door of the classroom a classmate stands and bars my way inside. He hands me my packed suitcase and tells me I am not allowed into the class.

I am expelled from school and sent home in disgrace but I am used to being excluded. I feel free. I don't have to go to school any more. I jump for joy at the thought of not having to go to school. But then I am scared, what will I tell Mum? She will be upset and worried, she will be cross with me. I feel guilty, she has enough to worry about. I don't have the courage to go home and tell Mum what has happened.

18
Hospital stories 1 – three bottles of pills

At night, when I close my eyes and go to sleep I wish that I will never wake up again. When I wake up, I wish I were dead. I long to sleep and sleep.

The gap between the outside world and my inner world widens. I fall through the gap into nothing, into a void, a faraway place.

I fantasise about killing the Special Branch men who follow me constantly whenever I leave the house. I will strangle them, shoot them, stab them, tear them limb from limb, stamp on their lifeless bodies and reduce them to a bloody pulp. As they draw their last breath I will gouge out their eyes.

❋ ❋ ❋

Mum finds a new school for me to go to. The Waldorf School has space for me, all the other schools said they were full. My new school is in a rambling old house and my class room is upstairs in an attic. The classes are small and the teachers are kind to me. There are not so many rules and regulations and I am no longer in constant trouble.

Some days my head feels fuzzy. When I say I am not feeling well my German teacher understands and drives me home and we talk in the car. I can tell that she understands about fascism and fear.

At home, when Mum calls me, up pops an obedient robot who goes through the motions of being alive. The robot goes to school dressed in her school blazer with her hair in ponytails or plaits, her tie neatly knotted. She tries to do her homework and get to school on time.

But it doesn't work, I can't do it. I hide, I run, I play the fool, I get drunk, I am a naughty, disobedient girl and my mother doesn't know what to do with me.

❋ ❋ ❋

On my fourteenth birthday, my latest boyfriend, Stephen, gives me a teddy bear, a black and white panda. Stephen is sixteen and goes to my school.

"What should I call my bear?" I ask him. "I don't know if it is a boy or a girl."

"Call him Tiresias," Stephen says. "Tiresias wasn't male or female." Stephen tells me the story of the Greek myth.

Tiresias was a hermaphrodite blinded by the goddess Athena when he saw her naked but Zeus took pity on him and gave him the gift of seeing into the future. I close my eyes and imagine I can see into the future.

❋ ❋ ❋

I am no longer a child. I stand outside my body and watch myself and I don't like what I see. I see clearly that I have a choice – that being alive is a choice and I can choose not to live. I have a way out. Relief floods through me. I feel happier than I have done in a long time. I can relax and enjoy myself because next week I will no longer be here.

Everything appears in sharp focus, the sky, the grass and the colours of the world around me. I smile at strangers in the street. I feel lighter as I say my good byes to the world.

Mum keeps bottles of pills in the medicine cabinet in the bathroom. I wait until everyone has gone to sleep and then I start swallowing pills by the handful. Three bottles of them.

When Mum can't wake me up she rushes me to hospital. I feel the rubber tube as it is inserted down my throat. My stomach is pumped and I vomit through my mouth and nose. I fight to tear the tubes out of my body, but the nurses and orderlies hold me down. I fight with superhuman strength before I pass out. I thought I would never wake up – it is a shock to open my eyes and still find myself alive.

I am kept in hospital, the after effects of the overdose are still coursing through my body. I wear striped hospital pyjamas and a towelling dressing gown. It feels like my feet no longer touch the ground and that everything is in slow motion and distant. There is a solid, but invisible barrier between myself and the world. I can no longer feel or touch the world around me. I float, far away in space, and the distance feels lonely.

I find myself in a small courtyard. I look through the glass of the window. There is the same invisible separation between me and the world, hard and cold, like the pane of glass. Very gently I break the glass, I put my fist through the cold hard separation. Tears run down my face as I feel a softening inside myself.

The nurses come running, there is blood and jagged, sharp, broken glass. They take me back to bed and I float up onto the ceiling. Visitors arrive, I talk to them from a great distance and hear strange words come out of my mouth as I look down at myself lying on the bed.

I breathe in the smell of the casualty department. The smell of disinfectant mixed with the smell of antiseptic is a familiar comforting smell. I wash my hands continually. The more nervous I am, the more I wash my hands.

My overdose is giving me a reprieve from the normal problems of trying to survive. I am suspended, taken out of life, out of time.

Lying in the hospital bed, weak, I feel a strange peacefulness as I let go. The pain was in trying to live but now I have given up trying. I can't do it anymore.

They send me to the psychiatric ward on the top floor of the hospital. The trolley lady does the rounds of the ward. It is early morning, 6 o'clock. The trolley is by my bed with a hot, strong, sweet cup of tea. I reach for a cigarette, and my day begins. I feel drugged from the night before, from my dose of barbiturates and I struggle to open my eyes. I light my untipped Texan cigarette and the nicotine courses through my body, along with the sweet strong cup of tea.

I don't want to get up. I open my eyes to the day and the familiar ward routine, breakfast, group therapy, coffee. The trolley is wheeled around again, this time for medication. Every day the nurses take our blood pressure and ask if we have had a bowel movement. There is table tennis, occupational therapy, lunch time, tea time, supper and bed time.

Brenda, Jay and I share a room, we talk late into the night. After the isolation of school, of being shunned like a leper, I enjoy their companionship. After bedtime Brenda and I climb out of bed and sit in the dark day room, smoking, sharing a cigarette, watching the tip glow in the dark, passing it backwards and forwards, sitting close together, close to the radio. We want to hear which song is Number One this week. The radio plays softly, if the nurse catches us we will be sent back to bed.

Brenda is older than me, she has left school and works in a shoe shop and spends her wages buying boots. She is fifteen. I try on different pairs of boots. My favourite pair is Brenda's black Dr. Zhivago boots, they lace all the way up to the knee. I want them. Sometimes Brenda lets me borrow them.

Brenda is petite and pretty, she wears sexy clothes and she cuts her arms. Her mother has left her father, their father mustn't find out where they are living. He was beating them.

Jay also mutilates herself but she does not cut herself, she bruises herself, she hits herself until her knee swells up black and purple. It has become infected. She breaks her arm deliberately. Jay is well behaved and quiet.

"Your gulls are calling you," Brenda shouts to me.

Every afternoon I feed the seagulls. I collect the stale bread from the kitchen and put it on the window ledge and they fly to the window and snatch the bread from my hands. The gulls swoop down, crying and mewing in the way gulls do, making wide circles in the blue sky with their dazzling white wings, gliding freely on the currents.

Mum comes to visit me and brings my favourite dishes from home to supplement the hospital food. She brings me dishes of chopped herring and chopped liver and blintzes stuffed with cheese covered with cinnamon. She brings me a carton of cigarettes even though she doesn't like me smoking.

Early in the morning, Brenda and I leave the ward and sneak away from the hospital while the nurses change shifts. Outside the confines of our ward the world is busy and unfamiliar, we are not part of this hustle and bustle. The outside world is full of forbidden promises, for months we have been carefully watched and monitored, we have not been allowed out by ourselves.

The dispensary door is open. Quietly Brenda and I go inside while no one is looking. It is like being in a sweet shop, we take some jars of brightly coloured pills. Later we plan to take an overdose, nobody will find us if we hide in a field.

First, we will go and have some fun, go to the bioscope and eat chocolate. Brenda buys a ticket and lets me in through the fire exit. Perhaps we could take the pills in the cinema? However, we decide to watch the film first. We are careful not to sit next to any men. We are two young girls on the loose, enjoying the delicious taste of freedom, of being on our own, unsupervised.

After the bioscope we are at a loose end, it is boring walking around, it starts to rain, and we are hungry. Today has been a good day. We decide not to take the pills. We go back to the hospital, the Sister calls us into her office she is angry, the police have been looking for us.

I feel safe locked up in the ward. The Special Branch do not watch me and follow me wherever I go. The psychiatrist tells Mum that I am suffering from paranoid delusions and that I am living in an imaginary nightmare.

"No," Mum says, "my daughter is not imagining the nightmares, these are not delusions, the things she is telling you are real."

The Special Branch want to come and ask me questions, they come to the hospital to interview me. Dr. Curry is my doctor. He went to Eton and speaks in a plummy British accent. He won't let the Special Branch question me. He calls my mother on the phone and says, "Ruth must leave the country as soon as possible, she must not go home again, it is not safe. Is there a friend Ruth can stay with?"

Dr. Curry wants to protect me, but he doesn't want to get into trouble with the Special Branch. He disappears, goes on leave and takes his family on holiday.

I go and stay with my school friend, Tessa, in Pinelands for ten days before I leave South Africa.

Me, aged fourteen, with Mum, Johnny, Lynn, Charles (Lynn's fiancée)
River Thames, Berkshire, UK.

PART TWO

United Kingdom 1967–1991
South Africa 1991–2000

19

London

At the age of fourteen, I cannot guess the consequences of stepping on board the aeroplane. It is not my decision to leave and go overseas – the adults in charge of my life have decided I need to go for my own safety. Theo, Mum's friend, has bought me a one-way ticket. Mum will join me in England when she has packed up and sold the house.

When I get to London and start my new life all my problems will be solved and I will be happy again.

I am dressed in my new pink dress with a matching pink hat. Under one arm I carry a roll of my drawings, the rest of my pictures are in my suitcase. In my other arm I carry my teddy bear, Tiresias.

Duncan's Mum fetches me from Pinelands and drives me to the airport. Duncan was my first boyfriend and now his mother is driving me to catch a plane that will take me to London. Mum sits in the front seat and looks distracted. Duncan's mum squeezes her hand as Mum looks straight ahead. I sit in the back with Duncan's little brothers.

At the airport Mum hugs me. "Have a safe journey and give a big hug to Johnny and Lynn from me." I wave goodbye to Mum as I cross the tarmac to board the aeroplane.

As the plane takes off, I see Table Mountain and the sea disappear into the distance and I am plummeted into exile. My life splits in two, a point of no return. I might never be allowed to go home again. I am flying to England, a new land, not out of choice but out of fear.

On the flight, I sit next to a man called Mr. Goodenough. He has been doing business in South Africa, perhaps he is a spy sitting next to me, put there especially to gather information from me. Under the blanket during the flight he feels me up, fingers me and fondles me. I fall asleep on his shoulder and the air hostess calls me his wife. I am old for my age, I have been like this since I was 12 and first developed breasts, jail bait I am called. I want love and warm touches, my 14-year-old body responds to opportunities.

❋ ❋ ❋

After a 24-hour flight, I arrive in England. I say good bye to Mr. Goodenough as he shakes my hand and gives me his business card. At last I am in London where the lights are bright and the streets are paved with gold.

At immigration, I am taken aside and interviewed, they ask me questions for a long time. I won't answer their questions. Men in uniform are not to be trusted. I hold onto my teddy bear, Tiresias, tightly and press my lips together, they won't get any information out of me. My sister waits anxiously for me on the other side. In my bag I have an invitation from a British family and a letter from Amnesty International. Eventually I show them the letters and they let me go.

Lynn meets me at the barrier with her fiancée, Charles. We drive through Richmond Park to get to Charles's flat. Charles is an English man, he is very proper and speaks the Queen's English. He works for a publishing house and his house is full of books. The roof comes off his car and I stand up looking out of the car, waving as we drive through the park. I have arrived in the land of the Queen and crumpets.

My sister lodges with an English family, the Huttens, near Highgate Woods in North London and works as a teacher at an East End school. She drives a Volkswagen beetle car, spray painted pink with swirling psychedelic flowers on it.

The buildings in London go on and on for ever. I cannot see any mountains or blue sky. Everything is strange and the colours are dull. London is not how I imagined it to be.

At four o'clock, I drink Darjeeling tea with Grandma Hutten and dunk a digestive biscuit in my tea. The tea is served in a bone-china cup that has been warmed. I notice that people talk quietly and laugh with restraint, they sit upright and are easily embarrassed. Nobody else is dunking their biscuits.

"What school do you go to?" Granma Hutten wants to know.

"I was expelled from school and then I had a breakdown and went into hospital," I tell her. I hear the sound of the china cups clinking. The room is quiet and nobody says anything for a while.

I make faux pas. That is what my sister calls them – I embarrass her with my loudness. I learn that it is easier to tone myself down and sit quietly unnoticed. After all, I am from the colonies.

Lynn takes me to stay with Johnny. He lives with the Glyns during the school holidays. The house is a large double-storey house with a big garden in Roehampton, an affluent suburb in South London. Dennis and Myrna Glyn have two teenage sons, David and Paul. Dennis is a doctor and Myrna works for Amnesty. They are very kind. They say I can stay with them for a few weeks while Johnny is on holiday.

Johnny and I don't have much to say to each other. He has grown his hair long and takes photos of the girl next door. I think he is in love with her.

I have heard about television, but I have never seen one. I can't wait for the television to be switched on so I can watch this small cinema screen inside the house. Exciting and mysterious, it is a novelty turning it on and changing channels and adjusting the volume. A cricket game is on the television, and soon I am bored. After all the build-up and excitement I fall fast asleep.

After supper I have a bath and go to bed. Myrna comes into the bedroom kisses me good night and tucks me in and asks me if I need anything. She reminds me of Mum.

Dennis gives me money, a blue five-pound note. I don't know what to do with my blue five-pound note, it is a lot of money. Dennis says if I go out I need to wear shoes. "The streets in London are dirty and you could pick up diseases," he tells me. David, who is sixteen, offers to take me into the West End for the day and show me the sights of London.

I travel on the underground for the first time. Escalators take me down deep into the earth. Under the ground is a network of tunnels where the air is dark and thick. When I blow my nose it leaves the tissue black, I breathe in a metallic dirty taste that sticks to the roof of my mouth and the back of my throat. The buildings are too big and too dense – they tower above me as people rush by. It is exhausting to see so many people in such unfamiliar surroundings. I long for home.

The London summer is hot, clammy and airless, it leaves me feeling dirty and sweaty. David shows me St. Paul's Cathedral and the Tower of London.

❊ ❊ ❊

In this city full of beautiful old buildings and big red buses, history weighs down on me, imposing a tightly established order. There are no cracks or chinks for me to crawl through.

David won't let me pay for anything. I still have the five-pound note that Denis gave me in my pocket. I put it in the hat of the long-haired busker playing his guitar outside the tube station. The busker calls me back. "I don't need your charity or your condescension." He throws the money at me and my face burns with shame and embarrassment.

David and I walk along the banks of the river Thames holding hands. We sit on a bench and kiss and David puts his tongue in my mouth. When we get home the table is laid and Myrna has cooked a leg of lamb. Dennis sits at the head of the table and carves the meat. David and I sit across the table from each other with our feet touching. Paul, the youngest son, gives me a funny look and passes the gravy while Johnny talks a lot between mouthfuls of roast potatoes and mint sauce. A few days later I move in with my sister at the Huttens. I sleep in the guest room but I can only stay there for a short time.

※ ※ ※

"We are going away for the weekend," Lynn tells me. "We are going to Littlehampton by the sea."

I am very excited, I haven't seen the sea since I left Cape Town. Lynn's friend has said we can borrow her cottage for the weekend.

We drive down to Sussex in Lynn's psychedelic Volkswagen and arrive at a tiny cottage with low doors and a low ceiling. I take our bags inside and Lynn puts the kettle on for a cup of tea. I am impatient to get down to the beach. Excited and full of anticipation, I run down to the sea. There in front of me lies a flat expanse of water. This is not the sea I know, this sea is grey and does not speak to me. The heavy sky presses down on me and the beach is made out of pebbles and not the fine white sand of a Cape Town beach that sings as I walk on it on a hot day. The dull colours disappoint me. I button my jacket up against the chilly drizzle of this English summer's day.

"We are going to Spain," Lynn tells me. "My friend Leo has invited us." Leo is a Jamaican artist living up in the mountains.

For our trip, Lynn and I buy paper disposable panties and paper dresses from a boutique in London. We drive to Dover and catch the ferry to Calais and drive through France to the Pyrenees Mountains. Lynn's painted Volkswagen Beetle takes us through mountain ranges that remind me of home, the sun is shining and the sky is blue. "The light, look at this light," Lynn says as she breathes in the mountain air. "You never get light like this in England."

We reach the village high up in the mountains where Leo lives with his American girlfriend. Leo towers over us and has a booming voice. He gives us both a huge bear hug and welcomes us with a glass of red wine.

For the next three weeks, I lie in the sun on the terrace in my bikini look-ing at the mountain, smoking and drinking rough red wine, reading *Diary of a Nymph* about a housewife who is unhappy and has sex with every one she meets. The book makes me cry, it is so sad that she is lonely and her husband neglects her.

In the middle of our stay, the quiet mountain village comes alive for the week with a Fiesta. A brass band leads a procession through the narrow village streets to the town square. We join in the circle and dance a traditional Basque dance. The wine flows freely. Charles, Lynn's fiancée, joins us during our last week and drives us back through France to England. We drive through Avignon stopping to eat at the roadside cafés where French lorry drivers eat. Charles practises his French. It takes us two days to get back to London.

※ ※ ※

In London, the weather gets cooler. The summer has ended and autumn has set in. The seasons are opposite to the seasons at home and the new school year starts in September not January. In September Lynn goes back to work and I start at my new school, King Alfred's, in Hampstead. I am staying with Lynn at the Huttens' house until Mum arrives next month.

At King Alfred's, there are not many rules and you can call the teachers by their first name and don't have to wear school uniform. Some of the children smoke and come to school barefoot.

Lynn takes me to school on the first day and shows me the bus stop where I must get the bus to school. On the second day, on my way to school, I get lost. For two hours I wander around, trying to find the right bus stop, but I keep going in the wrong direction. I am going round in circles. There are no mountains, there is no sea to act as a landmark – I cannot get my bearings. I ask people in the street for directions and they tell me turn right, turn left, but I have no concept of what is right or what is left. The bridge I have just crossed looks familiar. I give up looking for the bus stop, I just want to find the Hutten house, but I can't find it.

I see a phone box – perhaps I can phone someone to help me. I want my Mum and Dad, I want someone to look after me. I can't stop crying, I am very angry with myself, how can I cry like this? I am not a baby any more, I am fourteen, old enough to look after myself.

I calm down and manage to phone Lynn. She fetches me from the phone box.

※ ※ ※

This city is so vast and confusing, I feel like I could be lost forever. In London I expected to find bright colours and parties every day but instead I find the colour grey, and endless rain. I feel lost and rootless, struggling to find my way through this maze of buildings, traffic and cold, bad weather.

My fragile sense of self has disappeared and exile, and the loss of my country and family, fragment me. I lose all connection to myself in this strange city. How will I ever put the pieces together again?

20

The White Cliffs of Dover

Mum arrives on a cold October day. We drive to Dover to fetch her. The day is grey and overcast. She has travelled by boat from Cape Town to Dover.

"How is Dad?" Lynn wants to know. Mum said they wouldn't let her say good bye to Dad before she left. They only gave her permission to go to the docks. She said the Special Branch watched her get on the boat to make sure she was leaving. Mum has left on an exit visa. She is now a stateless person.

Lynn drives us to Hendon. Mum and I are going to stay with Esme Goldberg. Her husband, Dennis, is in jail with Dad in Pretoria. Esme has promised to look after Mum and me. The house is on a busy main road. All the houses look the same, drab and suburban. The winter trees have had their branches lopped off and look like people with their arms hacked off.

I have known the Goldbergs all my life. It is good to see familiar faces. Esme lives with her mother-in-law, Annie and her children, David and Hilary. Hilary and I played together when we were little and Annie was in jail with Mum during the emergency. We haven't seen them since they left South Africa after Dennis was sentenced to life inprisonment.

Esme and Annie have cooked us a feast, a mountain of rice and Esme's speciality, sweet and sour spare ribs. Mum and Annie exchange funny stories about their time together in Bien Donné when they shared a cell, when Annie would get dressed up in her pink bed jacket and sing Vaudeville songs in her Cockney accent and keep them all entertained.

Esme takes in lodgers to supplement her income and her house is always full of people. British friends and South African exiles are drawn to Esme and Annie's warmth and humour. I share a room with Mum. Mum sleeps on the single bed while I sleep on a mattress on the floor. Sometimes I just want to be by myself and left alone but I can never find a quiet corner to hide in. Outside the weather is cold and grey.

In the mornings, I stand and wait for a bus to take me to school. I am getting the hang of London transport. I don't have any friends at school. The other children can't understand my accent or what I am talking about. When I talk they give me polite, blank looks.

✳ ✳ ✳

My cousin, Roland, lives with his wife, Sue, in Clapham, South London. Mum and I travel by tube across London to visit them. They have invited us for supper. We sit on packing cases while Sue serves us spaghetti bolognese. Roland has made his own furniture out of packing cases and planks of wood. He is an art student and Sue is a nurse.

"We have some friends coming over later," Roland says to Mum. "They want to meet you."

The doorbell rings and Sue jumps up to answer it. From then on there is a steady stream of visitors, friends of Roland and Sue, students and young people. They crowd around Mum, sitting on the floor, drinking glasses of wine.

"What's the situation like in South Africa?" They fire questions at Mum. "Why did you leave?"

"How long is your husband in prison for?"

"When were you in prison?"

The questions go on and on. My stomach is in knots and I am white as a sheet, my hands are clenched and trembling as I hear another knock on the door.

This is not safe, why is Mum answering their questions? Perhaps we are being watched. The people here don't understand that this is a dangerous situation. Perhaps the police will raid the flat. I feel sick. More people arrive.

"Mum, should we go now?" I ask, but Mum looks like she is enjoying herself and doesn't hear me. I am trapped.

Lynn and Charles fetch us at the weekend and take us to visit John at his Public School just outside Reading. We sit by the river in Sunningdale enjoying a pub lunch in the English country side. After lunch we meander down country lanes covered in autumn leaves and pose for photos that John takes to send to Dad.

Mum says, "We are altogether now as a family." She smiles and looks happy. Charles puts his arm around Lynn. I feel blank inside myself.

✳ ✳ ✳

I write a letter to my father. It is the first time I have written to him in six months. I write it out over and over. I change words and sentences. I don't want him to know that I am sad, that I want to die, I don't know how to live. I can't say anything that might upset him, he has enough worries and enough to make him sad. But I do want to write to him, so I change my letter over and over again until it feels right and I can send it to him. "Dear Mouldybaldly," I say. I tell him about Christmas and the snow and seeing

Gone with the Wind. I tell him I like my school with its no-uniforms and sexy headmaster. I tell him all about my holiday to Spain and France with Lynn and Charles and seeing Dali, an old man with a handle-brush moustache. I tell him that I like Charles my new rooinek brother-in-law. I write a short letter because of prison regulations. My sentences are telegraphic, the images jagged. I am glad to send my letter to him, I need him to know that everything is fine. Light and breezy.

✳ ✳ ✳

I can no longer experience anything directly or relate to what I see. Everything I see, hear, taste, touch or smell is unfamiliar and I need to translate it back to myself, to understand it. I filter it through what I can remember, the clear blue skies and mountains surrounding Cape Town, and the wild sea with waves crashing on white sand. Here everything is tamed and muted. The landscape is flat and dull and the smell of car fumes in London assaults my nose.

21

Hospital stories 2 – suicide

I dress myself for school. I enjoy wearing whatever I like to King Alfred's. We don't all look the same like we did at Westerford in our boring blazers and school ties and regulation shoes. I wear a long jersey that Granny knitted me. It's black and red and I wear it like a dress. Around my neck is a string of beads. My boots are black, knee-high and my tights are red. They show off my legs, my jersey barely covers my bottom. My black hair is long and my eyes are green. I look older than I am.

I stand at the bus stop on Hendon Way outside Esme's house pretending to go to school. When the bus arrives I climb upstairs and sit at the front of the bus.

Today I will kill myself. Today is the day. It is 1967 and suicide has just been made legal in England.

"Fares, please." The conductor asks me, "Where are you going, luv?"

I am directionless, I only have one destination in my mind: death. I pay my fare and sit on the bus until I get to the last stop where I get off and wander around aimlessly. I wander into a park and find a bench to sit on.

I have no set destination. I only have one aim in my mind, annihilation.

A man comes to sit beside me, he looks evil and hard, with a bullet-shaped head and no hair. He wears a suit. He wants me to take drugs, he tells me I will feel much better if I do. He says he gives them to a lot of young girls and he says it makes them feel so good. I don't want him to give me any. I am scared. Maybe he wants to have sex with me. I don't like him or trust him. I want to get away from him, so I get up and walk away and hope he won't follow me. I catch another bus, I don't know where it is going to. One place looks the same as another.

In my bag I have my own medicine, pills I have been saving up, all different kinds. When I go with Mum to visit her friends I look in their medicine chests and take pills. It doesn't feel like stealing, they have so many bottles of pills, they won't miss one. I collect small pills, big ones, white ones, pink ones and brightly coloured capsules.

I catch a bus into the West End. In the centre of the city I am completely anonymous as people rush past me. At a cinema in Piccadilly Circus they are showing a film with Bridget Bardot in it. I go in and buy a ticket.

After the film, I go to the toilet and take the pills one by one forcing them down my throat. I go and sit in a café and order a cup of coffee and the room swirls around, making me feel dizzy. I hear someone say, "She must be on drugs."

I pass out on the floor. When I wake up in hospital the police come to interview me. They want to know my name and address and ask if anyone forced me to take the pills.

Mum sits beside my bed looking calm as she strokes my hair. "How are you feeling? They want to keep you in for observation," she tells me.

※ ※ ※

I am sent to a psychiatric hospital, St. Luke's, in Muswell Hill. The grounds are beautiful, with green rolling lawns and colourful rhododendron bushes.

At first I am put in an open ward called Cardigan. Crystal's husband, Natie, comes to visit me and brings me chocolates. Crystal and he have moved to England with Paul and Evelyn. Natie laughs and says, "Why have they named this ward after a mad general who led all his men to death?" I don't know who Cardigan is. Natie tells me that Lord Cardigan led the charge of the Light Brigade at the Battle of Balaclava.

Half a league, half a league, half a league onward,
All in the Valley of Death rode the six hundred.

Sonya Bunting is also in exile, living in London with her family. She comes to see me and talks about how much she loves the seasons and the spring time in England. I think she is trying to make me feel better about being so far away from home.

The ward is quiet. Some of the women on the ward are having sleep treatment for depression. They are put to sleep and given insulin injections at regular intervals. The treatment usually lasts for two to three weeks.

I feel like I don't exist and that I never did. This is much worse than feeling depressed. I am dead – I just go through the motions of being alive, like a robot.

My black and white panda bear, Tiresias, lies on my bed. He is supposed to be a comforting presence.

I sit by myself in my hospital room and I want to die. Tiresias sits and stares at me. I pick him up. I want to smash through my numbness. Rage rushes through me, pushing this horrible emptiness out of me. I tear Tiresias apart. He was already dead, now I want to make him really dead, so that everyone can see he is dead. I rip off his arms and legs, I tear out his staring eyes, I pull out his stuffing, and he lies on the floor in a heap. I cry. I cover his body in rose petals and make a shrine for him.

Mum comes to visit me, she takes Tiresias to the doll's hospital. She spends a week's wages to have him mended. He comes back all sewn up with a scar down the middle of his tummy.

❊ ❊ ❊

David is a patient in the same ward as me, he is a manic depressive. He is older than me, he is twenty three and I am fourteen. He likes to come into my room and feel my breasts and kiss me with his tongue in my mouth. He wants to go all the way, but I won't let him. I can feel his penis bulging in his trousers as he presses up against me.

One evening we decide to run away. We are bored. "Let's go the West End, to a Club," I suggest. We tell the nurse we are just going up the road to the shop to buy cigarettes.

It is getting cold and dark. We walk up the road and stick out our thumbs as lorries and cars thunder by. A lorry stops for us, the driver says he is going to Birmingham, to drop off a load of celery at the market. It is late and I'm feeling hungry. I don't know when I will next have a meal so I munch on celery sticks. The smell and taste is overpowering. We stop at a garage and David wanders off. He has decided to hitchhike back to London.

I carry on travelling with the lorry driver, he wants to have sex with me, he offers me money, I say no. We stop for breakfast. I am very hungry. I can't face the thought of more celery and my stomach is protesting. The lorry driver buys me breakfast, a large plate of bacon, eggs, chips and fried bread, and a mug of tea with plenty of sugar. But now he will certainly expect me to have sex with him.

I go to the toilet and see a pay phone, I phone the police and tell them I have run away from hospital and I don't know where I am. I tell them the phone box says Weedon.

The police come to fetch me and take me back to hospital. Back at the hospital I have a bath. The doctor is worried that I might be pregnant, even when I say I haven't had sex, not with David or the lorry driver.

❊ ❊ ❊

I am moved out of the open ward into a locked ward, the acute psychotic ward in case I try to escape again. The Beatles 'Sergeant Pepper's Lonely Hearts Club Band' plays on the record player, loudly, over and over again.

In the centre of the day room is a table tennis table. Patients sit around relaxing and chatting. It could almost be a youth club. The patients call it a holiday club.

At the hospital, patients are given ECT, electromagnetic shock treatment, sleep treatment with insulin injections, lumbar punctures, EEG for measuring brain waves, group therapy, occupational therapy, anti-depressants and tranquilizers. These are the treatments on offer at the holiday club.

A patient lies in her bed. Normally you are not allowed to lie on your bed during the day, but she has a headache. She is recovering from shock treatment. For the rest of the week she wanders around in a daze, her short-term memory gone.

I stand by the door and watch as patients are prepared for their treatment. The patients are dressed in white cotton gowns tied at the back and then they are strapped down on the bed where electrodes are attached to their foreheads. A rubber guard is inserted into their mouths in case they bite their tongues off as they convulse when the electric current is applied.

I am sent for an electroencephalogram. Electrodes are attached to my head and I watch as my brain waves appear on a screen. They want to find out if I am normal. I have an I.Q. test. It is abnormally high.

I know I am not mad, only bad, misbehaved.

There is a system of punishment and reward that I refuse to buy into.

"If you listen to the doctors, they let you out of here sooner," the other patients tell me. But I am scared of the outside world and I don't want to leave the hospital.

"When you are better you can go home," they tell me.

"Better than what?" I want to know, I can only be who I am.

※ ※ ※

Three times a week a nurse takes me on the bus to the Middlesex Hospital in the centre of London to see a Child Psychiatrist. The psychiatrist asks me questions. She asks me how I feel and sits motionless with a blank face when I tell her things about myself. I am not sure what I am supposed to tell her. I don't know what she is thinking.

On the way back to the hospital, I wait at the bus stop with the nurse for what seems hours, smelling the exhaust fumes of the cars and lorries. It is my first winter in London and it is icy cold. The cold and damp eat into my bones. My feet ache, my jaw aches from the cold. I am numb.

I go into an Off Licence and buy a bottle of brandy to keep me warm and sit on top of the bus drinking straight from the bottle. I talk loudly and the young student nurse gets very embarrassed. She doesn't know what to do with me.

The next morning, when I wake up in the hospital everything is transformed. For the first time in my life I see snow. The snow has covered the hospital grounds and created a fairy-tale scene. The world looks new and magical. Excited, I rush out barefoot into the snow. The cold snow hurts my feet and I am surprised. From inside, the snow looked so soft and inviting, like cotton wool.

In the evenings after work, Mum comes to visit me. She trudges through the snow and the slush to the hospital. We sit in silence. I don't exist. I have nothing to say.

Mum buys a house nearby the hospital so she can visit me more often. At weekends, Lynn comes to take me out.

❋ ❋ ❋

Sarah is George, she binds her breasts tightly – she refuses to have breasts. She cuts her hair very short and wears boys' pyjamas and will not answer to the name of Sarah.

"My aunt has a cat who barks," Sarah/George tells me. "The cat is really an Alsatian dog, we call her Prince."

"When I grow up, I want to marry a girl like you," Sarah/George says as s/he strokes my hair. He is more George than Sarah and this is how I start to see him. He wants me to buy him bandages to bind his breasts when I go out. For George, bandages to bind his breasts flat are illegal. The doctors have refused to let him use them. The doctors and nurses are determined that he will be a girl. He doesn't get dressed for a year because all they offer him to wear are dresses. We are the same age.

Margaret sits motionless on a chair. For months she has been sitting, frozen. Her limbs are wasting away and her skin is dry and flaking. A nurse sits with her all day. Tubes are inserted through her nose to force feed her. The nurses don't speak to her as they watch her and she never responds, not even by a flicker of her eyes. They say she is catatonic.

Every day, when her nurses take a break and leave her alone, I go into her room to say hello and to talk to her. She is a good listener and I am bored, I have nothing to do. I do not accept the labels the doctors and nurses use. I talk to the Margaret beyond the doctor's labels. It makes perfect sense to me that Margaret sits frozen in time and space, it is the perfect survival tactic.

I fetch two bowls of soup, one for me and one for Margaret and spoon soup into her mouth. Margaret whispers a greeting to me later on as I walk past her room. I never hear her talk to anyone else or eat the food the nurses try to offer her. I don't tell the nurses she has had some soup in case they put pressure on her to eat.

Mr. Biggerstaff has a large bulbous red nose covered in broken purple veins and pale, sad eyes. He spends his days shuffling around silently. It is one o'clock in the morning and he cannot sleep, his room has burst into flames and there are bugs crawling over his bed and down the walls, every inch of the floor is covered with bugs. It is the same every night. He cannot sleep when he gets the DTs.

I also cannot sleep. My system has grown immune to the double dose of barbiturates I am given each night, two at bed time and then another two when I wake up in the middle of the night. Sometimes they inject me and then I pass out.

I go into Mr.Biggerstaff's room and he cowers in the corner. "Don't worry," I tell him. "I will protect you, I am Zeus's granddaughter, and he is the god of Thunder and Lightning." I have been reading Greek myths.

The next morning in Group Therapy Mr. Biggerstaff tells everyone I am completely mad. His silent lethargy is gone and he becomes talkative and animated as he tells the other patients how crazy I am.

22

Hospital stories 2, continued

I cannot be contained by the hospital. When I am locked in I hurl myself against the door until it gives way. I smash the windows and tear the curtains and sheets to shreds. I throw whatever can be thrown and still I feel nothing. I am numb.

I cut my arms and the doctor stitches me up. I tear out the stitches and cut deeper till I reach the fatty tissue and still I feel numb. The physical pain reminds me I might still be alive, a real person might inhabit this body. I will do anything to take away this dead, numb feeling.

In the middle of the night, I run up and down the corridor, screaming, while the other patients sleep. The nurses hold on to me but I won't keep still or stop screaming. The nurse slaps me hard while the other nurse prepares the injection, they hold me down. I feel terror and complete powerlessness as the needle is injected into my arm. The drugs start taking effect. I try to fight but my energy drains out of my body. I cannot move my arms or legs or lift my head. I black out.

All my time and energy goes into wishing I wasn't here. I know I am not ill and refuse all labels and medication. I will take full responsibility for my bad behaviour and make my own choices. My madness is me, it belongs to me. I trust the logic of my craziness.

"There is melody in my madness," I sing to myself.

※ ※ ※

A new patient has been admitted to the hospital. Robert wears a long white flowing nightdress and hides behind the bushes. He jumps out and gives the Matron a fright as she does the ward rounds at night – Matron in her blue uniform with a crisp starched apron and the little hat perched on top of her head, her watch pinned to her breast. She wears nylon stockings with sensible shoes that don't make a noise.

Robert's intense brown eyes stare watchfully and miss nothing as he keeps his own truth and does things differently. He challenges what is boring and mundane and is ready to run for his life, to run from pain and to take his own life if necessary. He is ready to run to the edge.

Robert lives in a basement where he skips and dances across huge colourful canvases.

I understand the way he thinks.

In the ward kitchen, he is allowed to cook spicy curries, a change from the bland hospital food. Robert and I spend our time together covering sheet after sheet with drawings and paintings.

I fall in love. I understand Robert's moods when he suddenly switches and disappears behind his eyes. He is twice my age and he moves gracefully through my life. He is tall, lean and hard-edged and never sentimental. Our relationship does not taste sweet.

If you are well enough you are allowed out of the hospital grounds. The pints in the pub in the evening take the edge off our madness, the Guinness we drink is dark and bitter. The Strongbow cider in the woods in the afternoons tastes sweet.

Every afternoon, we walk to nearby High Gate Woods to drink. We lie in a secret place, on the leaves under the trees by the railway line, hidden behind the bushes. As we lie there, I sense a shift in Robert's mood.

He lies on top of me and I pull down my pants. He is inside me moving up and down, in and out. Before he comes he withdraws and ejaculates outside of me.

This is the first time I have sex. My first time and I am not sure what has happened. I don't feel anything, just slightly painful and uncomfortable, that's all. Is that it, is this what my mother warned me about, I ask myself. There is nothing much to it, so what is all the big fuss about, the fuss about being a virgin or not a virgin?

That evening we go to the pub, I drink pints of beer and I go and vomit in the alley at the back of the pub. Then we go back to the hospital where I do a striptease in the ward.

※ ※ ※

Something different is happening. I find I can say "I" to myself and "me" to myself. Being in love has given me back my "I" and my "me". Love has given me a reason for being alive and life begins to feel that it may be worth living. Robert is allowed to go home. The doctor puts me on the pill and when I am at home for the weekend Mum lets me stay the night with Robert.

Then Robert disappears. I don't know where he is.

Later I find out he has gone to stay in a therapeutic community to journey through his madness. In the hospital they want to take his madness away from him with drugs. But Robert wants to claim his madness and use it for his healing. That is what he says to me when I ask him where he was.

Everywhere I go, I imagine that I catch a glimpse of Robert. I walk up and down his road hoping to see him. But he is gone.

* * *

The ritual of taking an overdose has become an obsession, a habit, an addiction. I cannot help myself. Although my will to die is not as strong any more, I still need the ritual, the build-up to dying and the coming round again, the ritual of playing with death.

The ritual is satisfying. It begins with planning and setting a time and deciding on a method. Once that is settled, I can start saying my goodbyes. Then the world no longer feels so painfully empty and void, the separation between me and the world closes. The numbness I usually feel changes to openness and the colours around me become intense instead of the usual flatness around me. I realize I love the world and its beauty as I say my goodbyes.

After tomorrow or next week, the big bustling city full of people will disappear and I will disappear. I feel love for the people around me and this city and also a feeling of great relief that I am leaving.

* * *

The hospital has allowed me to go home for the weekend. Mum has agreed to supervise me. The nurse gives me enough medication for the weekend, sleeping pills, tranquilizers and anti-depressants. It is Friday morning and Mum is at work when the next-door neighbour gives me the key to the house. I let myself in, there is no one at home.

I switch on the gas oven but do not light it. I have been saving up my medication. I want to take an overdose and put my head in the oven as well. One by one, I swallow the pills between gulps of water. I put my head in the oven and breathe in the cold gas. I know it won't be long before I pass out and if any one finds me before the gas kills me, the pills will still have time to kill me. No one will guess that I have also taken an overdose, they will not think to give me a stomach pump. Also, I cannot change my mind halfway before the gas takes effect because I will have passed out. This time I know it will work, I will be dead.

Mum is due home at six and it is only eight in the morning, which gives me ten hours for the gas and the pills to work.

But something tells Mum she must go home early, she leaves work at lunchtime and goes home. She sees me with my head in the oven and calls the ambulance. My carefully laid plans were not so fool proof after all. I surface in the general hospital, I am still here, and feel happy to be alive. I do not know why it is different this time to all the other times. I surprise myself by my reaction.

The taste of the bitter pills I forced down my throat by the handful comes back, mingled with the acrid taste of bile and vomit from my stomach pump. My throat has been rubbed raw from the plastic tube threaded down it.

The psychiatrist sits by my bed. Calmly, and with great authority in my voice, I tell her to leave the room. I am tired of talking. I am tired of psychiatrists asking me how I am feeling.

She listens to me and gets up and leaves. I have my own room, a privilege that comes with being badly behaved. A nurse sits at my bedside twenty-four hours a day, guarding me.

The barbiturates have poisoned my body and in spite of the stomach pump the drugs are still in my body, affecting my nervous system. I am not conscious of what I am doing. I am told I ran naked and screaming through the men's ward, but I don't remember doing so.

When I try to light a cigarette my co-ordination does not work, I cannot focus, the match goes past the cigarette and I cannot manage to get the cigarette into my mouth. I try again and the cigarette goes in the direction of my ear. The nurse sits beside my bed and helps me put the cigarette in my mouth. She waits until I inhale, then takes the cigarette out of my mouth and puts it back in again. She feeds me and puts a bedpan under me.

The nurse leaves the room and I look in the small storage room behind my room. In the room are stored bedpans, bandages, syringes, sterile gloves, bed linen and a bottle of bright red pills. I cannot believe my luck that someone has left a bottle of pills unattended.

I could take those lethal looking red pills one by one and annihilate myself. Nobody will find them if I hide them away.

I hear the nurse's footsteps coming down the corridor, I will have to leave the red pills until later. The nurse spoons food into my mouth, I still cannot co-ordinate well enough to get the spoon from the bowl into my mouth. I haven't thought about how I am going to get the pills out of the bottle and into my mouth

The nurse is young and pretty, her hair is scraped back into a bun beneath her nurse's cap. Her uniform is crisp and starched. I could happily lay my head down on her starched breasts and be rocked to sleep. She feeds me bland, soft food: mashed potatoes, jelly, and custard.

I feel nauseous and vomit up my food, bright red chunks of jelly in a yellow liquid. The nurse cleans me and gently wipes my mouth with a warm damp cloth. My mouth has a bitter unclean taste and I ask for some water to rinse my mouth. The nurse brings me a glass and a bright red pill from the jar in the back room. I put the pill in the water and it fizzes and turns the water pink.

Those red pills are mouthwash pills. I would have been foaming at the mouth if I had swallowed them all.

＊ ＊ ＊

After I have been in hospital for a year, they decide to send me home. I have overstayed my welcome, other patients have come and gone and been readmitted, but I just stayed put. They don't know what to do about me. They tried their best and still I am not better. I am a hopeless case and there is nothing more they can do for me. If I fall off the edge in future, I must go to Friern Barnet, the Loony Bin for Hopeless Cases. I am more trouble than I am worth and they discharge me.

I don't care. I can't feel and I don't care. The earth must swallow me up. I want to sink down into the road, merge with it and disappear.

＊ ＊ ＊

I am sent to school. My class mates are two years younger than me. I have a lot of catching up to do and I struggle to keep up. I can't do Maths and I haven't got a clue about History – I don't know about the kings and the queens, the Vikings and the Anglo Saxons and the battle of Hastings. I only know about the Voortrekkers and the Boers and the Brits. I live on a different planet from my class mates. I struggle to get up in the mornings and to fit in at school.

At night, I dream no one can see me, my class mates look right through me, they look past me as if I don't exist.

It is late at night. I sit on the banks of the river Thames and I want to jump into the water and sink to the bottom. This city makes me feel invisible. I start to scream. I don't have the courage to jump in – the water looks menacing. I take out my razor blade and I cut my arms. I am lighter, I can connect to myself as the razor blade slices through my flesh and the blood starts to flow. A policeman finds me, but I refuse to give him my name and address.

23

Hospital Stories 3 –
Friern Barnet Asylum for the hopelessly insane

The police take me to Friern Barnet, a big old Victorian mental hospital. It is huge and sprawling with high walls. The large imposing gates are unlocked and I am taken to be examined. The doctor sews up the gashes on my arms. This is the hospital for the hopelessly insane, driven mad by too much of the world's craziness, the craziness of cutting and failed suicide attempts and of hallucinations, voices in the head and delusions of grandeur and guilt, terrible overwhelming guilt.

It is past midnight, when the nurse takes me to the ward. We walk down long underground corridors that are dimly lit. The ward smells of urine and stale cabbages. All the patients are sleeping, heavily sedated, except for one woman who walks up and down all night, wailing and screaming, repeating the same incoherent phrase over and over again. I find it disturbing. She mirrors what I am feeling inside myself and keeps me awake.

All night long, I lie awake. They have not given me any sleeping pills. My body disappears along with my name and anything else that might identify me. All I feel is complete darkness, but the darkness does not stay still, it rolls and heaves like waves.

In the morning, I find out that the woman in the next bed died in the night I wonder if the rolling darkness was her death, filtering through me by osmosis.

The ward is a mixture of geriatric patients who need feeding and bathing, and disturbed, psychotic patients, and in the morning it is in full swing. A woman runs up and down, screaming, fights break out. In the corner another woman squats on the floor and pees. Other patients sit and watch television all day, drugged and passive. This is the end of the road. Patients have been here ten, twenty, or thirty years, I learn, unable to function in the outside world.

The doctor wants to give me a lumbar puncture, he wants to insert a needle in my spine to draw some fluid out to see if I am brain damaged. Mum won't allow the doctor to give me a lumbar puncture, it is not altogether safe. If the needle is inserted incorrectly it can do permanent damage.

The food is terrible, inedible. We are served cold, greasy plates of food and given spoons to eat with. They don't trust us with knives and forks.

The food does not look clean, there are lumps of fat and gristle floating in grey water. I live on a diet of the milk, bananas and peanuts I buy from the hospital shop.

I make friends with a young woman who has been transferred from prison. She says the food in this hospital is much worse than the food in prison. We are allowed out into the grounds where we sit under a big old tree. The grounds are spacious and beautiful – we could be sitting in a hotel if the food was not so bad.

In this place, the men and women are kept separate and they put bromide in the tea to dampen our libidos. Soon after I arrive here I go outside to walk in the grounds. It gets dark and I can't find my way back to the ward. A man starts walking beside me, he has been a patient here for seven years. He wants to put his hand up my dress and down my knickers. I am scared and I push his hand away. The grounds are deserted and there is no one else in sight. I don't know where I am, I walk fast, but I keep going down the wrong paths. The man keeps saying over and over that I need a good fuck. He doesn't speak properly and pronounces words strangely, he slurs with the habitual slur of inmates who are drugged. I see a nurse in the distance and run to her, she takes me back to my ward where I am locked up for the night.

※ ※ ※

Madness provides me with a certain amount of freedom and I have time to explore my creativity. In the grounds of the hospital is a huge old barn. Birds fly in and out, and there are large tables with lots of paper and paints and crayons. All day I draw and paint my way through to the other side of the pain and alienation I feel. My drawings are colourful and harmonious, in sharp contrast to the turmoil and chaotic emotions I am experiencing.

I have had two choices: one, to go mad, and two, to die, but it seems I cannot deliberately go crazy – either it happens unexpectedly or not at all. I have tried hard at the second choice but have not succeeded. I am trapped in no-man's land neither crazy nor dead.

However hard I try, I can't destroy myself. I am still here, in spite of my best intentions. I tried madness and at first it was an escape, a welcome relief from my feelings of unreality. It used to feel good when I left my body but now it is tedious, it drains me to drag my empty body around. It is time to make another choice, a different choice.

I have a right to be alive, I tell myself. *My mother brought me into the world, she gave birth to me. That means I have a right to take up space on this earth, to live and to breathe.*

I am trying hard to convince myself that I am allowed to live and to be a real person. Most of the time, I just pretend to be a person. At worst, I am evil. At best, I am an annoying black dot, floating about, disconnected from reality.

✳ ✳ ✳

I am discharged from hospital so I don't have nurses watching me day and night any more. I go and see the doctor on the main road, he doesn't know me. I sit in the waiting room and fill out the forms with a false name and address and lie about my age and occupation. It is easy to lie and sign a false name. I tell the doctor I can't sleep at night and he writes me a prescription for strong, lethal Nembutal.

The chemist hands me my brightly coloured pills. I stash them away carefully, there are enough to kill myself. I decide to try out a few to test their strength so I take three Nembutal and catch the bus into town. I stumble around with my vision blurred and my limbs unco-ordinated, my speech slurring. It is like being drunk – the same unco-ordinated slurring and being out of control, falling about with blurred vision. I feel like I have been hit over the head with a sledge hammer, but I like the relief it brings from the vacuum I feel.

I pass the offices where Ethel, an old friend of the family works. Her brother was in jail with Dad. I go and say hello. Ethel makes me a cup of coffee and asks me questions. She watches as I try to lift my coffee cup and get it to my mouth with shaking hands that don't do what they need to do. She is talking to me, saying something about when she was young. She says, "Hang on in there," and offers me a cigarette. "I will get you a taxi home," she says.

That night, last thing before I go to sleep, I swallow the rest of the Nembutal. I know it won't be enough to kill me, that I will wake up the next morning. I don't want to die this time, but I must go through the ritual of self-destruction one last time.

For the last time, I will poison my body. I watch carefully as the familiar drama unfolds. I will not do this again, ever.

After this, I will accept the fact that I am alive.

✳ ✳ ✳

I have turned sixteen and for the past four years, since I was twelve, I have questioned waking up in the morning. Always at the back of my mind were thoughts of death, but now I glimpse other possibilities.

I realise in order to feel happy, I must allow myself to feel unhappy. However deeply I allow myself to feel sadness, is how deeply I will be able to feel joy.

I imagine my hair growing into branches, plants and flowers. I dream that I grow into a tree, strong and beautiful. I can feel each leaf of my tree-self growing and my roots reaching down into the ground. I realise I can make a decision, and the decision is very simple. I can fully accept the fact that I am alive.

Me, aged four, with Johnny. Newlands Forest, Cape Town

Pictures taken during the State of Emergency in South Africa in 1960

Me, aged seven, with Lynn and Johnny

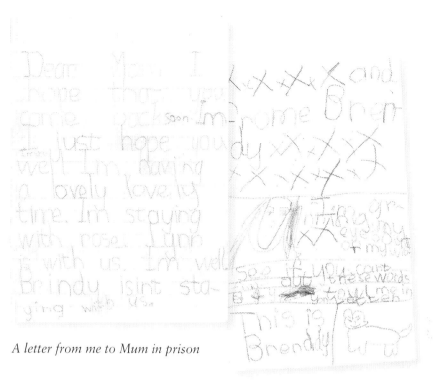

A letter from me to Mum in prison

Me at Goodhope Seminary School for Girls, Cape Town

Mount Pleasant.
Organjezicht, Cape Town

Me, aged ten, at Girl
Guide Camp

Me, aged 12, with Johnny,
Mum and Lynn at Mount
Pleasant after Dad was
arrested in 1965.

Me, aged 14, with
Mum. I was just out of
hospital and carrying
my book of poems. The
photograph was taken
by a street photographer
in Cape Town.

Pictures of me, aged fourteen, leaving South Africa for the United Kingdom

ABOVE LEFT *Me, with my friend Tessa, just before I flew*

ABOVE RIGHT *Me, with my teddy bear, Tiresias, and Mum at Cape Town airport*

*Me, aged 15,
on holiday in
Rimini, Italy*

Me, aged 14, at Aunty Bess' house in Hampstead Gardens in London

TOP *Me, aged 16, in our house in Annington Road, North London*
ABOVE *Me, aged fifteen, at Lynn's wedding in London*

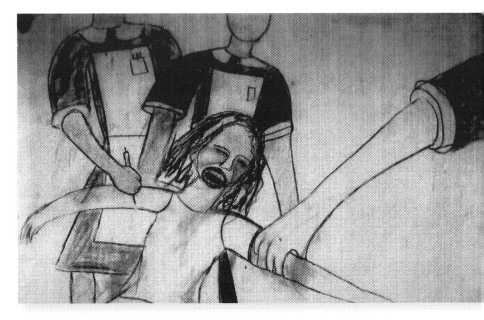

In hospital

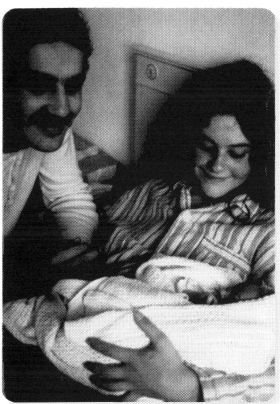

Me, aged twenty two, with Samson and Daniel in North London

Dartington Art College in Devon

Self portrait taken with a pinhole camera at Dartington

Dressing up at Dartington College

Me, in the centre, in Totnes High Street demonstrating against Apartheid in 198

My first solo art exhibition in Totnes in 1983

Me, taking the boat to Robben Island, where I was an artist in residence in 1997

Me, with fellow artists in residence, outside my house in Lighthouse Road, Robben Island

Lynn and Lionel's wedding at Suikerbossie, Hout Bay, Cape Town in 1999
(left to right)
Me, Nomvula (John's mother-in-law), Dad, Sipho (my nephew), Lynn, Lionel (Lynn's husband), Mum, Ntombi (my sister-in-law), John, Busi (my niece)

Me, with Mum and Dad, in Hout Bay harbour in 1997

TOP *The pre-school on Robben Island*

ABOVE *Me, with the pre-school children and colleagues, in 2000*

24

Samson

Barefoot, precarious, I walk on the wall, carefully putting one foot in front of the other, stretching out my arms to keep my balance. They have turned me loose from the lunatic asylum after two years and I am living with Mum in Fortis Green in North London. The scars on my arms are still raw red gashes.

A young man walks by looking like a friendly pirate with his wild curly black hair and bushy beard and rosy cheeks. He wears Wellington boots and a duffel coat. We smile at each other.

"I am an unemployed poet," he tells me, and I am suitably impressed.

"I am also unemployed," I tell him.

His name is Samson and he goes home and writes a poem for me.

I like ladies who walk on walls
Sometimes they walk in my dreams…

I buy packets of stars, red, yellow, blue, gold and silver and stick them on my wall in a circle until my wall is filled with stars. In the centre of the stars I put Samson's poem.

We are neighbours, just a stone's throw from one another. Samson comes by my house to ask me if I would like to join his political group. He tells me it's an anti-imperialist organisation, Tri-Continental, with its headquarters in Havana. Of course I want to join his group. I also want to be British and speak with a British accent like Samson's, a North London accent with a working class twang. I copy Samson, he is my role model. Later I learn that Samson is not British, he is Turkish, but for now I don't know the difference.

"Your friend is outside," Mum calls out to me. I look out of the window and see Samson standing outside playing his guitar as he serenades me.

On Saturday mornings, Samson calls for me and we go and sell Cuban newspapers outside Sainsburys, the local supermarket. The paper tells of the bumper sugar harvest in Cuba. The Saturday shoppers don't seem very interested in Cuba's sugar harvest and sales are slow.

During the week, we hold anti-imperialist meetings. We are rebels with a cause, we will save the world.

When it is time for our Annual General Meeting, a busload of miners comes to stay for the weekend. They sleep in rows on our living room floor. In the morning Mum opens the door and is surprised to see so many people.

I cook the men a big pot of porridge before we leave for the meeting.

I learn that Samson is Turkish, that he comes from Cyprus, a country that was at war, where soldiers moved into his home and he had to flee into the city with his family. There was no food to eat, only chaos. The Red Cross helped transport the woman and children out of the country, but the men were kept behind as hostages. Samson's mum did not know if his father was alive or dead. All her life his mum had led a protected, sheltered life – first her family protected her and then her husband. Her marriage was arranged when she was fourteen years old. By the age of seventeen she was married and by nineteen she had two sons. When she came to London, she arrived on her own with two children. She had to survive and earn a living in a strange country At school Samson and his brother were teased – they were foreigners, dark haired with strange names. They soon Anglicised their names and learned to fight.

Samson is like a big brother to me, he protects me. Mum trusts him to look after me and to see that I don't take drugs and that I get home safely at night. Samson understands that life can be turned upside-down overnight, that there is no such thing as safety. It is possible to lose everything in a flash – your home, your friends and your family. My British friends don't understand, they have lived all their lives in the same safe and predictable country where the police don't carry guns.

25
A suitable profession

In the summer of 1968, Lynn gets married to Charles. They have a Quaker wedding. Lynn dresses in a daring red velvet dress with a miniskirt. I dress all in white for the wedding. Lynn and Charles buy a house near Hampstead Heath and I visit them often, walking from East Finchley through the woods at Kenwood and across the Heath, past the ponds to their house. Charles always asks me how I am and if I am feeling depressed.

Johnny brings friends home from his public school on weekends and holidays. James stays with us often, his family are far away in America and he becomes part of our family. He falls in love with me.

Mum makes a home for us: gathering the family together again, and cooking large pots of spaghetti bolognese and savoury rice to feed us all. Even when the cupboards are empty Mum makes big pots of food out of nothing.

The miners go on strike and the Prime Minister, Edward Heath, declares a three-day week with power cuts to conserve energy. At home in the evenings it is cosy as we sit together in the dark playing cards by candle light.

At the end of the school year, Johnny leaves school and moves back home and James goes back to America.

❊ ❊ ❊

I want to go to Art College, but I am told, "You will never earn a living as an artist, you are good with children, and you should train as a Nursery Nurse. It is a nice job for a girl. You can do art as a hobby."

Mum thinks that at Art College the students take drugs and sleep around, and will be a bad influence on me.

At school I was never good at art, I found art classes boring and would try to skip them. To be good you had to be able to draw pictures that looked real and mine never did. Teachers said my drawings were clumsy and inadequate. But I loved drawing and at school I doodled and daydreamed, covering all my books with strange pictures. "This is modern art," I told my classmates as I passed my drawings around, joking and playing the clown.

The only artists who ever make it, I am told, are the really good ones, the ones who are born geniuses and can draw properly, and that is very rare, and practically never happens, and clearly I am not a genius.

I spend whole afternoons looking at art books. When I look at Kandinsky's work, I feel like I am travelling through space, the movement and shapes and colours in his work deep inside me. I relate to Picasso's disjointed and multi-faced paintings of women. These are real artists, in books, but their pictures do not look realistic, they come from their imagination. I take courage from looking at their work.

In my bedroom I have a long wooden trestle table, boxes of coloured pastels and sheets of paper. I draw and paint and then I pin my drawings on the wall so I can see them first thing in the morning when I wake up. I look at my drawings in the mirror and I see them better when I look at their reflections than when I am looking directly at the page. I make collages and assemble pictures in boxes. I work from what is inside me and wait for the images to appear on the page. I draw suns with faces and flowers with petals like sun rays. I draw because I need to keep my sanity, I need to keep the feeling of hollow emptiness at bay. Most days I draw.

Sylvia Plath is my favourite poet, at night in my dream I hear lines from her poem: A voice asks me what will happen when

> *The balled*
> *Pulp of your heart*
> *Confronts its small*
> *Mill of silence.*

In answer to the question I fall into a deep hole, an endless void, and feel a profound sense of peace.

※ ※ ※

I start my Nursery Nurse Course at Barnet College and work in a council day nursery for three days a week. The other two days I spend studying the theory of child care and learning how to cook and sew. I am not confident or articulate and can barely string two sentences together. My writing skills are almost non-existent and I have private English lessons to help me construct sentences and put them in paragraphs.

At home I draw and paint and at college I draw all over my note books. My bedroom floor is covered in piles of comics and I spend my time reading Marvel comics about Superheroes and their Super Powers. The Hulk is my favourite. When he is angry he changes from a normal person into the strongest man on earth. He can defeat the entire U.S.A. army singlehanded, but really, he just wants to be loved and understood. He is not a bad person.

I dress up as a Superhero in red tights and a cape with stars in my hair. I call myself Infra-Red and go out for the night.

In the mornings I wake up early to catch the double-decker bus to work and I sit upstairs smoking.

※ ※ ※

In the council nursery, the student nursery nurses wear pink overalls and the staff nursery nurses wear blue overalls. Matron has a special bone-china tea set brought to her office on a tray with a lace doily when it is tea time. At lunch time, when the children are sleeping, we sit around a large oval table with Matron at the head and the deputy matron at the other end. We say grace and then the student nursery nurses serve the staff before sitting down to eat.

On Mondays, we eat roast lamb with mint sauce and Yorkshire pudding and roast potatoes and two veg followed by steamed pudding – Spotted Dick and custard. Once a week we have Spam baked in tinned tomatoes and on Fridays we have fish and chips and jelly and ice cream.

The student nursery nurses start off working in the baby room. My job is to take the bucket of dirty nappies to the sluice room to rinse off, and then I boil the nappies in a big metal boiler. I take the steaming nappies out with tongs and put them in the spinner and hang them up to dry.

I put the babies on their potties at regular intervals and sing to them to keep them amused and to stop them straying from their potties.

After a while, I graduate to working with the bigger children. I don't like it when the children cry so I let them have their own way. I just like to play with them, I don't like to tell them what to do. One of the children won't eat. The child cries, she vomits out her food. The staff nurse in charge forces her to eat. Relentlessly the nurse spoons the food and vomit back into the child's mouth, she is determined the child will eat. A battle of wills ensues. I want to challenge the staff nurse but I am just a young student and I don't have any authority. I don't have the confidence or experience to challenge what I see. I look the other way.

※ ※ ※

Samson comes to visit. He reads his poems to us and plays guitar and makes us laugh. I run my hands through his thick, curly hair.

Samson has decided to stand for the local elections. He calls himself the 'All Night Party' and promises to give us everything we want. We can all have houses, cars and washing machines if we vote for him.

Samson and I become best friends and see each other most days. We visit the British Museum together, the day has a magical quality. We are in perfect harmony with each other and can read each other's minds. At the British Museum we enter the room where the statues of Buddha are kept. I see a tall Buddha with his palm outstretched and I place a penny in his open hand.

26
Drugs sex and rock 'n' roll

Samson thinks I am a sweet, innocent, virgin. The promiscuity of the 60s culture shocks him. He thinks I am different, that I have kept myself pure.

I discover hallucinogenic drugs, LSD and mescaline and I spin like a whirling dervish, spiralling out of control. Round and round and round I go, spinning faster and faster until my feet leave the ground and I am plummeted into outer space and the far reaches of the galaxy, with Dr. Strange and his magic orb, his all-seeing eye.

Back on earth Hulk rips the place apart, someone has offended him, but Hulk just wants to be loved. Roll another joint, just like the other one. I inhale deeply, inhale the sacred smoke deep into my lungs and float upwards. My senses are alert and the music plays deep inside of me.

People and events swirl in and out and make different patterns and colours in my mind.

I get the munchies and eat whatever I can get my hands on, I eat mountains of toasted cheese sandwiches and bars of chocolate, my taste buds are on high alert. And then I discover the perfect yin yang of brown rice and tamari and there is no looking back, I am eating my way to macrobiotic heaven.

I drop another acid tab and it is up, up, up and far away. I'm sweet sixteen and love is free and easy, I am on the pill, possessiveness, monogamy and marriage are outdated and oppressive. If you can't be with the one you love, love the one you're with and that goes for any one, friend or complete stranger. Anything goes and no one says no.

I walk down the street, stoned. Two young men pull up beside me in a car. "You want to come for a ride?" they ask. Why not? I have never seen them before but I am open to anything. They look like fun.

"You want to come back to our place?" one of them asks.

John works as a croupier in a casino, his friend is blond with a baby soft beard and blue eyes. He is slightly bewildered, quiet and shy. John and he share a room, a bedsit in Palmers Green.

The three of us lie on the bed entangled. John looks at his watch, he will be late for work. He gets dressed in black jacket, bow tie and white shirt, and goes out. The young man and I finish what we began. I leave and get the bus home.

❋ ❋ ❋

I meet Walter at a party. He is tall with a thin brown body and an Afro piled high on his head. He is also from South Africa but we don't talk about that. He lives with Stewart in Notting Hill Gate. Stewart is a heroin user, he stopped for a while, but now he is using again. He is strict about his diet and eats macrobiotic food, balancing out his yin and his yang.

A woman comes in and out of the house, as pale as a ghost. She is the drug dealer. I do not trust her. With the energy of a junky she sneaks in and out, her presence more of an absence than somebody real and solid.

Cherry, a young American woman is staying with Walter and Stewart. She lives on nothing but yoghurt.

We lie in bed together, naked, Cherry and Walter and Stuart and I. Cherry is shy and squeamish, she has never done anything like this before but I think nothing of it as I take my clothes off and we all tumble together on the bed.

In the basement it is dark and there is a red candle burning. Walter sits cross-legged on the floor and rolls a joint – Durban poison from South Africa. The dope is strong and hallucinogenic. The wax drips down the sides of the candle, and makes strange shapes. As I watch the red wax drip down I am disturbed, I think it is blood dripping.

Upstairs Stuart injects himself. He has needles and cotton wool and surgical spirits and his room smells strongly medicinal. I cannot understand how he can be so fussy about his diet and then inject himself with heroin.

I am very fussy about the drugs I take, I don't want to become a drug addict and would never take heroin. Sometimes to numb myself out I take barbiturates but not very often. Mostly, I smoke a lot of dope or take hallucinogenics. I don't even like smoking dope, it makes me feel disorientated and paranoid.

❋ ❋ ❋

I lose track of the men who try to pick me up, the many men I fend off and the chance encounters at bus stops or walking down the road or sitting on a park bench. I long for closeness and touch, but love and pleasure evade me. I do not like having sex, I do not feel anything. I end up with too many empty encounters in dreary bedsits on mattresses on the floor with the sweet cloying smell of joss sticks masking the smell of unwashed bedding and bodies. But I keep hoping that maybe this time, with this man I might feel something.

❋ ❋ ❋

North London Polytechnic has live music on Friday nights. Kerry plays the lead guitar and Mike plays the drums – rhythm and blues. The place is pumping. During the break Mike tickles me and pours beer over my head. I am dripping wet and I laugh as I pour beer over his head too. Mike comes home with me and sleeps on the couch downstairs in the living room. I barely know him but my body responds with unexpected pleasure to his kisses. Mike is not predatory, he is playful and I relax and have fun with him.

We go out with a group of friends to see a movie. The night is ours; we are stoned, drunk and outrageous and ready for adventure. A Rolls Royce pulls up at the traffic lights; a symbol of affluence and class oppression. We surround the car, knocking on the windows and pulling faces, laughing hysterically before the car hastily pulls away.

We are young, we are invincible. In Crouch End we have a night full of magic sitting in strange rooms listening to music and smoking dope. Just before dawn we start the long walk home up Muswell Hill. A milkman stops to give us a ride on his electric milk float. Mike and I share a cold bottle of milk as we watch the sun come up – a perfect ending to a magic evening. Mike has the magic touch and I am in love, in lust, obsessed. For a week I think of nothing or no one else, but he doesn't return my calls.

Agitprop is a revolutionary theatre company. They take culture to the masses in the form of street theatre. The members of Agitprop all live together in a large rambling house in Muswell Hill. When I visit the Agitprop commune I never know what to expect. Life is theatre and they constantly push the boundaries of suburban normality. The men wear frocks and the women dress in workman's overalls.

※ ※ ※

James phones me from America and asks me to marry him. I don't know what to say to him. His parents send me a ticket so I can go and visit them for a six week holiday. It is their way of saying thank you to my Mum for looking after James when he was in England.

※ ※ ※

A few days before I get onto the plane, James is at a summer camp out in the wilds where he splits his knee open with an axe and has to be airlifted to hospital. When I see him he is on crutches with his leg in plaster.

His parents reluctantly agree to us sharing a room, but not on a Wednesday night because the cleaning lady comes early on a Thursday morning and she wouldn't understand. After spending the night with me, James wakes up itching and scratching. Agitprop Andy has given me the crabs and I have taken them to America to give to James. His mother is horrified and polite as she hands me powder to kill the crabs. We shave under our armpits and our pubic hair.

Something flies into my eye and my eye swells up, I cannot see out of it. It is painful and I wear an eye patch. James hobbles along on his crutches, we are the lame and the blind.

I love America, the land of plenty, the land of the free, the land of the Vietnam War and draft dodgers. All that summer we listen to James Taylor singing "Fire and Rain" and Country Joe and the Fish with "I-Feel-Like-I'm-Fixing'-To-Die-", the anti-Vietnam War Song.

I am seduced by affluence – big cars and colour TVs and houses with big fridges and freezers stocked with every kind of food you can think of: litres of milk, and bottles of orange juice, and tubs of different flavoured ice cream. In America you can eat all day and all night and still not run out of food.

At home, we have a small black and white TV and no car and no freezer and a small fridge that is stocked up once a week on a Friday when Mum gets paid.

In the autumn, I go back to London and James and I lose touch with each other. During the week I work at a primary school as part of my Nursery Nurse training. I spend the weekends dropping acid and tripping.

※ ※ ※

I sit on the ground in the sun and look up at the sky. The clouds turn into shapes and letters of the alphabet. I cannot make out what the writing says. The sky has been taken over by adverts, the multi-nationals are taking over the sky, they have stolen the sky and colonised it. Stolen my sky and God's sky to advertise their crap and try to promote their worthless consumer goods.

I look at the trees and see the branches curling into letters of the alphabet. I have taken pure acid in a sugar cube and I am tripping for days, and for days after that I continue to have flashbacks.

※ ※ ※

One afternoon, I meet Nick in a park. He lives in a bed sit, he doesn't wash and he has no money for food. He wears a hearing aid and struggles to hear what is being said when he is in a room full of people talking. This makes him feel socially isolated. He makes friends with two guys who have come straight out of prison and they move in with him and steal everything he has. Every day he walks four miles to my house in time for supper, but Mum gets fed up with him, she thinks he is smelly and lazy.

Nick and I drop a tab of acid on a warm day towards the end of summer. I borrow Nick's hearing aid and turn up the volume and lie in the grass. I can hear the insects having conversations with each other. We walk through the graveyard and make love in the long grass. This is Nick's first time, he is a twenty-seven-year-old virgin.

We walk through woods holding hands. Bluebells carpet the ground, creating a haze of vivid blue. The scent of the flowers is like nectar. I kneel on the ground to look at a fairy-tale toadstool, red with white spots and watch the toadstool breathe in and out. The ground is also breathing and I watch the rise and fall of the earth's breath. The trees are breathing. Everything around me is in motion with the rhythm of the breath.

I keep very still, and then I notice lions and giraffes hiding behind the trees. They are friendly lions and look like cuddly toys.

❅ ❅ ❅

The Queens in Crouch End is a good place to score and get laid. I go there most nights. I meet Jack, the dealer from Glasgow there. He gives me some mescaline.

Mescaline is my favourite drug, it is gentler than acid. Acid is usually laced with speed and sometimes rat poison. I do not like the rush of speed.

On Saturday night, I go to visit Jack. He lives in a room down the road. Six of his friends share the small room with him, all young men from Glasgow. Everyone is tripping, each young man has a young woman with him. I lie on the mattresses on the floor listening to music. Jack looks at my pink paisley bellbottom trousers intently and so do I. The patterns swirl in kaleidoscope patterns. The colours have become intense.

Later in the week, I am having a drink at the Queens. It is closing time and Jack invites me to go and have a smoke with some friends. We sit in a circle and pass the joint around getting stoned. Jack and I go upstairs.

I lie under Jack wondering what on earth I am doing here. I do not feel a thing – I am profoundly bored and I am dead from the waist down. When will this finish? Why do I keep going to the same familiar, unsatisfying place repeatedly ending up with men I can't relate to? There is nothing I like about being there.

I grit my teeth and concentrate. Maybe, if I concentrate hard enough, I will feel a glimmer of pleasure. I wish this would end and Jack would get off me.

I wake up from my stoned passivity and realise I am not enjoying this. It's all déjà vu and repetition and I can't see any point in it. For the first time, it occurs to me that I have a choice and that I can say no to Jack, to all these men. I have been so passive it has never occurred to me before.

Jack wants to kiss me and to put his arm around me again. Next week, he tells me, he will be going to court on a drugs charge and he will probably be sent down for a few years for dealing. This is his last opportunity to be with a woman for a long time. But even after hearing his sorry story, I don't want him to touch me.

I walk home by myself and decide I want to be celibate. Perhaps I will become a nun and live out my days in a convent.

27
Dad comes home

Dad has served five years and nine months of his prison sentence and is coming home. The week before he gets out of prison I allow myself to miss him for the first time. When Dad was in prison I couldn't allow myself to miss him. Now that he is coming home the sadness of the last seven years catches up with me as feelings I have held at bay come to the surface.

When Dad comes out of prison, he is given twenty-four hours to leave the country and come and join us in England.

We get up very early in the morning to go and meet him at the airport. We wait for what seems like forever. Lynn holds a bottle of champagne, ready to pop the cork. I last saw Dad when I was a child standing waving to him from outside the barbed wire fence of the prison. I watch the passengers come through the gates pushing their trolleys but I do not see Dad in amongst them.

"Look, there is Dad," Lynn shouts.

"Where?" I scan the crowd. He is there, but I do not recognise him.

"There," Lynn points to a man with a bald head and round cheeks wearing glasses.

We all rush up to take it in turns to hug Dad. He hugs Mum for a very long time.

Lynn pours the champagne "Here is to your freedom." We raise our glasses and toast Dad before we walk to the car.

Dad has never been to England before. On the drive from the airport he looks out of the car window at the grey London day. We drive through suburbs where Dad sees row after row of terraced houses crowded together. Dad thinks these suburban streets are slums. He remembers a South African landscape of extremes of wealth and poverty, the wealthy white suburbs with plenty of space and gardens with swimming pools. He does not associate these drab semi-detached houses with middle-class comfort.

The world has changed, fashions have changed, and words have changed, while Dad's world has remained frozen in time. He does not know what the word discothèque means or duvet or mini-skirt. For the first time in his life Dad sees a television set.

At home, he opens and closes the front door repeatedly, and steps inside, outside, inside – and outside again. He switches the lights on and off, on and off. He takes such pleasure in these simple actions, enjoying the freedom and control he has not had for many years.

Crossing the road is more difficult and Dad feels like a baby as the cars whizz by, he has to relearn how to cross the road safely. Sometimes he says he wants to scream, the outside world is a bewildering place after being locked up and behind bars for so long.

We take Dad for a walk on Hampstead Heath. We find a pub and Dad drinks his first British pint – he hasn't had a drink in years. We enjoy seeing Dad's delight and amusement as he watches the young people in the pub, the girls in their mini -skirts and the boys with long hair and beards.

Dad makes a double bed out of pine for Mum and himself. He uses the skills he learnt in the carpentry workshop in prison. For the first time in years he sleeps in a double bed with a feather duvet. He lies next to Mum's warm body instead of by himself on a hard narrow bed with scratchy grey prison issue blankets.

Mum and Dad need time to adjust to each other again. They argue a lot. Dad wants to be the man of the house and Mum has got used to her independence.

I am also used to being me and living my life. I am a grown woman now with a job and a boyfriend. I have grown out of needing a father, I need to spread my wings and explore the world.

28
Samson and me

A large brown envelope arrives in the post. Inside the envelope are the names of the girls who have passed their Nursery Nurse exams. My name is on the list. I stare at it in disbelief. They must have made a mistake I think, and phone the College.

"There must be some mistake, my name is on the list of people who have passed."

"No, no mistake, you have passed, congratulations."

It isn't a mistake. After spending two years at Barnet College I am now a qualified Nursery Nurse. I am eighteen and free to leave home and head away from the big city.

※ ※ ※

The long summer of 1971 stretches ahead of me. I read Jack Kerouac's book, "On the Road", which inspires me and countless others to take to the open road.

I ask Samson if he wants to come with me. We head out to the nearest motorway in search of adventure and the meaning of life.

Together we hitchhike to Reading with a tent and two sleeping bags and spend the night drinking sweet cherry brandy and laughing before a friend shows us to the bedroom. In the middle of the room is a big double bed. I take my clothes off and climb into bed. I am not shy, Samson is my best friend. I am sleepy and Samson kisses me good night. I close my eyes and he puts his arms around me and gently strokes my body.

I am pleasantly surprised when our bodies merge and we cross the line from being just friends to being lovers.

The next day, we hitchhike to Cheddar Gorge, the home of Cheddar cheese, and meet up with Amy and Barry. They are also travelling the open road, with their small baby. We put up our tent in the field while Barry rolls a joint and Amy feeds the baby a jar of baby food. We are sitting around the camp fire smoking a joint when the farmer storms into the field and calls us "Bloody Gypos," and says, "Get off my land or I will get my shotgun and throw your baby onto the fire." We hastily pack up and Samson gets on the bus back to London and goes home to his Mum.

I hitch a lift to St. Ives and descend on St Ives with the usual influx of tourists. I join the Hippies camping in the woods for the summer months. The townspeople and all the other Straights call us Hippies, but we don't call ourselves that, we call ourselves Freaks.

St. Ives, with its pretty harbour and whitewashed houses and narrow streets has become an artists' colony. I love the winding streets and being near to the sea – after London the scale of the town is human and friendly.

We congregate at the harbour and spend our days getting stoned and dropping acid. In the evenings we go to the Light House, a Christian youth centre and they give us bread and soup. On Sundays we sing along with the Salvation Army, singing stoned and hallucinating – it's very moving. I run out of money. The weather is getting colder so I go back to London.

※ ※ ※

When I get back to London, Samson and I spend our days together. We become inseparable and can't even bear to be away from each other for just half an hour. We promise that we will never leave each other as we sit on a bench in the park kissing and holding hands, listening to the birds singing. The moment is perfect as Samson tells me he loves me. And I tell him I love him too.

He reaches over and slaps my face. It doesn't hurt.

"Why did you do that?" I ask him in surprise.

"Because I always wanted you to remember this perfect moment," Samson says, and we fall about laughing.

※ ※ ※

Samson lies in my single bed beneath the circle of stars with his poem in the middle, wearing my frilly nightie. My drawings are on the wall and my piles of comics are stacked on my bookshelf. We are playing, pretending to swap genders. I laugh at him. He looks so funny with his black beard and wild curly hair in my lacy nightdress.

"Do you like me as a woman?" Samson asks.

I put his cap and shirt on. "Would you like me if I was a man?" I lie next to Samson on my narrow single bed and kiss him.

"Would we still fall in love with each other?" I ask.

Mum knocks on the door and walks in. She glances at Samson lying in bed, half dressed.

"Hello Samson," she says matter-of-factly. "Are you staying for supper?"

"Yes, thank you," Samson says as he sits up in bed displaying the frills on my nightdress.

When Mum leaves the room, Samson and I get the giggles. "Won't your Mum be upset to catch me in your bed?" he asks.

"No, she thinks you are gay, she thinks I am safe with you. She asked me if you had a boyfriend."

* * *

Samson and I walk down the street holding hands. We walk past someone I know from the Queens. I smile at him and say hello.

"Did you sleep with him?" Samson wants to know.

"Yes," I say.

Samson is angry, he takes his hand out of mine. "You are a slag," he says.

"What's it to do with you? It's none of your business." I am angry. "How dare you call me names," I shout at him.

"Why did you shag my brother? He said you were a real goer."

Samson's brother works in a bank and is engaged to be married. I kissed him last year and his brother kissed and told Samson.

"I didn't shag him I yell!" I am angry that his brother is telling tales on me. *Smug bastard*, I think. I am caught up in the rivalry between Samson and his brother.

When we get back to Samson's house, I storm into his brother's room and write on the wall in big black letters. "Why did you say you shagged me and then call me a slag?"

Samson's mum locks me out of the house. She thinks I am a bad influence on her son. She tells Samson, "If you see her again, you are not my son any more."

"She is not coming in here again," she tells Samson.

Samson must choose between his mum and me. Beneath my stoned exterior I have a will of iron and nerves of steel and I drag Samson away from his mum.

When Samson's mum is out at work, Samson and I sneak back into the house but all the doors inside are locked tightly against me. I wait in the hallway while Samson packs his clothes. He moves in with me, into my room at home.

* * *

Samson and I have our daily routine, we stay in bed until 12 o'clock then walk down the road for the Chinese Lunch Special, a three-course lunch –

spring rolls, birds-nest soup, chop suey and banana fritters in syrup. We go back to bed and smoke a few joints and get the munchies. In the afternoon we buy yesterday's cream cakes for half price at the baker shop across the road. Then we buy extra cream to dip the cream cakes into.

We get a job in the same factory, the factory is a large bakery. My job is to wrap the bread puddings as they come off the conveyor belt and Samson's is to sweep the floor. We hold hands and kiss in the canteen during our breaks. The workers get half-price bread and cakes to take home. We are saving our money to go travelling.

After a few weeks, Samson's mum, makes peace with him. They are talking again. She doesn't want to lose her son. She unlocks the doors and I am invited for Sunday lunch. The table is groaning with food.

Every Sunday, she prepares a feast for the family. Dolmades, vine leaves stuffed with savoury rice, humus and homemade olive bread. Roast potatoes and lasagne, roast meats and vegetable dishes and afterwards homemade baklava and Turkish sweets, layers of pastry with honey and nuts.

We sit together around the dining room table, Samson's brother and his fiancée and Samson's mum and her new husband who she met at the factory where they work as machinists. After lunch the men watch football while the women clean the kitchen.

"I was fourteen when my parents called me inside to meet my husband," his mum tells me in the kitchen. "That was Samson's father. I didn't want to get married, I wanted to stay at school." She passes me a plate to dry. "I locked myself in my room and wouldn't come out, I wouldn't eat. My parents agreed then that I could wait until I was sixteen until I got married. I was seventeen when my first baby was born and eighteen when Samson was born."

Eighteen is the same age I am.

29
On the road

Before we got together as a couple Samson saw an ad in the *Time Out* personals column saying:

> Wanted, a man to father my baby.

Samson applied to be the dad and wrote a letter saying he was a poet who loves children, and sent a photograph of himself. In reply a woman called Judy wrote back and invited Samson to come and stay in her commune in Cornwall.

But now Samson and I are a couple and he writes back and tells Judy about me. She says that it's fine, we can both come and stay in the commune.

Samson and I hitchhike to Cornwall with five pounds in our pocket and arrive at the address that is on the letter. Judy has moved on and all that's left of the commune are two people, Zak and Hazel and their baby, Sky. They say we can sleep on the floor and Hazel offers us supper – a bowl of brown rice mixed with a tin of tomato soup.

The next day, we go and find Judy who has moved to a cottage on the edge of the cliffs of Pendeen with her two cats. It is a wild and desolate place. The cottage has two bedrooms and Judy says we can stay with her. The autumn days are getting shorter and there is a chill in the air. We run out of money and Judy spends all her dole money on cat food. We are hungry. With my last few shillings I buy a box of porridge and we eat porridge three times a day.

I suggest I make stew with a tin of cat food but Judy and Samson turn their noses up at the idea. I pick wild blackberries on the cliffs to give the porridge a bit of flavour but the blackberries are past their best and are no longer sweet and juicy.

Judy says she has found a man who will father her child. She has been writing to him in prison and he will be coming out of prison in six months' time.

The house is in darkness, we have run out of electricity and have no coins for the meter. Outside the wind howls and the rain pours down. Judy has the only candle in the house. The candle lights up her face, she looks at us with a dark intense stare as she holds her hands behind her back. Maybe she is holding a knife behind her back, maybe she wants to kill us. Samson and I look at each other and lock ourselves in the bedroom. There is nowhere to hide, we whisper to each other about how scared we are.

We leave early the next morning, as soon as we can, and hitchhike to Camborne where we have an address of a commune. The commune is run by a nasty drug dealer who makes us feel unwelcome, especially as we don't have money to buy his drugs. It is time to move on.

Samson goes back to London and I go to the Employment Exchange and find a job in Falmouth cleaning at Cliff House, an old people's home. In the paper I find a bedsit to rent nearby in Wood Lane, a tree-lined street filled with large old houses. The houses have been turned into bedsits for holiday makers and students.

I phone Samson from a call box and tell him the good news. He says he will come and join me as soon as he has saved up the coach fare.

※ ※ ※

I start work at Cliff House. The wages are twelve pounds a week and I have to work a week in hand and will only be paid in two weeks' time. I have spent the last of my money on paying the rent and deposit. There is no money left to buy food and I am hungry. I take home the crusts of bread from the kitchen at work before they are put in the pig bin but the matron sees me and tells me off for taking food home from work.

One of the carers gives me food that she brings from home, tins of soup and other small scraps. She is discreet and kind, she says she doesn't eat this sort of soup and would I like it.

I sit in the staff room during tea breaks feeling shy and invisible amongst the boisterous banter. The cook calls me "me luvver" or "me handsome" when she talks to me and puts her arm around me.

Each morning I wake up early, and walk to work. My first task at work is to take a cup of tea to each of the residents in their rooms. I help clear the breakfast tables and wash the dishes before I clean the bedrooms and bathrooms. I sweep, I mop and dust, and scour out the toilets.

At four o'clock, I leave work and walk home along the empty beach. At the bottom of Wood Lane is the Art College. On my way back from work I go in and wander around the empty studios. The smell of oil paint is like nectar to my nose and an intense longing overtakes me. How wonderful it must be to be an art student and spend all day painting.

One day, in the supermarket, I pick up a packet of tea and a tin of sardines. I am wearing my long blue velvet coat with a lining and a hole in my pocket. I put the tea and sardines in my pocket and feel them slipping down to the bottom of the lining and head for the door. A heavy hand lands on my shoulder and my heart sinks as I look up into the face of the store detective.

"Come with me," she says, as she leads me off to the manager's office. I want to die of shame and wish I could fall through the floor. I am shaking and my face grows bright red. The police are called and I am charged with shoplifting. A probation officer comes to visit me and my court date is set for three months' time.

Samson arrives by coach from London, and we settle into our bedsit, in our first home together, with a large double bed and a table nestling in a sunny bay window. The rent is four pounds fifty a week and we share a bathroom and toilet with the other tenants.

Samson waits for me to come home from work. He has cooked chips and an omelette on our Baby Belling cooker. I feed the electric metre with fifty pence coins. We sit and eat and Samson reads me the poems he has been writing while I have been at work. We live on omelettes and vegetable stews. I try to make Cornish pasties but my pastry is hard as nails and inedible. On Friday nights after I get paid, we eat fish and chips and get drunk at the local pub on the local brew, Triple Vintage cider.

※ ※ ※

The date for my court case has arrived. I dress up in my best clothes and hope I look respectable. The Magistrate fines me five pounds and gives me a stern warning. A small paragraph about my crime appears in the local paper. I hope no one at work sees it.

Samson is getting bored and restless, he complains that his days are aimless and he needs to go back to London and find a job. I hand in my notice and we pack up our few belongings and go back to London.

30
Shrewsbury

Amy and Barry have moved to Shrewsbury, and Samson and I hitchhike to go and see them. They don't have a phone for us to tell them we are coming to stay. Shrewsbury is a small market town in Shropshire on the Welsh borders. The town is neither small nor big – it is an unremarkable rural English town. Amy and Barry's flat is on the corner of the main road, opposite a supermarket.

We find their flat and knock on the door, but nobody answers. The back window has been left open. We climb through the window. Inside is chaotic, with chairs turned upside down and dirty dishes strewn about the floor. Dishes are piled high in the sink, food is plastered on the walls and the bin is overflowing.

We wait for Amy and Barry to get back home. We don't know when that will be. Maybe tomorrow or next week. After a few days they arrive back from Glastonbury music festival. A woman called Carol has moved in with them and Barry is with her now. He is no longer with Amy, his wife. Before they left they had a fight and turned the place upside down. Barry and Carol have claimed the large front room as their own while Amy sleeps by herself in the back bedroom with the baby.

Amy has a new boyfriend, Derek. He is married, with two children. He keeps us up the whole night, telling us jokes and making us laugh at things we shouldn't laugh at. He has a very dark sense of humour. He is just out of rehab, he was addicted to morphine. He says his wife is always nagging him and doesn't like it when he spends money on drugs.

❋ ❋ ❋

Samson says he feels sorry for Amy sleeping by herself, she must feel lonely, she should come and sleep with us on the nights when Derek is at home with his wife. Amy is my best friend. Lying on the mattress under the covers it is warm and friendly and close between Amy and Samson and me.

We are easy with each other, we laugh the whole night long, making love, entangled, not knowing whose lips are whose and whose arms belong to whom.

Amy and Samson and me. There are three of us against two. Barry and

Carol demand housekeeping money. Then every day they go across the road to the supermarket where they load up a shopping trolley and 'liberate' the groceries. They walk confidently past the cashier without paying and flash her a smile and spend our housekeeping money on drugs and Chinese takeaways. They don't share their takeaways with us. Carol is in charge of the cooking and every day we eat exactly the same food, vegetable curry with peanuts and sweet and sour sauce and brown rice.

✳ ✳ ✳

Samson and I are in the kitchen cooking mashed potatoes and fish fingers with tomato sauce. We sit down to savour the warm buttery mash and the crispy fish fingers.

Barry walks in, he is annoyed with us. "How can you waste your money buying that consumer crap?" he asks us, and gives us a disapproving look.

Samson keeps quiet.

"We are sick of eating the same food every night," I tell him.

"Can't you get something different for a change when you go shopping?" Amy asks Carol.

Carol looks like she wants to slap Amy. "I am the only one who ever does the cooking around here," she says, and storms out of the kitchen.

Barry goes into the front room and pumps up the volume on the stereo. The Rolling Stones shout through the speakers, "I Can't Get No Satisfaction".

Derek lies on the double mattress on the floor smoking a joint. He passes it to Barry who takes a long slow draw on the joint and smiles.

"I am not made for a nine to five job," Derek says.

Barry agrees with him. "Neither am I," he replies.

Amy sits on the floor and plays with the baby. Barry passes me the joint while Carol sorts through a pile of dirty washing in the corner of the room looking for something to wear.

"I am wasted on work. I have other talents," Derek says. "I don't want a boss, I want to be the boss."

Derek is proud that he has not worked a day in his life. "I am going to start my own business," he boasts. "I am going to be driving fast cars and buying a villa in Spain by this time next year." He has big plans and dreams. Shrewsbury is a town with no work, there are not many opportunities for anything.

Barry rolls another joint and Carol lights up some joss sticks. The sweet smoke curls into the air and masks the smell of the dirty nappies that need washing.

"What are you going to do?" I ask Derek.

"I am going to be a dealer, I am going to sell heroin – you can make a lot of money," Derek says.

I am horrified. "How can you be a merchant of death and profit from other people's destruction?" I ask him.

Smoking dope is one thing but crossing the line into using heroin is another.

I don't want to be around that kind of energy, watching young junkies come and go like ghosts. Once you are hooked on heroin you become desperate enough to sell your own grandmother.

"If I don't sell heroin, someone else will," is Derek's logic.

It is time to move on.

"I don't want to be surrounded by junkies," I say to Amy and Samson and start packing my bags.

Samson wants to go back to London and find work and I want to go to Wales. I want Samson to come with me. I don't understand why he doesn't want to come – I would rather die than be trapped in London again. Samson and I argue and pull each other's hair and hit each other. I walk out the door and up the road to where the turn-off for Wales is signposted. In my pocket I have the address of a commune in Cardiff.

31
Ruthin

After half-an-hour of standing at the side of the road, a lorry stops for me.

"Where are you going?" I ask.

"Wales."

I get in and make conversation. I tell the driver I have never been to Wales before.

"How far is it to Cardiff?"

"You're travelling in the wrong direction," he tells me. "This is the way to North Wales, you will have to go back to Shrewsbury."

I don't want to go back to Shrewsbury, it is bad luck to go backwards. I decide to carry on in the direction of North Wales. It is all the same to me.

The lorry driver drops me off at the side of the road and soon after I get another lift with a travelling salesman. The signpost points towards Llangollen.

I make polite conversation. "Are you married?"

"Yes."

"How many children do you have? Where do you live?" I ask him

"How old are you? Do you have a boyfriend?" he wants to know.

He stops the car and we look at the view. He says he wants to have sex with me. "I will give you five quid," he says.

"No, thank you," I answer him politely. I ignore him and look out the window at the magnificent view.

❄ ❄ ❄

In front of me the hills and valleys stretch out into the far distance. The mountain road winds up and down and around and the sight before me takes my breath away. I have not seen such beauty since I left South Africa. I drink in the wildness of the mountains with my eyes, hungry and thirsty for the untamed space. I did not know such an unspoilt, wild landscape existed in Britain. The landscape I have seen in England has been tamed, cultivated and flat and contained by fences and hedges.

The salesman drops me off in Llangollen, a town with a strange name that I can't pronounce.

I stand on the bridge and look down at the river and up at the mountains that surround the town. I like the peace and the beauty of this place. Why do I need to go anywhere else? I can stay here, this can be home.

I buy the local paper. A flat is advertised for rent in the next town, Ruthin, and I hitchhike over the mountains to go and have a look. The landlady doesn't like the look of me and tells me the flat has already been taken.

Ruthin is a medieval town on the Welsh borders with an old medieval castle where banquets are held with singing waitresses serving venison and mead. I book in at a local bed and breakfast next door to the castle and go down to the Employment Exchange to look for a job.

They are looking for staff in a hotel on the outskirts of town. It is spring time and lambs, white and fluffy, play in the fields, bleating and skipping. The hotel is at the bottom of the mountain with a stream running by. I get the job and I think I am in heaven, the views from the hotel are breath-taking.

The job is a live-in one. From early in the morning until past midnight I work in the kitchen washing dishes. When I finish working, I sleep in the bar after it closes for the night. The bar smells of cigarettes and stale beer and the bench I sleep on is hard and narrow. The other women who work here are from the Philippines and they send money home to their families. They are grateful to have work. It shocks me how badly paid and exploited they are by the hotel. But then I realise, I have not asked how much I will be paid.

Friday is pay day.

"How much will I get?" I ask, while I am busy scrubbing the kitchen floor.

"Seven pounds a week," I am told. This is too little money for working from early in the morning until late at night. All we get to eat is bacon and egg sandwiches – I am told off for taking a lettuce leaf to eat. I stop scrubbing the floor.

"I want my money now, I am leaving." I leave the floor half scrubbed and walk out.

I need somewhere to stay and go back to the bed and breakfast. The police come to interview me. I think the owners of the hotel have reported me out of spite. The police say somebody said they saw me in Denbigh, the next town, where some money was stolen from a pub. I have never heard of Denbigh, let alone been there.

I sit in the town square, watched by hostile eyes. I want to scream. What if the police lock me up and I fight them and lose control and start screaming? They could take me back to hospital and inject me with a chemical straitjacket and throw away the key. My freedom and sanity feel fragile and precarious.

At the Employment Exchange I see an advert for a live-in job at Llysfasi, an agricultural college nearby, as a domestic worker. I apply and get the job. On a Saturday we are paid time-and-a-half and on Sundays and public holidays we get double time. I work in the kitchen and clean the student's hostels. Living in at work and getting my meals means I can save a lot of money. The other girls speak Welsh. I am sure they are talking about me behind my back. I learn to say "Bore da" and "Sut ydych chi? – "Good day and how are you?"

✳ ✳ ✳

I phone Amy from a public phone and she tells me, "Derek and his friend Mike have been arrested. They broke into a chemist shop and stole cocaine and heroin. They drove to Torquay and were giving away free samples but someone miscalculated the dose and overdosed and died. Then everyone in the room panicked and ran away, nobody wanted to be caught with the body."

"I will phone you later, my money is running out," I tell Amy and go and get some more coins to feed the phone box. When I phone back, Amy tells me that Derek threw all the drugs into the sea before he drove back to Shrewsbury. When he got home, the police came to question him. The only thing was, he didn't know that the police only wanted to ask him questions about a speeding fine. He was scared and he told them it was not his fault, it was his friend's idea to break into the chemist shop. He gave the game away.

"Now they are both locked up," Amy says.

I am worried about Amy and I miss her, she sounds lonely. Carol and Barry have moved to London. I go and visit Amy and find Lee and her sister living with Amy. Lee is Derek's friend Mike's, girlfriend. She is sixteen and pregnant and spends all day knitting for the baby and writing letters to Mike in prison to tell him she loves him and will wait for him. When Amy is out of the room, Lee and her sister bad mouth her and laugh at her behind her back, even though she looks after them and feeds them. Amy is soft-hearted and they are taking advantage of her.

Amy has made friends with Derek's wife and they go to court together to Derek and Mike's trial. The judge sentences the two men to two years but they get time off for good behaviour.

✳ ✳ ✳

When Derek comes out of prison he goes back to live with his wife and children. By this time Amy is living in Wales. She writes to me to tell me some shocking news. Derek's wife has killed him. She stabbed him to death, says Amy, and she doesn't blame her. In court his wife said he beat her and called her a whore and took the food money to buy drugs. Amy says the judge has sentenced her to fifteen years for his murder. It's sad because the children have been taken into care. It doesn't seem fair. It wasn't their fault that he was a bastard.

32
Back to nature

I have saved up enough money working at the agricultural college to start travelling again. I leave my job and buy an arctic sleeping bag filled with duck down that will keep me warm in all weather. I pack my rucksack with essentials – bread and cheese, a bottle of water and a change of clothes and roll up my sleeping bag and set off while the grass is still wet and the world is fresh. Around my neck I wear a small St. Christopher on a chain to keep me safe.

I have a map of the mountains and am heading for a small village up in Snowdonia. It will take me a day to walk there. For the next few weeks I walk over the mountains, exploring Snowdonia, staying in Youth Hostels. I want to put my feet firmly on the earth. Walking slows down my pace so I can see, smell and hear the landscape all around me with its trees and fields and animals. For hours I sit and stare at plants, trees and flowers. I stare at the grass and at the sky – I am trying to get inside the blades of grass. I watch as a tiny insect crawls up a blade of grass. My eyesight touches the surface of what I see, but I want to feel each blade of grass and leaf as it moves.

While I was tripping or stoned, the world became vivid and interesting, each sense was heightened. But in between I got bored with the blandness and emptiness of life. The more I thought about filling the space with drugs, the less I could settle into the present and the more disconnected I became. Alone in the mountains I can be myself without interruption.

The silence and beauty of the mountains feeds the empty spaces inside of me.

※ ※ ※

Gentle and generous Emma, an old friend from London, has moved from London to Scotland with her four children. Emma is renting a Forestry Commission house for thirty shillings a month. She lives alone with her twin boys, ten-year-old Max and Manny, her seven-year-old daughter, Francis, and the baby, Ben, who is two years old. The children have different fathers.

"Come and stay whenever you want," Emma had said when I last saw her in London at the Queens in Crouch End. Her cottage is off the beaten track in Dumfriesshire. Emma doesn't have a phone for me to let her know I am coming and I hope she is still there.

I leave Wales and hitchhike to Scotland. It is late at night when the lorry driver drops me off in the small Scottish town of Lockerbie. It is too late for me to continue on the road so I sleep in a bus shelter on a narrow bench. When I wake up it is daylight and I set off down the road to Emma's house. I get a lift some of the way and then walk the remaining eight miles. Emma's house is a morning's walk to the nearest road, twenty miles away from Lockerbie. I see no other houses or cars or people until I reach her cottage. Scotland is so quiet – all around me is a deep silence.

After my long walk, Emma flings her arms around me and welcomes me warmly. She makes me a cup of tea and cuts slices of fresh homemade bread for me to eat with jam. A goat wanders into the kitchen. "That's Daisy," Emma tells me. She shoos the chickens out of the kitchen. "They always shit in the kitchen," she says. Ben, the baby, comes and sits on my lap and then follows me around like a puppy.

In the cottage there is no electricity. The Scottish autumn is chilly and the fire is kept going all day. I spend hours chopping wood for the fire. In the barn are piles of logs that need to be chopped. I lift the axe up and swing it through the air and crack! the log splits open. The trick is to hit the log dead centre with just the right force to split it in half. After the first few hours I get the hang of it. I pick up the heavy basket of chopped logs and carry it indoors to the fireplace in the living room. Sandy, the dog, is curled up in front of the fire and Emma has put some loaves of bread to rise near the warmth of the fire.

The children have come home from school and the house is no longer quiet. The evening light is fading and Emma asks me to fill the lamps. Manny and Max show me how to pour paraffin through a funnel into the small hole on the side. We light the lamps and they give a warm glow to the kitchen and living room. By seven o'clock the rest of the house is in total darkness. I go to bed early, my bed is up a steep ladder in the dusty attic on a mattress underneath the eaves.

✳ ✳ ✳

Emma's aunt has left her some money and she needs to go to London to sort it all out. On Friday she says, "I will be back on Wednesday, can you look after the children?"

I make pots of soup and bake bread and make puddings for the children. At night I tether the goats and shut the hens up in the barn so the foxes won't eat them. In the morning I coax Daisy the goat into the barn to milk her. Little Ben wanders in wearing his pyjamas and a very wet nappy and watches me from the doorway. I squeeze and pull Daisy's udders rhythmically and the warm milk squirts into the bucket. Francis, Emma's seven-year-old, collects the eggs and feeds the hens while the boys clean out the fireplace. On the stove a pot of porridge is simmering.

On Monday morning, I get the children ready for school and take them to the school bus at the bottom of the road.

Wednesday comes and goes, but Emma is not back. She didn't say which Wednesday she would be back and I am running out of food. I don't have much money and the nearest shop is a long walk away.

The goats break into the vegetable patch and create havoc. Daisy is a difficult goat, she won't keep still and steps in the bucket when I milk her. The milk tastes sweet at first but after a few hours, when I give it to the children, it tastes goaty and they refuse to drink it. The Billy goat is in heat and gives off an overpowering smell. When I touch him the smell stays on my hands and clothes the whole day.

Emma arrives back from London with lots of groceries. She is driving a Land Rover, bought with her aunt's money. She has brought us treats and the children devour white sliced bread and peanut butter with golden syrup.

Sandy, the dog, comes limping into the kitchen. She has spiked herself on a poacher's trap. Her nose is hot and dry and her leg has become infected. She lies in front of the fire in pain, not eating. I pray that I can take on her pain. I cannot bear to see a dog suffering like that.

It is getting dark. I fill the oil lamps, light them and go to the barn to shut the chickens up for the night. In the twilight, I don't see the nail sticking out of the wood but I feel it as it goes through my boot and into my foot. I pull it out, but I don't look at the wound. I ignore it, but I feel the blood seeping into my boot.

The next morning, my foot is a strange colour and has swollen to twice its normal size. I limp to the road to see if I can get a lift into town to see the doctor. The doctor wants to give me an injection. Terror takes hold of me and I want to run. The doctor says she will forcibly restrain me if I refuse to have the injection.

Memories of hospital and feeling powerless and out of control are triggered by the doctor's voice of authority. I manage to control my fear as she gives me an anti-tetanus shot.

We put ointment on Sandy's leg and her wound heals. Next time I must be more careful about taking on somebody else's pain.

33
Wild Wales

Five miles from Ruthin on the road to Wrexham, Derwyn Llanarch lies nestled in a valley surrounded by Welsh mountains. In October, when the weather turns colder and the nights are growing longer, I go back to Wales. I walk the five miles from Ruthin to Derwyn Llanarch to ask a local farmer, Mr. Williams, if I can rent a caravan on his farm. I need somewhere to stay to keep warm and dry for the winter months.

Mr. Williams agrees to rent the caravan to me for three pounds a week and the next day I walk back along the lanes with my sleeping bag and a paraffin heater and settle into my new home for the winter.

The caravan is on its own in a field hidden behind a hedge. Sometimes I spend over a week not seeing anyone or talking to anyone. To get water I walk across the field and climb over the gate and walk down the muddy lane until I get to the place in the hedge where the water gushes out from a stream. I fill my water bucket and walk back down the lane over the gate and across the field to the caravan.

Winter sets in, and in the mornings the condensation on the inside of the window turns to ice and my glass of water freezes solid overnight. Outside, the branches of the trees bend under the weight of snow. On stormy nights the wind rocks the caravan and the heavens open up and the rain pours down onto the thin roof of the caravan.

I try not to get undressed – it is too cold. In the mornings when I climb out of my sleeping bag, I just put more layers of clothes over the clothes I have slept in.

Once a week, I warm the caravan with my paraffin heater and boil water and strip off for a wash. The caravan fills with steam as I pour hot water in the bowl and soap my flannel. I scrub my body from top to toe before I rinse the soap off with the warm water. Last of all I wash my feet in the bowl.

Once a month, when I can afford it, I go to the public bath house in Wrexham which is twenty miles away. The lady who works at the baths hands me a bar of soap, a large white towel and the plug for the bath. I lie in a bath filled with hot water, enjoying the luxury of the warmth enveloping my body and the smell of shampoo and soap.

✳ ✳ ✳

In the caravan, I start to lose track of time and of myself. I feel guilty about eating when I think of the starving children in the world. What right do I have to have a full stomach? When I look at my jersey I wonder about the sheep that the wool came from and who sheared the sheep and where the factory where my jersey was knitted was situated. What did the person who knitted my jersey look like? Was she bored or sad or happy? Was she badly paid?

I wander around in my head for days and when I go into town I feel light-headed with hunger. I buy chocolate bars and eat them guiltily, ravenously, one after the other. The sugar rush leaves me feeling fuzzy-headed.

At night when it storms I go for long walks across the fields to experience the wildness of the weather on dark moonless nights. On clear nights I look up at the stars and get lost in the immensity of space.

I am careful about how I use things. I don't use toilet paper because I worry about the trees that need to be chopped down to make the paper. I recycle what I can and use as little as possible. I pride myself on what little rubbish I leave. The bread I buy from the baker shop is wrapped in tissue paper. I carefully smooth out the paper and save it and wrap up leaves and straw in the paper. When I menstruate I use this home-made pad to catch the flow of my blood but the paper is unbearably scratchy between my legs and I walk the five miles into Ruthin to buy sanitary towels.

In Ruthin I fall asleep by the river and wake up to find a strange man sitting next to me. He starts talking to me and tells that in the forests on the other side of the river live bears and wolves. People who have entered the forest have been known to disappear, he says, never to be seen again. I want to go and explore the forest. I ask a friend, Susan Jones, why no one has told me about this forest and she laughs at me. She says the man who told me is the village idiot, that he is not quite right in the head.

Halfway down the hill, in the lane that leads from the farm to the main road, sits a red phone box. I phone Samson from there as often as I can, whenever I have the coins. We write letters to say that we will love each other for ever. Samson has a job and is living back at home with his mum. He saves up money and buys a motor bike, a Honda 50, and comes to visit me in Wales.

✳ ✳ ✳

Samson is my best friend, my twin soul. I tell him everything – I have no secrets from him. My heart is completely open to him and we read each other's minds, even from a distance. People ask us if we are brother and sister, they say we look like twins. We will never leave each other, not ever.

We fight though. I want him to move to Wales. "We will find a house to live in and you can get a job," I tell him. "You don't need to go back to London."

But Samson feels like a fish out of water in Wales and he always goes back to London – to his Mum and his job and his family.

I tell myself I don't need any one, I like to be by myself. I will die a slow death if I move back to London, away from the wildness and peace and quiet of the Welsh mountains. In London I will be trapped by buildings and traffic.

Once a week, I phone Mum and Dad. Mum has a knack of knowing when I don't have money, even though I don't say anything, and when that happens she sends me a cheque for five pounds in the post. Mum and Dad say they want to come to visit me to see how I am. I book them in at a nearby bed and breakfast and fetch them from the station in Wrexham. I am happy to see them. We travel by bus back to the caravan. It has been snowing heavily and the bus creeps slowly along the country lanes. The trees on the side of the road are heavily laden with snow. When Mum and Dad have settled into the bed and breakfast, they walk up the hill to visit me in the caravan. Dad cannot understand why I choose to live in an isolated caravan with no running water or electricity – he says it's like being in prison. I tell him I don't like to be cooped up in a house in the city – I like to live close to nature.

Samson is visiting me in the caravan at the same time as Mum and Dad. We walk Mum and Dad back to the farm house where they are staying and then head back to the caravan. The full moon shines brightly on the snow-covered fields and mountains. Samson and I laugh as we run, then roll over and over in the virgin snow.

"Imagine," Samson says, "No one else has ever made footprints in this snow before us."

"I am the first woman of the universe and I will never lose my madness," I shout, my arms outstretched in the midnight snow.

The moon reflects on the white snow and lights up the field. Midnight is as bright as day as we play in the dazzling snow.

34
Newcastle brown

The Claimants Union is holding a conference in Newcastle-on-Tyne for people claiming welfare benefits. Unemployed people on the dole are fed-up with how they are being treated. I hitchhike from the caravan to the conference. People have arrived from different parts of Britain for the conference.

In the evening, after a day of intense debates and discussions, a group of us go to the pub and after a few rounds of Newcastle Brown the room starts to spin round and round. Newcastle Brown is deceptively strong. I sit on the floor in the ladies' toilet feeling disorientated, I don't know where I am. Miraculously I manage to find my way back to the group of people I have come with.

After the conference, before we leave and go our separate ways, we exchange addresses with each other and I invite my new friends to come and visit me in Wales.

The following week, Dave, an older man I met at the conference, turns up unexpectedly at my caravan. His face is interesting and looks like it has been weathered by a hard life He has recently come out of prison after serving a two-year sentence for dealing drugs. He tells me he has stopped, but the police are watching him. They come to see what he is doing here in my caravan. Rumours are going around that we are having hippy orgies and selling drugs, but the reality is very different. I am living a very sober, chaste life in my hermit's retreat.

Mr. Williams, the farmer, wants to see me in private. "The police came to see me." He looks embarrassed and looks down at his feet. "They say I must ask you to move out. They say your friend is selling drugs to school children. You will have to be out by tomorrow."

The caravan has been my home for the past six months, my time here in the Welsh mountains has been a special time and it breaks my heart to leave. Sadly I pack my bags and hitch hike to Mid-Wales to stay with Amy. She is renting a cottage on a farm. I hope she will be there – she doesn't know I am coming.

The cottage is off the beaten track but the farmer who gives me a lift knows exactly where I am going even before I tell him. This is a small close-knit Welsh community who don't trust the English, but Amy has settled into the local community. Her son is three years old now and being a mother gives her a measure of respectability. A steady stream of people visits Amy from London and Shrewsbury.

❋ ❋ ❋

On Saturday nights, dances are held in the village hall. Amy and I dress up and go with Bronwyn, our friend and neighbour, to the dance. Bronwyn is married to a farmer and has four children and lives on the farm down the road.

Beer and cider flow freely. As the evening progresses the band plays faster and faster and the dancing becomes wilder and wilder, whirling and twirling as round and round we go, doing traditional country dancing. I am dizzy with all the whirling and twirling.

After midnight, we start walking to the car. The local lads follow – we are easy game, everyone knows hippy girls have easy morals and are just begging for it. The boys try to put their hands up my skirt and feel my breasts. I hold on tight to Amy and fight them off.

"Get in the car," Bronwyn shouts to us and locks the doors. The boys crowd around, banging on the roof of the car. The boys are laughing, jeering, leering in at the windows. This isn't simple rowdy fun. They come closer and closer, get louder and louder. Their lips are wet and shining, they make crude thrusting gestures with their hips. They would like to pull us out of the car and rape us. I hate them. I want to shoot them.

But Bronwyn opens the car door for two of the men. She says she knows them, they are her neighbours. Bronwyn and Amy sit in the back of the car with the two men who kiss them and fondle them. I sit on the front seat by myself and feel sick. Eventually they climb out of the car and we drive home.

When we get home the lights are on. Amy and I are scared that they have followed us home. We stay in the car as Bronwyn strides purposefully into the house – she knows all the local boys, she can sort them out. But she comes running out to tell us that it's just Michael, a friend who has arrived from London. We are more than pleased to see him. We tell him he must sleep in the bed with us to protect us. I sleep with a knife under my pillow and the fire poker next to me.

❋ ❋ ❋

Amy gets sick and is rushed to hospital in an ambulance. She has an infection in her ovaries and Barry comes to stay with his new girlfriend, Lee. He is here to look after their little boy. They have been living in a squat in

London, a semi-derelict house, and Lee has been working as a prostitute to support her drug habit.

While Amy is in hospital the house is full of people from London. Now Michael, Barry and Lee are staying in her house. But then Lee and Barry argue and Lee walks out.

The farmer's daughter is fourteen and wants to break free. She is intrigued by our lifestyle, and likes spending time with us. Barry takes her under his wing and she follows him around. And then she disappears – she runs away to London with Barry to live in a squat. Her dad is frantic. He wants to know where she is and when we tell him he comes into the cottage with his shotgun and tells us we must leave the farm immediately. We are nothing but trouble.

We pack our bags hastily. The other people in the house disappear and Bronwyn says she will look after Amy's little boy until Amy gets out of hospital. I stand in the rain outside the house wondering where I will sleep tonight. The farmer and his wife take pity on me and invite me in for supper and say I can stay the night. They are very worried about their daughter and there's not much I can say to reassure them.

35

On the road again

I'm hitchhiking – England, Scotland, Wales, Scotland, Wales and England –
going around and around in the same circles, and around and around again,
locked inside cars and lorries on soulless motorways. There is no money in
my pocket, I am open, and vulnerable.

My days are full of possibilities, but the nights are full of
danger. I toughen up, my foolishness and sense of adventure keep me
going. I have nothing but myself and my trust that I can survive on
nothing.

I walk by myself over the mountains and discover lakes and valleys and
forests. I eat wild strawberries and gooseberries and pick wild garlic and
nettles from the hedgerows to make soup. At night I sleep in a field and I
look up into the dark, travelling further and further into the night sky. I
travel through the stars and feel the ancient earth beneath me, and the presence of the silent hills and the river. I am so tiny and insignificant compared
to the infinite space I stare into. Why do I ever worry about anything at all
in my small life? I feel comforted by this feeling of insignificance. It takes a
weight off my shoulders.

❊ ❊ ❊

Mum puts some money into my post office account. I cash it in and write a
poem on a five-pound note:

> You go by car,
> I go by night
> You have your carpets,
> I have my constellations
> You are petrol,
> I am a star

I go into a pub hoping to find warmth and company, but feel alienated
and bored with the drinking and pub talk all around me. I take money out
of my pocket and look at it. Should I buy myself another drink? I roll myself
a cigarette and take out a match to light it. The flame burns brightly. I strike
another match and put it under the corner of my pound note.

"Are you mad?" the man sitting next to me shouts, and tries to grab hold of the burning money. I laugh as the note goes up in flames.

"Money is only bits of paper," I tell him and put the ash in the ashtray. I hand him the five-pound note with my poem on it.

※ ※ ※

I am rootless and restless, drifting. If I do not get a lift in one direction, I cross the road. Maybe I will have better luck going in the opposite direction. One place is the same as another. I hitchhike through the night. Truck drivers want to have sex with me. I fend them off and try to dress like a boy. The routine of fending them off becomes predictable and boring.

I get a lift to Cornwall and sleep on the beach in Falmouth while I look for a job. It is the summer season and they need staff for the hotels. I get a live-in job as a chambermaid. It is not an ideal job, but it will give me somewhere to stay. The job starts in a few days' time.

I spend the day walking on the beach and in the early evening I walk through the town and look through lighted windows into people's homes. Tables are set for supper, there are pictures on the walls and family photographs on the dressers. At the fish and chip shop, I buy a packet of hot chips with salt and vinegar and take my chips down to the beach to eat by myself.

Night comes, and it becomes chilly but I have my arctic sleeping bag. The tide is coming in and the wind has come up. I feel vulnerable on my own and lonesome in the dark, but I won't admit it, not even to myself.

I feel restless and vulnerable in the dark on the beach and decide to catch the train to London to stay with Mum and Dad, just temporarily. At the station I wait for the last train to London. The ticket inspector walks through the carriage and I pretend to be asleep. If I had seen him coming I would have hidden in the toilet. He asks for my ticket, but I don't have one and I don't have any money. He says I must get off at the next station, which is Redruth. I have never been to Redruth. It is past ten o'clock when I get off the train.

I walk into the warmth of a pub as they call "last orders please" and look for a friendly face. I see two long-haired, bearded men drinking pints and laughing. Their faces are friendly and they look like they are having fun, so I go over and talk to them. At closing time we leave together, into the chilly night street.

"Do you know of somewhere I can sleep tonight?" I ask them.

"Come with us," they say.

Perhaps they think they will get lucky later.

We go to a flat nearby. Inside, music plays loudly and a group of people sit in a circle passing a joint around. As soon as one joint finishes another one is rolled. There is no shortage of dope here. The familiar warm fug envelopes me as I float off into the music of Pink Floyd. The two men want to talk to me, can I come outside for a minute?

"There is a problem," they say. "We are sorry, but you won't be able to stay the night. You see, this isn't our place, we are just crashing on the floor. The chick who lives here says it will cause problems if you stay. Her husband is in prison and if he hears strange people are staying over, he won't like it. You could be an undercover policewoman."

I fetch my rucksack and sleeping bag. "No, problem," I say as I head out the door and walk to the edge of town. It is past midnight and the sky is clear and full of stars, the road is dark and quiet. I know I can trust that life will present the right person in the right place at the right time. I see headlights coming towards me and stand where the car can see me and put my thumb out. I am in luck. The car stops and I climb in the front seat.

"Do you need somewhere to stay?" the man asks me. "I know some students who have a house just outside Falmouth. I can drop you off there."

It is past two o'clock and I don't want to wake anyone up. I don't know what to expect.

When I get to the house, I see lights on and hear music playing. I knock on the door and it is opened by a young woman with a big smile. The women in the house are awake and busy cleaning, sweeping and scrubbing the floor even though it is so early in the morning. Their parents are coming to visit the next day. They make me a cup of tea and show me where I can sleep. The room at the top of the stairs is clean and tidy and I sleep between clean sheets and soft blankets, feeling safe.

After a good night's sleep, I go back to Falmouth and start work in the hotel, part of the transient seasonal work force but making beds and cleaning toilets is boring and mind-numbing. After a few weeks I have saved some money and I decide to pack up and leave.

I go back to London. Mum and Dad have kept my room for me and I want to spend time with Samson. Lynn has had a baby and I go to help her look after the baby. Johnny is also at home – he has been working in Portugal and comes home briefly before he goes to teach in newly liberated Mozambique.

But after a few weeks I feel oppressed by the big city. I long for the peace and quiet of Wales and Scotland and I pack my bags and go hitch-hiking again, hoping to get to Wales and Scotland. On my way there, I explore Suffolk, staying in youth hostels and cycling around the small market towns and villages looking for somewhere to rent and a job. I could live here, out in the rural quiet. Suffolk is nearer London. Perhaps Samson would agree to move there with me. But I don't find anywhere for us to stay and in the winter time I go back to London.

36

Barefoot and pregnant

I turn twenty-one in January and Mum has a party for me. Samson gives me the perfect gift, a beautiful Swiss Army penknife. The next day Samson and I hitchhike to Scotland to visit Emma and arrive in the middle of the night.

It has been snowing and there are no cars to be seen on this isolated country road. We sleep in a field wrapped up in Samson's fur-lined leather jacket. We hold each other close and Samson dreams that his body heats the entire field. That night we sleep soundly, warm in each other's arms.

We stay at Emma's for a few weeks and then move on. Scotland is bitterly cold in the winter. Samson goes back to London and I keep travelling, down to Cornwall this time.

❋ ❋ ❋

Samson and I continually pull each other in opposite directions – we disrupt each other's lives. I drag him away from his mother and London, and he pulls me back.

"Why don't you marry your mother?" I scream at him. Samson wants to be in London where he can be warm, secure and well fed, with a job.

We hitchhike to Essex and Kent looking for a home near London, a compromise. We argue in a tent in the rain, overlooking fields and hills. Samson is tired of eating stale cheese sandwiches in a wet tent. I am angry that he doesn't share my enthusiasm for leaving London. He wants to go home.

I accuse him of being too soft, of giving up too easily.

"Look at the view," I say. "At least we are out of the city."

❋ ❋ ❋

Our child is conceived on a windy hillside in Wales, and Samson goes back to London, to a home, a job and his mum. I carry on travelling. After a few months I am pulled back to London. My breasts are tender and I have missed my periods. I travel by bus to the doctor with a urine sample in a milk bottle.

"You are pregnant," the doctor tells me.

Samson and I lie under the stars, thinking of our unborn child. We are excited, we feel so proud of ourselves – we think we are the cleverest two people in the world for knowing how to make a baby. We don't tell anyone our news, not yet.

Samson gets a job working in the library of the British Museum and we go and stay with my sister and I look after her eighteen-month-old baby while she is at work. She has a self-contained flat downstairs at her house that Samson and I can live in. I don't want to be in London, but at least we have somewhere to live, Samson has a job and I have a resting place.

My nephew has a rash, maybe it is measles. I am worried about how it might affect the baby in my womb, I know German measles can cause blindness and deafness in an unborn child. I go to see the doctor. She gives me a blood test and a few days later she phones with the results. My sister's husband answers the phone and she tells him I don't have to worry – the results are negative. He is furious, he didn't know I am pregnant. My sister is angry too, why did we lie and not tell them? Samson and I decide to leave.

We find a room in an attic with a small skylight in the ceiling where we share a toilet and bathroom with the other people in the house. The house has a strange smell. The young men who live in the house play loud reggae music all day and all night and smoke ganja.

I am woken in the middle of the night by the sound of a woman screaming. "Please, God, help me," she screams. The scream goes right through me and chills me to the bone. I want to go downstairs to help her, but I am scared. Samson says I mustn't, I could get hurt.

We hear footsteps outside our door, someone bangs on the door. It is the police asking, "Did you hear anything?" It appears that a woman was held against her will. After that I am scared to be on my own in the house. I think the woman was raped.

※ ※ ※

I get a job cleaning in an old people's home across the road. It is depressing working there. I make the beds, mop the floors and scrub shit off the walls of the toilet. The old people are not treated with respect, the carers shout at them and give them the wrong medication, but I keep working there and save up enough money to pay for a midwife to come and deliver my baby at home.

One day, I come home from work, tired and hungry. I heat a can of soup to eat and am about to pour it into a bowl when I look down and see a dead mouse on the floor. This is a bad omen. I don't want to eat the soup – I don't want to live here anymore.

Immediately Samson and I pack up and move out and go and stay with

Samson's mum. I feel trapped staying with her and after a few weeks I pack my bags and hitch-hike to Ruthin. I hope to find a house to rent. My stomach is growing huge. Samson follows me to Wales and we stay in a bed and breakfast, but after a week the landlady says she needs the room and we need to move out.

We don't know where to go. It is too cold and wet at this time of year to sleep out. Samson says, "Let's go to Denbigh today."

"Why Denbigh?" I ask. "What's there in Denbigh?"

Samson says he just has a feeling we should go there. We pack up my small suitcase and hitchhike to Denbigh.

Wednesday afternoon is half-day closing, and by the time we get to Denbigh everywhere is shut. We walk in the rain, holding a list of bed and breakfasts and knock on the doors, but they all say they are closed for the winter season. There is no room at the inn.

A small child runs in front of us and trips and falls. He starts crying and we pick him up and comfort him. His parents are not far behind him. We are getting wet in the rain so we go into a café for a cup of tea and to warm up. The café is steamy and filled with cigarette smoke and the smell of bacon and eggs frying. We order large mugs of strong sweet tea. The couple we saw earlier are sitting with their child in the café. The children in the café run up and down playing, making a noise while their parents sit and smoke.

It is still raining when we go outside and we take shelter in a shop doorway, wondering what to do next. We see the same couple again. They ask us if we need somewhere to stay.

"Wait here," they say and come back with a man wearing a builder's hard hat. He is working on a building site round the corner.

"I have somewhere you can stay," he tells us. He has an empty house. We travel on the bus to the small village where they live and stay in his house until we find a cottage to rent in a small village nearby. I pay the deposit on the cottage and we move in. I find a job. I turn twenty-two. Samson writes me a poem and we eat a packet of Jaffa Cakes.

❋ ❋ ❋

The cottage is full of frills and ornaments, everything is pretty and in place, neat as a pin. Samson and I do not fit. We are strangers in this doll's house. The landlady and her husband live next door. She has been looking at our mail and has noticed that we have different surnames and are not married.

"You are living in sin," she says. "You can't stay here. The people in the village will talk." The woman who has taken me on for the job is my landlady's friend. She phones her and tells her not to give me the job. Once more we pack our bags and go.

I must find a home. I cannot go back to the city defeated, but I am not feeling as strong as usual. I want to be taken care of, I am angry with myself for being so weak. My mantra is *I am strong and I don't need anyone*. But I do need somewhere to stop and rest. My baby is due soon and I do not want to go into hospital to give birth. I want to have a home birth but first I need a home.

We go back to North Wales, to Ruthin, and find a house to rent but it is unfurnished. Samson and I sit in the empty house, we have no money after paying the rent. I do not have the energy to furnish the house, or to get a job. I want to be taken care of.

My stomach is huge. I feel the baby kick inside me – I can see the baby's knees and elbows making bumps and shapes in my belly. Usually I am strong enough to take on anything. I cannot understand why I feel so weak. I go for a long walk, I must make a decision about what to do. I cry, I have a craving to eat sweets, but I do not have money to buy any. I am unable to do what needs to be done to provide a home for our child. I feel defeated.

We decide to go back to London.

We stand by the side of the road and I put out my thumb. A lorry stops to give us a lift and Samson helps me climb up into it. The lorry driver buys us breakfast in a greasy roadside café: eggs, beans, tomatoes, fried bread and a mug of strong sweet tea, and then we are on the road again, singing the blues.

※ ※ ※

In London, we stay with Samson's mum. Samson and his mum are very close, they speak in Turkish, which I can't understand and it makes me feel lonely and excluded.

A week after we arrive back in London, I go into labour and our baby arrives prematurely. At one o'clock in the morning I wake Samson up. Water pours out from between my legs. Samson tells me to go back to sleep, maybe I have wet the bed. I wonder what this water is, it must have something to do with the baby coming.

"Where is that book, *The ABC of Child Birth*?" I ask.

Samson and I page through the book, looking for clues about what is happening. "Look, it says waters breaking – call the midwife. Time the contractions."

The midwife arrives and I breathe through my contractions. I breathe in and out and focus while Samson holds my hand. We light candles and in the soft candlelight the room feels peaceful. I am excited, I am not scared at all. I am confident and powerful as I breathe through my labour pains. Samson and I feel so close, there is so much love between us as we get ready for the birth of our baby.

The midwife calls the doctor, she is worried there may be complications with the baby's early arrival. My contractions have become stronger and more painful. Mum arrives and our two mothers keep each other company downstairs as they wait for the baby to arrive. Samson's mum paces up and down while my mum calms her down.

"You are like a peasant giving birth," Mum says to me because I am so calm. I push, feeling powerful and fully in control and I wonder why nobody has told me how strong I would feel giving birth. It feels as if I could just lie there and the baby would pop out on its own.

I have entered a different time zone. I know that no matter how painful my contractions are, the pain won't equal the responsibility of bringing new life into the world. I will not always be able to protect my child from what life brings, the inevitable cycle of birth and death. As I concentrate on my breathing I tell myself that compared to the weight of this karmic responsibility my pain is insignificant and it is only temporary.

I have chosen not to take any painkillers, I want to be fully present while giving birth and my excitement outweighs the pain I feel. The doctor holds a mirror up for me so I can see my baby's head emerging. I give one last push and Samson catches our son, Daniel, as he flies through the air and into his arms.

Our baby is tiny and thin and blue and he feels cold as I hold him to my breast. The umbilical cord is wound round his neck. The midwife gently unwinds the cord and waits until it stops pulsing before she finally cuts it.

We feel such intense love for this tiny person we have never seen before. As I hold my baby for the first time everything makes sense and I feel I know all the secrets of the universe and the meaning of life. The room fills with light, the light is bouncing off the walls. Everything I look at, I see as if for the first time. A bird sits on the window ledge and sings to me and my baby. I look at the small face of my baby and his face fills with light. I am looking straight at God – not at physical matter, but at pure spirit.

I smell the top of my baby's head and breathe in deeply, the smell of my womb. The doorbell rings and I go downstairs to open the door. The doctor's wife has arrived with a huge bunch of flowers. All day people come and visit us and our new baby, bringing gifts. Dad takes the afternoon off work and arrives with flowers and a cake. I feel special, like the Virgin Mary with baby Jesus when the Magi came bringing gifts.

37
The joys of motherhood and domesticity

After giving birth I come back down to earth with a bump. Motherhood grounds me, but my dreams are of floating, of flying and of desperately trying to get back down onto the ground. I dream I am left stranded far off the ground in a high-rise building. I jump up into the air and spring higher and higher off the ground. I cannot get down, I am weightless in space. Then I spiral slowly, slowly down again.

My days are no longer carefree, I am not free to come and go as I used to be. I am lonely and long for the freedom of the Welsh mountains. My mornings are spent boiling nappies in the big metal boiler Samson's mum has given me and going for long walks. I push the pram through Cherry Tree Woods and Highgate Woods. The weather is very hot and I sit in Highgate Woods with my baby in the shade under the trees breastfeeding him and eating ice cream. I don't know how to cook and am always ravenously hungry. In the morning I eat a big bowl of porridge and for supper I eat cheese on toast. After my baby is born I become very skinny, the weight just drops off me. In the morning my breasts are like two huge melons, swollen and heavy, leaking sweet thin milk, but by the time the evening comes my breasts hang flat, like pancakes, like two deflated balloons.

We are still living with Samson's mum and on Sundays she cooks large Sunday lunches. The table is laden with homemade olive bread and humus and dolmades and salads and then comes the main course – lasagne and roast potatoes and chicken and vegetables followed by homemade pastries made out of nuts and honey. I eat huge platefuls piled up high, I eat for the week.

Samson and I are exhausted, at night we don't sleep. The baby wakes us up to be fed every two hours and I walk around like a zombie. I would give anything for a good night's sleep. My body aches with exhaustion but I need to get up and feed the baby and change his nappy and walk up and down patting him on the back to wind him and rock him to sleep when he has the colic.

Samson works as a cleaner in a local school, he gets up at six in the morning to clean the classrooms. The pay is not very good. He has always wanted to work with people in a caring profession and he decides to study so he can get a better job to support his new family. He thinks of becoming a nurse but he can't stand the sight of blood. In the paper he sees an advert for a Youth and Community course in Sunderland, up North.

He goes to an interview and is accepted on the course. We will be moving out of London at last.

When the time comes to go we pack our belongings into the baby's pram – mainly nappies and a sack of brown rice – and catch the train up North. Sunderland is a ship-building town but the shipyards have closed down and the men are out of work and rows of shops are boarded up. We see streets of houses with their front doors facing directly onto the pavement.

Our flat is on the top floor of an old house opposite the beach. It is winter in Sunderland and icy cold.Some days it is wild and stormy and it is impossible to go out. I am very lonely – I don't know anybody and Samson is out all day studying. A Jehovah's Witness knocks on the door and I invite her inside. I am desperate for company. The poor woman wants to leave, she has given up trying to convert me, but I insist she drinks another cup of tea. I don't want her to go.

When my baby is asleep I spend my time drawing and painting or taking him for long walks along the beach. Women look at me in disgust when they see me breastfeeding my baby, it is unacceptable to breastfeed your baby in public in this Northern town – strictly taboo. I am in the minority, only ten percent of women in Britain breastfeed their babies.

❋ ❋ ❋

Samson wants to marry me. I love him and want to be with him forever and ever, but I feel trapped.

"Who do you think I am? I am not a suburban housewife," I tell him. I burst into tears, I can't imagine being a wife. I have lost track of myself and the trivial, mundane world has taken over my imagination.

I open up an old carrier bag, a bag full of memories, filled with my old letters, scribbled notes and doodles and pages of pictures I have drawn. In the bag are poems I wrote in hospital. My memories come flooding back and I feel excited. I've been feeling as if I was invisible, and just another boring housewife, but I have done other things. I have written poems and drawn pictures and walked over mountains and been a lunatic in an asylum. I feel a sense of relief as I look at my mementoes and remember who I was.

❋ ❋ ❋

I phone Mum and Dad from a call box. "Have you heard the news?" they ask.

I don't read the newspaper and we don't have a television so I haven't heard the news.

"They are shooting the school children in Soweto," they tell me and I can hear the horror and outrage in their voices when they tell me about what has happened in the streets of Soweto. The news shocks me as I stand in the telephone box on a bleak Sunderland afternoon.

At home on the radio they are playing music from South Africa – *Blue notes for Mongezi*, an album produced in memory of Mongezi Fezi a young South African musician who died in England, far from home. I listen to the musicians playing out their grief and homesickness. Outside it is cold and raining and the tears stream down my face as I allow myself to remember home and South Africa.

✸ ✸ ✸

Our friends visit us in Sunderland. Seymour comes to stay with us and brings his new Japanese wife who cooks us miso soup and tempura. Seymour is a poet and an artist who inspires us with his outrageous imagination. We walk on the beach and watch the clouds.

"Why don't you go to Art College?" Seymour asks me as I watch the extraordinary shapes and colours of the clouds.

"I will never get in, I can't draw," I say.

"Just try," he says.

38
Noah and art

I apply to do an art foundation course at the local college and am accepted. Daniel gets a place at the local day nursery and I start at college. A whole new world opens up to me and my days are full of making things and drawing and painting and exploring my creativity, but it is very hard to leave my baby in the care of strangers. He cries when I leave him and then I am pregnant again.

After the first term, I have to leave college because I can't afford the fees and I am not eligible for a grant. When I leave college I spend my days drawing pictures on our kitchen table while Daniel is at the nursery.

Our second baby, Noah, is born at home in Sunderland. He slips out easily and I enjoy the sensuous feeling of giving birth. He is born at night and all is quiet outside as I breathe in the scent of my new baby and listen to the sea across the road. I look at my baby's face full of light and keep him close to me.

I have my hands full with a new baby and a jealous toddler. Our two babies take it in turns to keep us awake at night and during the day I am exhausted, my energy divided between feeding and changing the baby and running after an energetic toddler.

❋ ❋ ❋

After two years, Samson finishes his course and gets a job as a community worker in London. I have become used to Sunderland. I have made friends and I like living by the sea. I don't really want to move back to London. Samson is promised a house with the job and the pay is good so we pack up and move to London. The house we were promised doesn't materialise and we end up staying with Mum and Dad in their small two bedroom house.

After six long months of waiting to be housed, we eventually get a flat in Tottenham, a run-down area with a bad reputation and busy main roads. Our house in Vicarage Road is near the Tottenham Football stadium and I can hear the chants of the football fans on Saturday afternoons. We have a big three-bedroomed flat with a garden. I move my long brown trestle table and my art materials into one of the bedrooms and turn it into my art room. I wake up early in the mornings before Samson and the children are up and go into my art room to do some work.

On days when the rain is endless and the landscape outside the window is dreary, I escape to my art room and fill pages and pages of paper with bright colours. I play music and dance while I work and forget about doing housework. The dishes pile up and the kitchen floor is left unwashed. I draw obsessively whenever I have the time. When I don't find time to draw I feel incomplete.

* * *

In our flat in Tottenham, I sit at home with the children and wonder who I am. Fragments of myself are flying through space and I do not feel solid. I am scared to be alone but when I am with other people I cannot be myself – I feel too self-conscious. I feel misplaced as I wake up in the morning. Where am I? Who am I? What is this strange life I am leading as a housewife? I push the double pram down the high street and breathe in exhaust fumes as lorries and buses thunder by.

I take the children to the park to play. It is full of dog shit and broken glass and alcoholics sit on benches drinking, muttering and swearing incoherently. They stagger over to the playground and pee in the grass. I must get out of the city – this is no life for our children. However, we have a flat with three bedrooms at an affordable rent and Samson has a good job.

Samson is out all day and has meetings in the evening. Most of the time I am on my own. We don't have much to say to each other when we are together. But I would give up all this security because I feel like I am dying inside.

"It is your turn to stay at home and look after the children," I tell Samson. "I want to go to college."

My mind is fixed on wanting to study – I want to improve my life. I am tired of being stuck in this dead-end repetitive Tottenham life. My dream is to study art. I fill in application forms and dress carefully and take my pictures to interviews. But I do not make the grade – I do not pass and I am not accepted. I am Cinderella's ugly sister trying to squeeze myself into a shoe that is too small, that does not fit, but I refuse to cut off my toes or bind my feet.

* * *

All the art colleges I have applied to have rejected me, but I have one last chance, I have applied to do an unusual course in Devon, perhaps I can fit in there. But they write back and tell me I do not have the right qualifications, they cannot accept my application. All the doors have been slammed shut, firmly shut in my face.

I write a letter and unload my anger and frustration on the page. "How can you judge me by what I don't have, instead of by what I do have? What are these qualifications? Empty pieces of paper, what do they prove? You have not seen what I can do."

I mail the letter, it will surely end up in the bin, but I have to get my feelings off my chest.

A letter arrives inviting me to an interview at Dartington College of Arts in Devon, a reply to the rude letter I wrote. They have given me an assignment to do, I must make a hat.

I make a bridal hat with two sides, front and back. At the back is the fantasy with roses, lace and smiles and in the front is the reality of chains made out of nappy pins and a crown of clothes pegs symbolising domestic drudgery.

I am very excited as I put my work in my portfolio and prepare for the interview. I take the train from Paddington station to Devon. The college is in a rural setting and all the spring flowers are out. I look down at the river below me and walk along carrying my bridal hat and art work in my new black portfolio.

When I get to Dartington College, I am shown into a small office where I am interviewed by three men who shake my hand warmly. They like my hat and laugh at it, but I am worried that I might be exhausting them, I have so many pictures to show. I see that my letter, the one that was meant for the bin, is lying on the desk and feel embarrassed.

"We will be pleased to see you when the term starts," they tell me and I leave, walking on air.

39
Like a fish out of water

After much discussion, debating and arguing about giving up our flat, Samson leaves his job and we pack up and move to Devon, into the great unknown. We rent a flat, a temporary holiday let, we will have to move out at Easter time. The flat has a musty, damp smell. The building was an abattoir before it was turned into flats. I imagine the smell of blood and the hanging carcasses and the fear in the cattle's eyes as they were slaughtered. The flat is furnished. We sleep in beds other people have slept in.

However much I scrub, the flat never feels clean. It never feels like home – it is just a temporary place to stay. The town is on the edge of Dartmoor and we hear plenty of stories of ghosts.

Next door to where we live used to be a pub, the Valiant Soldier that has now closed down. An old lady lives there but she never comes out. When her husband died, she closed down the pub and kept everything exactly the same, untouched, frozen in time.

There are no jobs in Devon and Samson is out of work. He feels aimless, like a fish out of water in this small English town, drifting, with no money and no work. While I blossom at college, Samson stays home and gets depressed.

In the evenings when I hitchhike back from college in the dark Samson doesn't greet me when I come in. As soon as I come in he goes out, down to the pub with his mates. The children spin round and round, making me feel dizzy. I hardly have time to catch my breath before I see to their demands. They need to be fed and to be bathed, they need to be heard, to be seen, to be read to, to be sung to sleep. I fall asleep next to the children, exhausted.

Samson doesn't greet me when he comes back from the pub, he is withdrawn and silently resentful.

Samson and I share a long year of resentment and distance, living in the same house, not eating together, not sharing the same bed and not talking.

"Can we spend some time together?" I ask. "We can get a babysitter and go out somewhere."

"You colonise enough of my time already," Samson tells me angrily.

He is standing looking out of the window upstairs when a lorry thunders down the high street and crashes into our window. He feels the ground shaking and jumps back just in time. The ground disappears from beneath his feet and the side of the house is ripped off.

❈ ❈ ❈

The lease for the flat is up and we need to move, to make way for summer holidaymakers who will pay double the rent. We are homeless, once again, so we buy a caravan in a field on Windmill Down Farm just outside Totnes.

The caravan has one double bed but no toilet or running water. The nettles sting my bum as I squat down to pee behind the hedge. When I climb up the hill to fetch water from the cattle trough the view is magnificent and makes up for the other inconveniences. We have run out of money, but luckily I discover a field of huge potatoes the farmer has left in the ground after harvesting, they are a godsend. We eat baked potatoes, fried potatoes, mashed potatoes and roast potatoes on Sundays. When our dole money arrives we have eggs, chips and beans. But chips are our staple diet.

Samson takes the children to London for a week and I feel like I have been let out of a cage. I go to the pub and get drunk on the local scrumpy.

❈ ❈ ❈

"Would you risk it for a biscuit?" Alan, a man I have just met in the pub, asks me. He flirts with me and I enjoy the attention I am getting and yes, I risk it for a glass too many of scrumpy and Alan comes back to the caravan to spend the night.

Samson comes back from London and looks at my face. He can see there is something I am not telling him. I cannot lie, but I am also scared to tell him. I sit mute, frozen in time and space. Eventually his accusations wear me down. I am too tired to hold my secret close any longer and I tell him what I have done.

Samson is angry, all night we fight. I am out of my mind with exhaustion, I am a scared rabbit caught in the headlights of an oncoming car. I freeze up, unable to respond to Samson's anger, or defend myself, or answer his questions.

There are no houses nearby only me, the children, and Samson's uncontained anger in the dark field. The love, the hatred, the anger, the betrayal fly around the dark field. How could I, how could he? We make love. There is a desperation to our intimacy, a fear of losing each other. We lie on the ground, the children are asleep in the only bed.

❈ ❈ ❈

That summer is tough – the water in the cattle trough dries up, we have no food, no electricity, no money, and no house. But I look at the view and enjoy the beauty of the hills stretching in front of me, the lush green and the rich, red earth.

Samson goes to London to visit his mum for a week and Harvey, the farmer, comes to visit me. He tells me I don't have to pay rent if I will come and sleep in his bed once a week. I refuse.

Later, Harvey comes striding across the field in his old cloth cap, dirty jacket and muddy boots. My son of three years has left the gate open, he's let the cows out of the field. Harvey wants to beat him to teach him a lesson. He wants to beat him with his belt. Noah hides. I look for him everywhere, he has disappeared while my back was turned and now he is nowhere to be found. I search behind hedgerows and in the fields running up and down the lanes calling his name. It has been an hour since I last saw him. The worst must have happened.

I run down the Old Roman Road but there is no sign of him. I look everywhere for him, the landscape is shrouded in mist, I fear the worst.

I knock on Harvey's door at the farm house. "Please can I use the phone?" I ask. The policeman on the other end of the line says to phone back in an hour.

An hour is too long, I phone back in ten minutes. I am frantic. "Please send someone immediately." The policeman calms me down. They have my son, I can come and fetch him.

I rush down the Old Roman Road into town. Noah is sitting in the police station enjoying himself, eating a bar of chocolate and wearing a policeman's helmet. "Mummy, Mummy, where were you? I was looking everywhere for you."

40
Splitting

Samson has been my best friend and my soul mate for more than ten years, but anger and resentment have driven a wedge between us. Mistrust takes over and we compete for who has hurt who the most or who has suffered the most. I hate him – I want him out of my life, I no longer feel safe with him and he feels betrayed by me.

Winter is coming, and I don't want to live in a muddy field in the cold weather with two small children and the tension that is between Samson and myself. A man from the council comes to visit me in the caravan and puts me near the top of the housing list. He gives me extra points for no electricity, no running water and no toilet. However, he says I must wait, the housing list is long and local people get priority.

While I wait for a house, I rent a flat in Buckfastleigh and move out on my own with the children.

Samson stays on in the caravan.

＊ ＊ ＊

The flat is small, but it seems huge, like a palace, after the caravan. It has one bedroom, a tiny living room, a bathroom and a kitchen. We can stay here until Easter.

Samson comes to visit us, he is struggling to come to terms with losing his family. He has no money and he is depressed, living in the caravan on his own. I feel guilty and I open my purse and give him what I have – and then I also have no money.

After the children are asleep at night, I lie alone in bed. I am twenty-seven years old and I can't imagine ever allowing myself to be close to anyone else again. I will be celibate for the rest of my life – I will never live with a man again. They are bastards, all of them, bullies, and not to be trusted.

It is too difficult to carry on going to college now that I am on my own with the children and I decide to leave. The children are unsettled and need a lot of my attention. May be next year, when they are older, I can go back.

＊ ＊ ＊

Samson has met someone else, a woman with two children. He comes to fetch the children to take them out. I stand by myself at the side of the road, smiling and waving. They are all going on a family outing together. Our children, Samson's and mine, laugh and play in the back of the car with the other woman's children. They are like one big happy family. The other woman sits at the front of the car, in my seat.

I stand on the curb and wave good-bye. I feel sick, I run upstairs and vomit in the toilet. My heart is breaking, but I won't admit it. This is what I wanted, this is what I have chosen. I have left Samson. I hate him but that doesn't stop half of me feeling like it has been ripped off, leaving an open wound. I feel as if I won't survive this raw pain. I can't eat, I can't sleep. I can't tell anyone. I am a strong independent woman and I don't need a man – this man, any man. My heart is a heavy weight, it shatters.

I am set adrift. After ten years and two babies, I am floating. I must rely on my anger to get me through this heartache.

Samson comes to see me, he drops the children back after he has taken them out and we sit silently, like strangers, with an awkward silence between us, an empty space. We don't know how to be with each other from this distance. When Samson leaves, the children cry themselves to sleep, they are inconsolable. I shut the door to shut out their crying. I don't have it in me to comfort them, I feel too angry.

At Easter time we move again, to make room for holidaymakers who pay double the rent for the flat. We move into a cottage down the road. The landlady is selling the cottage and after a few months we have to move out. This time I don't know where to go. I am at my wits' end, I phone the council to find out how far up the housing list I am.

✵ ✵ ✵

A letter arrives from the council to say I have been allocated a house, a two-bedroom house in Totnes on the edge of the council estate near the river. We go and visit the house and I walk around. I feel like I have won the lotto – this is my castle. Nobody can ever tell me to move again, as long as I keep paying the rent, this is my home, Number 16 Parkers Close, Totnes.

We have no furniture and move into an empty house. We sleep on a mattress on the floor and hang sheets up at the windows for curtains. I apply for a furniture grant from Social Security: for beds and blankets, curtains, a table and chairs and a stove. A cheque arrives for a substantial amount of money. I furnish the house with some of the money and the rest I save up to go travelling.

We settle into Totnes, a small English town nestled in a valley, surrounded by soft green hills. It feels womb-like and safe, with a river flowing through the middle of the town. I walk down country lanes with hedgerows and wild strawberries and spring flowers growing along the side of the lanes.

Devon feels like home. Now that we have a house and I know where we will be living I can go back to college to complete my course. As part of the course we do placements in the community and I have chosen the Woman's Centre.

This is at the height of feminism, the honeymoon period. We are all sisters and love each other and support each other. We are powerful women, reclaiming our space and our women-defined identities. We are separatists and men are not allowed inside the centre.

The children go to school in a nearby village. The school is small and friendly with a stream running through the playground. A lot of the other mothers are also struggling single parents.

In the morning, while the children are still asleep I walk along the riverbank. The river Dart becomes a constant presence in my life. Very early in the day it is time for the birds and the animals to claim their space. Fish jump to the surface of the water to catch flies, and otters play in the water. The colours are soft and quiet before the busyness of the day begins and I have time to centre myself without distractions. I forage for food. Wild spinach grows along the riverbanks in the mud, and celery, and sometimes tomatoes and cabbage. In the autumn, there are blackberries and chestnuts to pick.

The river is used as a dump and Daniel and Noah bring home treasures they find, an old wheelbarrow, plastic containers and pieces of wood. I fill the plastic containers with earth and grow flowers and vegetables in them. We find beautiful fragments of china and crockery, old bottles and ornaments that I make artworks with. These are our treasures.

✳ ✳ ✳

The heavens open and the rain comes down – all day long it rains. It rains for days. Cooped up inside the house the children grow bored and restless and fight with each other, competing for my attention. I want to smack them – they won't stop fighting and the noise escalates. We dress up in our raincoats and Wellington boots and go down to the river in the pouring rain where we jump in puddles and run in the rain. The rain wakes me up and makes me feel alive and helps the children get rid of their pent-up energy.

41
Tanzania

At the end of the summer, I finish my course at Dartington College and manage to put together enough money to buy the cheapest ticket to Tanzania, an
Aeroflot ticket via Moscow to Dar es Salam. I have dreamed for a long time
about putting my feet down on African soil again. I want to go and visit my
brother who is working as a teacher in Tanzania at the ANC school. Noah is
coming with me but Samson and I decide that Daniel will stay behind with him.

I am not allowed to go back to South Africa, but at least in Tanzania I
will be closer to home. We leave on a plane to Moscow, wrapped up in coats
and hats and scarves. In Moscow we stay in the Aeroflot transit hotel on the
edge of the city. The hotel is surrounded by a forest covered in thick snow.
Noah and I go into the forest and make a snowman and throw snowballs
at each other. The next day we fly to Dar es Salaam.

The journey takes more than twenty hours, we stop and start, off-loading
and re-fuelling. In Dar es Salaam we get off, carrying our heavy winter coats
and hats and scarves. John meets us at the airport and we collect our luggage
and step into steamy, hot, tropical weather.

After fifteen years of being away from home, my feet at last touch African
soil. Steam rises from the tropical rain puddles and Noah strips his clothes
off as fast as he can and splashes in the warm water.

It is so hot I feel as if I am hallucinating, the colours are vibrant and
bright in contrast to England's muted landscape. Lush bushes are covered in
brightly coloured flowers, and people are dressed in vivid, patterned clothes.

At sunrise and sunset, when the weather is slightly cooler, I find it possible to go outside. In the heat of the day the heat is too intense. After so
many years I have become accustomed to English weather. I know how to
bundle up against the cold. My blood is sluggish and I battle to cope with
the thick, sultry heat.

In the early morning, John takes us to the beach for a swim and the sea feels
like warm soup. I am thirsty and want to buy something to drink but in Dar
es Salaam the shops are empty. There is nothing to buy and the Tanzanian
shilling is worth nothing. There are no supermarkets with shelves stocked
up with bread and cheese and milk. Instead we buy a green coconut filled
with cool refreshing coconut milk from the side of the road.

※ ※ ※

After a few days, we drive inland to Morogoro and from there to the School in Mazimbu where John teaches. Mzimbu is surrounded by mountains and the heat is a dry heat, not the debilitating humidity of Dar es Salaam or the biting cold of England. The school has been built on an old sisal plantation and has become a well-developed community of South African exiles.

I am surrounded by young South Africans who have fled to safety and constantly dream of going home. England seems far away and I feel closer to home here amongst other homesick South Africans.

The students greet me warmly with a "Hello, comrade." Many of them will be going on to do military training or study in socialist countries. In the evenings the students gather in the hall to hear news briefings about the situation at home and to sing inspiring struggle songs.

There is no water in the camp, the pump is broken and they are waiting for the parts to arrive from Germany before the pump can be mended. Someone from the school needs to drive to pick the parts up in Dar es Salaam, but there are no tyres available for the communal car, so we must all wait for water. A tank comes every day and we rush out to fill up buckets and bowls with water. I learn to bath with one cup of water.

Supplies are brought round twice a week and shared out. We get four tins of Russian sardines, two cabbages, half a dozen eggs and samp and beans.

※ ※ ※

During the day, I work at the pre-school. Six-year-old Noah comes into work with me. The other children stroke his smooth hair and rub the skin on his arm to see what lies beneath his paleness.

For breakfast, the kitchen sends over big pots of mielie meal porridge for the children and for lunch the children eat beans and rice. After lunch in the afternoon heat they sleep on small mattresses on the floor. Malaria is rife and some of the children will lie on their mattresses all day, weak with a fever. Not all of the children have parents.

Noah makes friends with a young student who works with the chickens and feeds him boiled eggs. At night in the dark Noah catches frogs and fireflies.

At Christmas time, we are given a live chicken to pluck and eat. Noah feels sorry for the other chickens tethered outside waiting to be slaughtered. He releases them and they go running down the road. Our fellow housemate is not amused to see his Christmas dinner running down the road and gives Noah a good smack.

I would like to stay here, it feels like I am closer to home, but I miss Daniel and Noah misses his dad. It is time to go back to London.

※ ※ ※

We drive from Morogoro to hot, humid Dar es Salam and stay over for the week before we board our flight to icy Moscow. The plane stops to refuel at the tiny airport in the Seychelles. In the distance I can see the turquoise sea shimmering in the hot sun. The people here look the same as the people in Cape Town. They let us off the plane to stretch our legs and Noah fights with a little girl the same age as him. She belongs to a family from the Sudan with nine children.

In the airport shop, I see Eet-Sum-Mor biscuits, tempting me with the forbidden tastes of home. Guiltily I buy two packets. One packet to eat now and one packet to savour, bite by bite, in the middle of the cold Devon winter I am returning to. I shouldn't be buying them – there is a boycott on South African goods. I buy Noah an ice cream with a chocolate flake in it, the first ice cream he has had in a long time.

I don't want to leave this rock in the ocean with its blue skies and soft breeze and forbidden biscuits. I want to step out of the airport and lose myself in this small town. "Come, Noah, let's run away." We could slip out of the side door – the security is very lax here – and run across the tarmac and down the road that leads to the sea. The plane can leave without us. I can find a job and a house to rent and Totnes with its endless rain and living on the dole can vanish like a puff of smoke. I can stay and make a life here.

I offer a biscuit to the woman sitting next to me on the airport bench and take my first sweet, buttery bite of my forbidden Eet-Sum-Mor biscuit. The sweet taste of home. I close my eyes and savour each mouthful.

A woman's voice interrupts my thoughts.

"All passengers for the flight to Moscow please board now."

※ ※ ※

After spending a few days in Moscow at the transit hotel, we arrive in London. Samson is there to meet us and we make our way to catch the bus to the train station to get to Totnes.

Samson tells me he wants Daniel to live with him. We stand at the bus stop and argue, our voices raised. The children fight. "Stop it, behave yourselves stop fighting," I scream at them, my tears flowing.

"He is coming home with me," I shout at Samson.

"He doesn't want to, he wants to come with me," Samson shouts back at me.

The bus arrives and I try to pick Daniel up. I try to pull him onto the bus but Samson holds onto him tightly. Daniel wriggles free and runs away while Noah stands beside me crying.

42

Tug of War

Over the next year, we engage in a tug of war, a fight to the death. Samson threatens to take the children away. I want to buy a sharp knife and plunge it into his chest, and see the blood flow bright red, dark red. I put a curse on him and in my mind I picture him slipping, breaking his neck. When I next see him he is wearing a bandage on his knee. But I don't really want him dead, I just want my children to stay with me.

Instead of cursing him I begin to pray. I light a candle and I pray for protection for myself and my children. I hold on. Without my children, I will be nothing, and have nothing.

I hold on, afraid that they will want to live with their father. I spoil my children, giving in to all their whims and wishes. I let them do what they want and they run wild without boundaries. This time round I win the battle and the children stay with me. There is an uneasy truce between Samson and me.

* * *

In the holidays, the children go and stay with Samson and I am left out on a limb. My daily routine is aimless and meaningless. The children give my days a structure – getting up early, washing, shopping, cooking and bedtime. Without them here I can stay out as late as I like, I need not worry about paying a baby sitter.

I don't need to cook three meals a day. I go to the pub and on the way home I buy hot chips from the fish and chip shop. The grease and salt soak up the beer. I feel sick. Someone suggests we go back to their place for more drinking and smoking. I smoke a joint and it makes me feel strange. Is this freedom?

My senses are not to be trusted. Reality nose dives. I miss my children.

* * *

Daniel and Noah come back home after the holidays. They don't want to go to school and I am too tired to force them, too tired to get out of bed. I look out of the window. The sun is shining.

"Let's go to the beach today," I say to them.

On the bus, I lie about the children's ages. Noah is six and Daniel is eight, but children under five go free. "No he is only four, he just looks big for his age," I tell the conductor. "Whatever you do, don't tell the conductor how old you are, otherwise we will have to walk. I can't afford to pay all our fares," I say to the children.

We spend the day playing on the beach and climbing over the rocks and catch the last bus home. The next day, the alarm clock goes off, but I do not hear it. We oversleep as usual, we have to rush and the children are late for school.

※ ※ ※

I rush to work. I have a job working in an office as a tea lady. The offices are within walking distance of the children's school.

"Do you take one or two sugars?"

"Would you like tea or coffee, hot or cold milk?"

I push the trolley along the corridor to the next office and ask the same again.

"One or two sugars?"

"Tea or coffee?"

Then back again, to collect the dirty cups and saucers.

I go into the toilet where there is a stack of pink toilet paper. Sometimes I take a roll home with me and a bar of soap, hidden in my bag. It all adds up and saves me money when we run out of soap and toilet paper.

I find a place to do my art work nearby. In between my job and fetching the children from school in the afternoons I have a few hours to spare where I can draw, but I am ambushed by lack of time and long for an uninterrupted hour, for the space to drift and do nothing and let my imagination go where it needs to go.

※ ※ ※

On my birthday, I feel very sorry for myself, no one has wished me happy birthday or sent me a card. The postman delivers a gas bill instead. Obviously nobody loves me. Oh, poor me! The world has forgotten that I exist … but by the time the afternoon comes my friends and neighbours arrive, bringing birthday cards and gifts.

Daniel turns ten and Noah turns eight. Their birthdays fall in the same month. We make a huge cake in the shape of a house with a roof made out of smarties and green coconut grass. We invite all their friends. At their party two clowns perform magic tricks.

※ ※ ※

I want to be a good mother, like the mother in the Janet and John books, or the mother in the washing powder advert, calm and perfectly in control. I never quite manage to get it right. I shout at the children and the house is always untidy. I feel exhausted by my outbursts of anger and frustration, tired of my conflicting feelings.

My life is an endless round of housework, shopping, washing, cooking, and going to work. Untidiness, dirt and chaos lurk in all the corners. There never seems to be any let-up from the relentless demands of my daily routine. I am alone and everything falls on my shoulders as I walk the straight and narrow path of daily demands.

I want to let go. But to let go I need to be in control of my life. I over-eat when I don't want to, I smoke when I don't want to. I need a clear purpose, to be able to shape my life the way I want it to be.

I work to make money to pay the bills. I have no shoulder to lean on, and I don't want one. That would only make more work for me – to have to see to someone else's needs. Sometimes at night, I wake up with my heart screaming in fear.

In this small English town, where people go about their daily business peacefully, in the early morning before dawn, in the dark and the quiet, my life catches up with me. It gets me in the small of my back and the stiffness in my neck. My body aches with stored tension. Memories of prison visiting rooms and the man who sits and takes notes of what we say and the woman who locked and unlocked the door when we visited Mum come flooding back to me.

Every moment I can, I draw and paint, covering hundreds of sheets of paper. Strange images emerge, shedding light on my shadowy places. I find magic and healing in creating something out of nothing and discovering the unexpected. I hide my pictures under my bed and defend my space from intruders.

The house is looking shabby and I decide to paint it from top to bottom. It is a huge job but I am undaunted. First I strip the old wall paper off the walls. There are layers and layers of wall paper, going back twenty years. The wall paper sticks stubbornly to the wall as I scrape and tear the paper. I steam it off using my iron and a solution of vinegar to melt the glue. The house smells like a fish and chip shop. The process takes forever. When I am bored of tearing strips of wall paper off the wall, I go upstairs and draw on the pieces of wall paper and the patterns show through the crayons and paint.

＊ ＊ ＊

The Totnes Women's Centre has become a central meeting place for women. In the front of the building is a women's bookshop and at the back is a canteen where we take it in turns to cook communal vegetarian meals for each other.

The many rooms of the Women's Centre house businesses, all run by women. Greenshoes is a successful hand-crafted shoemaking business and Charlotte from Denmark designs and hand prints fabrics. Dragonfly Tofu makes tofu burghers and tofu ice cream and Diana uses vegetable dyes to dye wool to knit into exquisite jerseys that are works of art. Diana invites me to share her workshop and I draw prolifically in our shared space.

"Why don't you have an exhibition?" Diana asks, and gives me the phone number of Birdwood House which hires out rooms for holding exhibitions. I book the space and spend the summer framing my work, staying up late into the night cutting mounts and putting my pictures behind glass. I frame over seventy pictures. When I am done I want to cancel the exhibition. I will just make a fool of myself.

My pictures are up on the wall and the people in the town come to see my work. My pictures are selling fast – as soon as I turn around another picture has been sold. I feel strangely well-off and I spend the money on a vacuum cleaner and taking the children on holiday.

43
Exhibitions and protests

A gallery in London has invited me to have an exhibition. I take my pictures out from under my bed and dust them off. This time I get a professional framer to frame my work. I screen print all the invitations – a slow laborious process of making the stencils by hand and squeezing the ink evenly through the screen before cleaning the screens. The heavy oil-based inks need to be cleaned with toxic solvents. My head feels dizzy from the toxic fumes of the solvents and I go home with a headache but feeling satisfied with the work I have done.

In London, at my opening, the gallery is crowded with people talking and drinking wine. People want to talk to me about my work – they want me to explain it to them. A journalist wants to take photos and interview me. I drink too much wine and my face is flushed. I want to hide in a corner. I don't like to talk about my work. I have no idea what it means, it is just something I do, like breathing.

At home, next to the window in my bedroom that overlooks the River Dart, is the long wooden trestle table where I work. I paint and draw, listening to music from South Africa, dancing and connecting to the rhythms of South Africa. This is my way of travelling back home. I listen to struggle songs and have a poster of the Freedom Charter on my wall.

"There Shall Be Peace and Freedom and The People Shall Govern." The words inspire me and I paint a series of colourful pictures illustrating the Freedom Charter.

The paintings show both the ideals of the Freedom Charter and the suffering of people under apartheid. I ask myself, What is the value of beautiful pictures if they are not connected to the Struggle? I draw pictures of prisons and barbed wire and faces behind bars.

My work keeps me busy. I donate my work to the ANC and they produce cards and calendars of my paintings to raise money. Oxfam asks me to do art workshops about South Africa in schools across London and I exhibit my work in Devon and Glasgow and Amsterdam and London. But I am shy and not very confident and would rather hide away and stay at home.

※ ※ ※

I stand outside Barclays Bank in Totnes High Street holding a placard. "Boycott Barclays Bank. Blood Money." I am a lone voice, handing out leaflets, trying to bring attention to the bank's support of the Apartheid regime. The response is slow. Passers-by ignore me and an employee from the bank asks me to move to the other side of the road as I am causing an obstruction.

For many people in Totnes, South Africa is just another exotic country in darkest Africa, full of wild animals and happy tribes living in mud huts.

I plod on, protesting, spending a huge amount of time and energy for results that seem very small and insignificant.

But all of a sudden things take off. The news is filled with shocking images of violence and injustice in South Africa. I watch obsessively. The Totnes anti-Apartheid group grows from a small group of one to become a busy hub of activity with many members. We organise festivals and fund-raising discos and pickets outside businesses who are supporting the Apartheid regime.

The local Labour Party joins our protest outside Barclays Bank and the bank manager comes outside to introduce himself. He invites me inside. He sits me down and offers me a cup of coffee and hands me a glossy brochure explaining how Barclays is helping black people in South Africa. Students have been boycotting Barclays Bank in significant numbers and the bank is starting to take their protests seriously. In the end Barclays Bank decides to withdraw its investments from South Africa.

※ ※ ※

At home, my nerves are on edge. I am suffering from pre-menstrual tension. I walk down the road to the phone box to make a call and come back home with a bag full of barley wine and tobacco to keep me going. When I get home, I cook chips for the children. I'm exhausted, I have not stopped all day. I am working as a char two days a week and in a fish and chip shop the other three days.

I am lonely, but relationships are complicated and painful. My heart says it wants to be loved, not just safe. I want to choose warmth and connection, but my head tells me to stay clear of relationships – it is safer to be alone. Emotions are messy and I can't afford them. I have two children to bring up, I can't fall apart again.

I am strong I don't need any one. I am strong I don't need any one. I am strong I don't need any one. I repeat my mantra over and over.

※ ※ ※

I carry my shopping from the supermarket over the bridge. I am laden with heavy bags.

"Can I help you?" a woman asks and gives me a smile.

"Thank you," I say as I hand her a heavy bag.

When we get to my house she puts down the shopping and holds out her hand.

"My name is Anna."

On Friday nights, at the Women's Centre, we let our collective hair down and dance. I am surprised and pleased to see Anna on the dance floor, shaking her sexy body. She tells me she has just come back from Kenya where she was working as a volunteer helping a midwife to deliver babies. She needs a place to stay for the night.

"You can come and stay with me," I tell her.

I fall in love with Anna and Samson says he will take me to court and tell the judge I am a lesbian and get custody of the children. It is a high price to pay for love, but I will risk it.

It is the height of feminism in Britain, and all women are sisters and women are not afraid to love each other passionately and erotically. It is politically correct to be a lesbian and woman-identified. Men oppress women and one does not want to be caught sleeping with the enemy.

Anna leaves for America to work at a summer camp for a few months, but promises to be back at the end of the summer. She leaves all her belongings at my house. But on her way back to England, on the way to the airport, Anna changes her mind and turns around, she won't be coming back to England. I am left in limbo, waiting, and my heart grows an extra layer of scar tissue.

44
No males allowed

The children go and stay with Samson during the summer holidays and I go camping at a women's summer camp in Glastonbury. No males are allowed – not even male dogs or boy babies. Only women's energy is allowed.

I unpack my small single tent. The heavens have opened and it is raining heavily. Between me and the outside elements there is nothing but a thin fly sheet, but miraculously I keep dry in my tent. I lie in my sleeping bag listening to the sound of the rain drumming down on the tent. I feel safe and with my sense of safety comes a sense of freedom that I have not felt before. I become aware of how I usually hold myself in and guard my body, vigilant against predatory eyes and predatory hands.

The years of fending off lecherous men have taken their toll and it is a relief to let go in this safe women's space with no undercurrents of male violence or sexual abuse. My body expands into this space and I enjoy the luxury of not having to guard it.

But then my peace and quiet is interrupted by the sound of women shouting at one another.

"We want to sleep, turn that fucking noise down."

"Why didn't you stay at home if you wanted to sleep? You middle class wankers, we want to party and enjoy ourselves."

If you can't beat them join them, I think. I give up trying to sleep. It has stopped raining and I go and sit with the drinkers, but secretly I sympathise with the sleepers.

"We came here to get away from the city, we want peace and quiet, just turn the music down," the women in the tents shout.

The women at the camp fire turn the music up.

The exchange becomes very heated and it looks like a fight is about to start until a woman with a reputation for being a witch joins the camp fire and casts her spell over us all and tames the situation. A compromise is reached between the women and harmony is restored once more.

I spend a week at the camp enjoying the wine, women and song. We have nights under a full moon singing and dancing and I go back home feeling strong and inspired.

"Fuck off," I tell men in the street, as they undress me with their eyes or whistle at me as if I am a dog.

✳ ✳ ✳

A group of women and their children have walked from Wales to Greenham Common to bring attention to the American nuclear weapons base at the common. The women set up camp outside the base and Greenham Women's Peace camp grows until there are women from all walks of life and from all over the world setting up camp on the common. Totnes Women's Centre has an active Women's Peace Group and organises coaches to go to Greenham Common on a regular basis.

A day of action is planned for Greenham and women have been asked to make banners to put on the fence around the American Base. I spend the week sewing a banner with bright yellow sunflowers and birds of peace. At five o'clock in the morning I run over the bridge with the children to catch the coach from the Women's Centre to Greenham.

The camp at Greenham Common, is a women-only space and women gather outside the American missile base to bear witness to the weapons of mass destruction housed inside the base. The children play in the woods, climb trees and gather firewood while the women spend the day sewing all the banners together to make a long rainbow-coloured dragon. The dragon is nine miles long – long enough to circle the entire base. We dance around the base and the day culminates in drumming and singing and dancing as the magic dragon weaves in and out of the gathering.

Women from all walks of life, from vicars' wives to lesbian separatists, gather together. There are women from all over the world camping outside the American military base enduring freezing British winters in tents and benders – round shelters, made out of sticks and canvas.

On New Year's Eve, I visit Greenham. It's the middle of winter and the weather is icy cold. Women huddle outside around the camp fire, sharing food and wine and singing. From inside the base where the missiles are kept, we think the army is transmitting electromagnetic waves into the women's camp, zapping us, and tampering with our energy. The low level dosages of radiation make the women ill. The mood of that New Year's Eve is low and sombre.

✳ ✳ ✳

Sisterhood is becoming undone, the honeymoon period is over. Women splinter into small groups competing to see which group is the most oppressed.

I travel to Brighton with the children to a Lesbian Custody conference. The conference is very well organised and the children have a wonderful time being looked after and enjoying the different activities and outings laid on for them. We have a day of intense workshops where lesbian mothers share their experiences. Women tell of tragic experiences – having their children taken away, not being permitted to see them, purely on the grounds of being a lesbian and deemed an unfit mother.

In the evening, we have a disco and let off steam after the day's workshops. The music is pumping as we dance and flirt.

The DJ plays "We Are Family" and we dance together in a circle. Then she plays "I Will Survive" and we all sing along together.

A woman takes the mike and sings a moving solo. "Dream Lover, where are you?"

I am having a great time.

But on the other side of the room a woman from up north bumps into a woman from down south and asks her: "Where did you get your ethnic outfit from?" The woman from down south takes offence, she is insulted and an argument and a scuffle ensue. I don't notice and carry on dancing.

The next morning, we splinter into groups, we are supposed to take sides. Jewish and black women sit in one room discussing their oppression while the other women sit in another room discussing their guilt. The lesbian mothers sit and listen silently while the conference degenerates into an argument about class and race.

What was meant to be space for lesbian mothers to support each other has been hijacked by egos and the opinions of women who don't have children.

I go back to Totnes feeling profoundly disillusioned and disturbed.

❄ ❄ ❄

In Totnes, the bookshop at the Women's Centre is losing money and someone suggests that we turn it into a computer shop. Many of the women distrust computers as a patriarchal tool whilst others say computers can empower women.

At the meeting to decide whether to close down the bookshop, women turn against each other and polarise into working-class lesbians versus middle-class married women. The craft-based businesses are pitted against the invasion of technology.

In the end, the Women's Centre closes down and the building burns down one night under mysterious circumstances. Rumour has it that a property developer wants to get his hands on the land.

45
Totnes, trials, and therapists

Totnes is a town of therapists, there are at least two therapists to every person. People believe in past lives, and aliens, and world events are measured by the line-up of the planets and the influence of astrological energy. Totnes has the highest percentage of vegetarians in Britain. But on the council estate where we live, it is a bit rougher around the edges and people are narrow-minded and wary of foreigners.

My neighbour in Totnes walks out on her husband and her children and runs off with a biker covered in tattoos, with long greasy hair and dirt encrusted nails. George comes to look after her heart-broken husband and help him through his misery.

George has been in prison for the past seven years for dealing heroin. He has a motherly quality about him and is like a clucking hen. He drives me around in his car and takes me shopping and cooks spicy Red Dragon pie for me. He is playful and brings out the childish qualities in me. We get stoned together and giggle. He lives on a boat on the river, but the boat is leaking and sinks.

"I luv ya," he tells me and I am caught in his net. He wants to move in with me and the children. They call him Georgie Porgie Pudding and Pie. I am scared. I don't want to get too close to George. I know the hazards of his life, what might happen to me. Georgie Porgie is a motherly clucking hen, but he will want to take my life over and tell me what to do.

We go for a drive and a drink, a liquid lunch he calls it. The pub is in a small village and in the church yard is a yew tree that is a thousand years old. According to local legend if you make a wish and walk around the yew tree backwards seven times with your eyes closed your wish will come true.

I close my eyes and walk backwards and wish very hard not to get involved with George. Round and round I go seven times.

My wish comes true and I am saved just in time by his ex-girlfriend who turns up out of the blue. She has been arrested for driving an illegal car and being in possession of drugs. George goes to her rescue.

He puts his arms around me, "I luv ya, but I have to go," he tells me.

As he walks out the door I breathe a huge sigh of relief.

George and his girlfriend, Tina, spend the winter together living in a freezing cold shed on a farm, fighting and drinking. When I bump into Tina in town she can hardly walk, she is covered in bruises and looks like a ghost. They are killing each other and themselves, but they can't get free of each other until Tina gets a new boyfriend and moves into a flat across the road from me.

The people in the flats across the road are always fighting – there are always dramas happening. Police cars and ambulances pull up outside the flats on a regular basis to collect the casualties.

One morning, an ambulance is parked outside Tina's door. She sits in the ambulance with her head bandaged and watches as her boyfriend's body is carried out of the flat.

The neighbours stand around talking, whispering and gossiping. Tina is charged with murder but she is acquitted. The court rules that it was bad luck that her boyfriend died in the middle of their fight. The coroner's report shows that she didn't kill him after all – the cause of his death was a combination of alcohol and drugs.

※ ※ ※

I organise an anti-Apartheid meeting with Dumisani, a speaker from South Africa. At the meeting Dumisani tells us how he fled to Botswana where he had to sleep in a different house every night in case the Apartheid government bombed the house. We go for a drink and swap South African stories with each other. We are both far from home.

Dumisani is studying nearby in Exeter and he comes to stay for the weekend. The men in the road make fun of him and talk to him in fake West Indian accents. The men are drunk. We hear them knocking on my door late at night, hear them in my yard, pissing up against my kitchen wall. We switch off all the lights and keep quiet, not wanting to draw attention to ourselves.

The neighbour across the road says to me "You are a nigger lover and a foreigner. People here don't like you." The children in the neighbourhood throw stones at my windows and post swastikas through the letter box.

"It's like the Klu Klux Clan," Dumisani says.

I wish I had a machine gun and could mow down these small-minded people.

I sit by the river Dart and cry. I am a long way from home and a song plays in my head:

By the rivers of Babylon, there we sat down;
oh how we wept, when we remembered Zion.

It looks like I will never get back home again.

✳ ✳ ✳

On the radio I hear Winnie Mandela saying, "We will light a fire, we will surround this country with a necklace of fire. We will put an end to this oppression. The exiles can come home." I am ready to pack my bags and go home immediately.

I go with an ANC delegation to a cultural conference in Amsterdam. There are emotional reunions as exiles and people from home meet each other after being separated for many years. South African exiles from all over the world are at the conference and we hold long heated debates about "When we go home" – how we will change things, how we will run the institutions in a post-Apartheid South Africa.

We don't sleep for ten days, we are up all night talking and dancing and catching up with each other. I fall in love with Bheki, an MK soldier who is studying in Bulgaria. We walk along the Amsterdam canals at three in the morning holding hands as he tells me about his difficult times in the camps. After an intense and exhausting ten days I go back to my life in Totnes.

46
Night walks and poverty

In the Devon summer time, when the sun rises very early, I wake up before dawn. I am in a hurry to climb up the hill and see the sunrise.

"Where are you going, Mum?" The children wake up and want to come with me.

"Be quick." I tell them. "Get dressed and put on your boots."

The fields are wet and muddy and the sky is just beginning to get light as we climb to the top of the hill and see the sun rising over the far hills. We stand in a circle and hold hands.

Wisps of mist curl around the hills in the distance. "Look, there is the magic serpent curling his tail around the mountain," I tell the children.

One night Noah wakes up and comes into my bedroom. "I can't sleep, Mum," he says. I have also been lying awake.

"Let's go for a walk and look at the stars," I say.

The night is cold, we dress warmly, putting layers of clothes over our pyjamas. Quietly we open the front door and walk down the road in the still dark. Everybody is sleeping and the lights are out in all the houses. We see the moon as it emerges from behind the clouds and the stars bright in the dark sky. We walk home and eat breakfast. It's four o'clock in the morning.

On a full moonlit night we go up to Dartmoor with friends and take food and wine and make a fire and watch the moonrise.

Noah takes all his clothes off and runs naked over the moors. "Mum, Mum, I'm moon bathing," he shouts as he gallops over the moors with the wild ponies. Packed with fiery energy he is in his element, at one with the freedom and the wildness of the moors.

※ ※ ※

On the first of May, the children wear garlands of spring flowers on their heads.

Brightly coloured ribbons are attached to the maypole, the headmaster wears traditional Elizabethan clothes. The children dance round the maypole, singing. I have a lump in my throat. My children are part of this English spring ritual while I watch as an outsider.

My son changes his name to an English name, he is tired of having his father's foreign-sounding name and of being teased, he wants to be English.

Meanwhile, I am in dire straits. We live on a diet of porridge, rice and lentils and wild spinach I pick from the river. I pay the milkman with the last of my money and fall out of love with my boyfriend, Bheki, when he writes from Bulgaria to ask me for money.

I think of selling my body, but there is not much call for that in this small town where everybody knows everybody. Perhaps I could sell my body parts? A kidney, perhaps, to raise some money. I am tired of being poor and of running out of money mid-week. Every Monday morning I stand in line at the post office to collect my welfare benefits before I can buy something to eat.

The cows have been over-producing milk, there is a milk lake and a butter mountain. Single mothers, pensioners and the unemployed are eligible for free butter and cheese. I stand in line to collect my voucher to take to the church hall where the butter and cheese is being distributed. It all helps. I go home and make a bowl of porridge with dark brown molasses sugar that melts into my creamy bowl of steaming hot porridge. I warm the teapot before I put in fresh tea.

At the moment, there does not seem to be any work available, except for a job picking mushrooms on a nearby farm. I make a phone call. "What are the rates of pay," I ask, "and is it cash in hand?" The rates are too low and it's not cash in hand. If I declare my earnings, I will lose my welfare benefits. I cannot afford to take the job, the money I earn will be less than the money I am getting from my welfare benefits.

In the morning when the postman delivers the mail, there is a letter from the council saying they will stop my housing benefit and my rent will not be paid as my circumstances have changed. I cycle to the council offices to find out why.

"You have someone living with you and you no longer qualify," they tell me.

Someone has seen my new boyfriend sleeping over and reported me to the council.

I am furious. Which nosey neighbour has told on me? If I have a man living with me, the law says he must support me and they will not give me my welfare benefits. I will not be able to pay my rent.

"Who has not got anything better to do than spy on other people?" I ask the neighbour across the road.

"You are not allowed to have men staying with you," my neighbour says.

"I can have as many men as I like, as long as I don't have the same man in my bed more than three nights in a row," I reply. "That is what the cohabitation law says. Besides which, I am not going to have any one move in with me and tell me or my children what to do."

I cycle up to the council offices and sort it out. I tell them there is no truth to the malicious rumours that I am living with a man and they promise to re-instate my benefits.

✳ ✳ ✳

In the springtime, Daniel and I go for a walk over the rolling green hills of Devon. Below us is a view of the river Dart and Totnes becomes a picturesque country town. We can see our house in the distance at the very edge of the town. The spring flowers are out and the sun is shining.

"Mum, I want to go and live with Dad," Daniel says.

47
Daniel leaves

Daniel has wanted to live with his Dad for a while and I know I can't ignore his wishes any more, but I want to hold on to him more than anything in the world. He is old enough now to articulate and choose where he wants to be. He has turned eleven and will be finishing primary school in the summer and starting high school.

Samson has a small flat and a good job in London. Samson's fortunes have improved and we are getting on better with each other. Reluctantly I agree to Daniel going to live with Samson, hoping and trusting that I won't lose him if he goes.

When he goes to London I am devastated, my feeling of loss is extreme. I wake up in the mornings with a heavy heart. For years I have been holding onto my children. My worst fear has been losing them. At night I dream my children have died. In my dream I open the window and scream my grief into the night, a bloodcurdling endless scream. I wake up scared and shaken. I fear this is an omen that my children are going to die.

London swallows Daniel up and instead of two sons I am left with only one and I hang onto him for dear life. Our home is now too quiet with just Noah and myself left. The sounds of Daniel and Noah playing and fighting, the noise that at times would drive me to distraction has now become a painful absence. Noah refuses to go to school and stays at home. I homeschool him until the truant officer visits us and puts pressure on me to send him back to school.

✳ ✳ ✳

Daniel visits me in the school holidays. He has always wanted to go to Bath and we go there on the train for the weekend. He is dressed in his white Miami vice clothes, a white jacket with white trousers. I wanted to make our time together special. But nothing is right. He wants me to buy him new clothes and a toy, but I don't have money. It is as if I don't love him or love him enough. I buy him something cheap and useless to try and compensate, and fail dismally as a mother. My time with him is measured in hours and days before he goes back to his father.

48
Planting pennies

It's Christmas, and both the children are with their father. I spend my days in my dressing gown. I cannot be bothered to wash, I cannot face going out. I am missing the children. I could take an overdose, no one will find me. But because of my responsibility to my children this is not an option.

I travel to London on the train to spend time with my family and fetch Noah from his dad. While I am there I go to visit Daniel, and Samson tells me I am a bad mother and will not let me in the house. Noah stands and watches us shout at each other on the doorstep. Samson's mum is causing mischief. She lies and says I slapped her. At the end of the school holidays I go back to Totnes with Noah, feeling devastated and angry.

Noah goes back to school and we settle into a routine at home in Totnes. The worst of the winter is over and the days start becoming longer and slightly warmer. In the spring time I work in the garden. First, I clear the ground and pull out the old roots and the weeds, then I dig the ground over and feed the soil with manure and rotting decomposing matter, old vegetable peelings and grass cuttings to make the soil rich and fertile. The soil is heavy with clay, so I dig in peat and rake the earth to make it fine and crumbly and ready for planting.

I plant my seeds out in furrows and water them. During the winter I planted seedlings indoors, carefully nursing lettuces and sunflowers, but when I plant them outside the slugs eat them overnight and my hard work is wasted. The bulbs I planted in the autumn have lain dormant in the earth, but now it is springtime and everything is flowering – bright yellow daffodils, deep red tulips, brilliantly blue forget-me-nots. Small hearts-ease flowers grow in between them all.

I dig up the small patch of lawn in the front garden to plant vegetables. Last year I planted potatoes and this year I am growing peas and beans. The slugs like to eat everything, I go to war with them and have no mercy. Usually I do not like to kill things, I am reluctant to weed as I do not like to destroy anything growing, but I make an exception for slugs.

I wrack my brains thinking about how I can make ends meet and earn some money. There are no jobs available.

"You cannot believe everything people tell you," I tell myself. "People say money does not grow on trees, but what about the farmers and their apple orchards? Their money grows on trees."

Today I will plant something different. I will plant pennies and watch them grow. I go to the bank and ask the teller to change a pound coin and come home with a bag of one hundred shining new pennies. I make a circle out of my pennies and sit in the middle of the circle. I build them into piles and scatter the pennies randomly, looking at the patterns and shapes the scattered coins make on the floor.

I take my pennies outside into the garden and with my spade I dig a small hole. Plant a penny. I dig a hundred holes and in each hole I plant a penny. I concentrate and make a wish as I plant each penny. I have faith that my pennies will bear fruit. They have to – it is the only option I have left.

49

Communal living in London

Woman and child wanted for
vegetarian communal house
in London. £60 pm.

I am in London, visiting Mum and Dad. I walk up Muswell Hill, past Alexandra Palace, feeling like damaged goods, struggling to make sense of my life. The sun is shining and I dare to ask myself, "What if?" I dare to consider the possibility of my life being different.

I tell myself that my childhood was extreme, it was not normal, but over the years I have taken my pain for granted and hold onto it as part of my identity. But *what if* I had been secure and rooted and confident? And *what if* I had finished my education instead of being locked up in a mental hospital?

Maybe I could have been successful. Maybe my life would have been easier and I would have known how to be a good mother and make a safe home for my children, instead of feeling this constant restlessness and always messing things up. Maybe I would have had a husband and security and a safe suburban home. Perhaps this is who I could have been instead of being crazy and wild. Maybe.

What if my childhood had not been stolen from me? I ask myself, and at that moment, I look down and see money lying on the ground in front of me. Pound coins, one, two, three, four, five, six, seven coins. I pick up the seven coins and wonder what this means. Does it mean I would have been rich?

I pay attention to omens and dreams. One night I dream that some people have advertised for a person to join their commune and children are welcome. In my dream the house is large and spacious, but I am not sure I want to give up my privacy as I walk from room to room to room, unsure of what choice to make.

On another night, I dream I am in the hallway of a large house. I am renting a room for myself and the children. The rooms in this house are let only to women and children. I am pleased that only women are allowed in the house, and I turn to a shadowy woman standing behind me and say I will feel safer. I go into one of the rooms, it is large and comfortable. The room is divided by a sofa. One half of the room is a bedroom and living room and the other half has a television and a kitchen. I wake up with the images fresh in my mind.

That morning I sit in the sun and read the newspaper. I turn to the 'Property to Let' section and see an advert that intrigues me.

> Woman and child wanted for
> vegetarian communal house
> in London. £60 pm.

The rent is ridiculously low for London. Out of curiosity I phone the number at the bottom of the advert.

"Is the room large?" I ask the woman on the other end of the phone. "And is there a garden?"

"Yes," she answers to both questions. "When can you come and look at the room?"

"This weekend," I say.

I have no intention of moving to London permanently but my curiosity has got the better of me. I am not ready yet to give up my life in Totnes. I forget all about the room.

❋ ❋ ❋

A few months later, back home in Totnes, the phone rings.

A woman's voice asks, "Are you still interested in moving to London? We are looking for someone to live in our communal house." The opportunity to move to London is here again, handed to me on a plate. Perhaps I should consider it?

❋ ❋ ❋

On a cold December evening, I go to look at the house in Stapleton Hall Road. I look at the numbers of the houses to see which house is the right one. All but one of the houses in the road have their curtains tightly drawn and this one – a house with no curtains at the kitchen window – beckons me. Light shines through the plants growing in profusion in front of the window, creating a welcoming glow. I have arrived at the right house. I walk up the steps and knock on the door.

The house is large, an old Victorian with six storeys and many rooms. The rooms have high ceilings and in the living room is a fireplace. I am shown into the room that could be mine. It looks like the room in my dream and sends shivers down my spine.

I dream about a plant that is dying and when I look to see why, I see the roots are tangled up and the pot is root bound. The plant needs to be re-potted into a larger container if it is to survive.

* * *

Decisions in the house are made democratically and after a long process of house meetings and visits, Noah and I move into Stapleton Hall Rd. Margaret and her daughter, Jade, and Lucy and Bridget are our house-mates. It's an easy, effortless move. Totnes has become too small and limited and London with its busy mix of people is being held out to me like a gift.

On the day I move to London, Albie Sachs, a man I have known all my life, is blown up by a car bomb. I watch the news on television as the scene is replayed over and over in slow motion. The explosion has happened in faraway Mozambique.

Nearer to home, in Paris, Mum's friend, Dulcie September, is assassinated. Mum and Dad's address book mysteriously disappears and the newspapers talk of a hit list targeting exiled South Africans in London. The net is closing in and Europe is not safe anymore.

I am glad that I am close to Mum and Dad now. I can spend time with them and Lynn. London is not as lonely as Totnes.

Daniel and Noah go to the same school in London. They are back together, instead of living separate lives in Totnes and London.

There is more work in London and I get plenty of jobs as a nursery nurse through an agency. When I am working late Noah goes to Mum and Dad's house and I don't have to worry about who is looking after him.

The exile community has become our family and there are endless funerals, memorial services and celebrations to attend. I rush around from ANC meetings to anti-Apartheid rallies to pickets outside South Africa House.

* * *

The communal house in Stapleton Hall Road is run efficiently. We all put money into a kitty to cover the bills and buy groceries and we take it in turns to shop and cook. After living on my own with my children I enjoy having adult company and sharing the responsibilities of running a household.

On Saturday nights, free food arrives from Marks and Spencer. It is shared out and distributed amongst the houses in the housing co-operative. As single parents we qualify for free food and feast on out-of-date cream cakes, salmon and strawberries.

My room is in the attic. I have a view over London and at night the city lights twinkle like jewels. During the day the sun streams through the long sash windows. Foxes and hedgehogs live in the large back garden that stretches all the way to the railway line. The view of lush greenery and trees make living in London bearable.

※ ※ ※

Daniel has become a teenager. When he visits me he is awkward and at a loose end in this house full of strange women. It is not clear where there is space for him in the house. Together we paint the small attic room next to mine for Daniel to use. I have to negotiate his status in the house with my house mates as everything has to be a communal decision.

In the new school year, Daniel and Noah go back to school in Highgate and I go back to art college to do my BA Honours in Fine Art. I have been credited for the course I did at Dartington and will be able to complete my degree in the next two years. To earn money I work part time looking after a baby while her mother works. At college I spend my time in the print-making room, engrossed in making etchings, screen prints and collagraphs. I make my collagraph printing plates out of cardboard, tissue paper and sand and print them through the etching press. The work is physically demanding and labour intensive.

50
Hospital stories 4 – teenagers

After a year, Margaret and her daughter, Jade, move out, followed by Bridget and Lucy. Beth and her daughter move in. Beth has run away from her husband – he mustn't find out where they are. The house becomes entirely focussed on Beth's fears. Her daughter eats more and more and grows larger and larger, she misses her Dad but can't mention his name in front of her mum. Her mum says her father will come and snatch her away and steal her if he finds her.

The house is taken over by Beth's friends and relatives. Her brother comes to stay. First thing in the morning I go downstairs to make myself a cup of tea. He is talking about The Multinationals and how they have colonised the world. I am just waking up as he talks about the latest atrocities in Indo China, in Africa and the Middle East. I escape to the peace and quiet of my room.

❋ ❋ ❋

I still have my house in Totnes. It is a safe place, a place to go to in the holidays with Daniel and Noah. I want my children to come with me to Totnes to stay in Parkers Close for Christmas, but Samson's mum says they must stay with her over Christmas. It is another tug of war.

Daniel is torn – he can't make up his mind where he wants to spend Christmas. He falls ill and is taken to an old Victorian hospital with pneumonia and I wonder whether the tension has manifested itself in his body. Daniel lies in the hospital bed with a drip in his arm. I sit at his bedside day and night and only go home to change my clothes and have a bath when Samson sits with him. The hospital has fold-up beds for the parents to sleep on at night in the huge dimly lit ward with high ceilings. I doze off fitfully listening to Daniel's breathing.

Directly opposite us, I watch a small baby being rocked in the arms of her parents, they pace up and down anxiously holding their sick baby. On the bedside table a candle burns. Its soft glow is warm and personal in the big impersonal space of a hospital ward.

Samson and I put our differences aside as we wait by our son's bedside. Deciding who is going to be with which parent for Christmas no longer seems important and I wonder why we spent so much time and energy on fighting about something so insignificant. I cannot concentrate on anything else while Daniel is in hospital. After a week of drips and antibiotics he is strong enough to go home. I feel eternally grateful for antibiotics and shudder to think of what would have happened without the wonders of modern medicine.

✳ ✳ ✳

When Noah is twelve, he decides he doesn't want to go to Highgate Wood school any more – he doesn't seem to fit into a conventional schooling system easily. He wants to go to the White Lion Free School instead. Without telling me, he phones up the Free School and arranges for an interview. I am surprised by a phone call from the school asking us to come in for an interview.

At the school, the children run riot, there appears to be no discipline. The school is tucked away in an old semi-derelict building at the back of King's Cross in an area rife with prostitution and drugs. I worry about Noah travelling to school, the area is not safe, but he is determined to go there.

The school is run democratically – the children make the rules and lessons are not compulsory. The children at the school swear and smoke and steal. They steal a passing stranger's new mountain bike. The owner is devastated, he looks everywhere for his bike. Noah feels sorry for him and shows him where the children have hidden the bike. The other children are furious. They run after Noah and threaten to kill him. He is scared to go back to the Free School and instead goes back to his old school.

✳ ✳ ✳

In January 1990, the Americans invade Iraq. I can feel the bombs inside my head pounding Baghdad and am sickened by the self-righteous war fever in the media, but become obsessed reading newspaper reports of the horrors being perpetrated in Iraq. I feel powerless in the face of such military might. For my degree show I create a huge panel made up of forty-four individual collagraphs printed onto newspaper collages. At the bottom of each print I write a diary of the war taken from the newspaper reports showing the cruelty and contradictions of war. I spend days standing in the icy cold outside the War Office protesting against the war.

I read Mills and Boon romances obsessively, escaping into the comforting predictable formula of the stories, beautiful woman meets very rich man and there is chemistry between them, as well as obstacles and misunderstandings.

But the ending is always happy as he holds her in his arms and asks her to marry him and promises to love her for ever.

❄ ❄ ❄

In the summer time, after I complete my degree in Fine Art, the children and I go back to small, sleepy Totnes. I feel like a snake stepping back into my old skin as I walk down the high street greeting people and having familiar conversations. I have changed, but Totnes has stayed the same.

I go down to the river with my friend Avice. Usually she likes to talk a lot, but this evening the peace and stillness have stilled her tongue and we walk in silence. Fish jump to the surface of the water to catch flies to eat. The colours are soft as the sun sets on the water and the hills. As it becomes dark the moon rises, perfectly round and full. We sit on the bench at the end of the path and a fox comes down to the water's edge. We watch the fox with his bushy tail beneath the full moon. The fox disappears into the bushes and the stillness. A boat lit up with fairy lights sails down the river. Sounds of music float over the water and people dance on deck as the boat sails on its way. This has become our river and our special place and our perfect shared moment.

"My children don't want to go out with me any more," I tell Avice. "I want to take them to the beach but they don't want to come." I am in tears. "What's the matter with me? Why don't they want to go to the beach with me?"

Avice has been through this herself, she understands.

"Your children are growing up," she says. "You have to let them go."

My children are growing up, but I don't realise that teenagers need as much attention and care as toddlers do. You can't take your eyes off them for a minute. There are dangers all around that teenagers are not aware of – drug dealers, unprotected sex. Looking after teenagers is like having a toddler who wants to run in the road or put their hand in the fire. They seem unaware that they are walking straight towards danger. I spend sleepless nights waiting for my children to come home, my nerves on edge, expecting the worst if they are late. I want to hold them close, to keep them safe, stop them burning their fingers in the fire. But when I try to mother my sons they push me away.

"Where are you going?" I ask them.

"Out," they reply.

"When will you be back?"

"Later," they tell me, shutting me out.

I am lost, I have no role model to go by. When I was their age I was completely out of control and mad. I don't know what normal is for teenagers, what they should or shouldn't be doing.

❋ ❋ ❋

Back in London, in our big house with its many rooms full of women, Noah hides down in the basement, smoking, scared to come out into the world. He sleeps all day and stays up all night. Why is he so pale, so scared of the world, so over-cautious? As a small child he was outgoing and full of energy but now he has withdrawn into himself. He hides under this large house in the city and won't get up to go to school in the mornings. His headmistress calls me into the office to fill in forms for a truancy centre. She intimidates me. I can understand why my son wants to hide all day and avoid the world.

During the next school holidays, we go back to Totnes. Noah says he is going to visit a friend, but doesn't come home. I wait up all night for him. Where is he? I search everywhere for him. I knock on door after door. At each house I am told a different story. I begin to panic. I phone Daniel in London. He says he doesn't know where Noah is. Their Dad is away on holiday.

"He was last seen on the road to London yesterday," my friend tells me. I phone Daniel again.

"Where can he be?" I ask my son. I am frantic now. "I will have to phone the police, I'm worried about him." I hear muffled noises at the end of the phone.

"He is here with me," my son tells me at last. "Don't phone the police, he will be back home tomorrow."

My anxiety grows, how can I keep my son safe when all he does is push me away? When Noah comes back from London he refuses to talk to me and I can't find a way in. I can't communicate with him. He is unfocused, something is not right. His head keeps nodding in a strange manner. But I can't keep him at home. He goes off again, in a van with friends to a music festival. How long will he be gone? What will he eat? Where will he sleep?

The police phone me a few days later. "Your son is with us. He wants to come back home, will you pay his fare if we put him on the train?" I am hugely relieved. I meet him at the station, but I am at a complete loss – I don't know what to do, what boundaries I should put in place.

My debts mount up and my sons are out of control. Nothing has prepared me for teenage sons or the many sleepless nights of waiting and expecting the worst.

When Samson comes back from his holiday, I phone him. I am at my wits end.

"I don't know what to do. My nerves are shattered, I haven't slept for days. I don't know how to be a mother any more," I tell him.

"Noah can come and live with us if you like."

I am relieved and grateful when Samson tells me this.

※ ※ ※

Noah goes to live with Samson and Daniel in their tiny one-bedroom flat in Islington. Samson seems better able to contain Noah and keep him safe. Noah listens to his Dad, but he is angry with me, and hurt. He feels rejected. He won't talk to me. I tell him I love him, but I don't know how to look after him, how to keep him safe. Although I miss him, it is a relief not to worry through sleepless nights, wondering where he is, what he is doing.

After sixteen years of looking after my children, there is an empty space in my life.

5 1

Coming home

Nelson Mandela has been released from prison, the political organizations have been unbanned and de Klerk says the exiles can return home. I rush down to Trafalgar Square with my friend, Rebekah. Thousands of people have gathered spontaneously in Trafalgar Square to celebrate this historic occasion and emotions run high as the crowd sings and dances together.

There is a flurry of weddings in the exile community as people prepare to go back home. I imagine that we will all fly home together – the plane full of exiles singing freedom songs and arriving home to a rousing welcome. I see us falling to our knees and kissing the earth. The reality is somewhat different. The tight-knit exile community scatters and people return home in dribs and drabs.

Mum and Dad are among the first to pack their bags and return home to South Africa.

Dad says that whatever happens, he does not want to die on foreign soil. He is going home.

Mum says, "What if? What if it all goes wrong?" She does not want to go through all that tension and danger again. . She will miss the grandchildren.

Dad said if needs be he will fight to the bitter end. But I am worried and Mum is too. Is de Klerk planning to do what Dingaan did, I wonder. Will he invite us back in with false promises, lure us in, make us drunk and give us a false sense of security and then, when we are trapped and asleep, slaughter us in our beds?

But in the end it is all fine. The promises seem real. It is safe to go home. When Mum and Dad arrive at the airport, they are greeted by crowds of people singing freedom songs and toy toying.

❋ ❋ ❋

Home. The word makes me cry. I thought that I would never get back home again and that I would be stranded in Britain forever. Now that my dream has become reality my emotions are like a tidal wave crashing against the rocks. I can hardly believe it as I make plans to go back to Cape Town.

Before I leave, I hold a "Going Home Exhibition" where I fill five rooms with my work. I invite everyone who has supported me as an artist over the years to come to my exhibition and I sell enough work to buy my plane ticket with money to spare.

I am going back for three months. I wish I could go back permanently, but it is difficult to leave Daniel and Noah behind. My children don't feel connected to South Africa. They have watched anti-Apartheid documentaries showing the police shooting school children and to them South Africa is a dangerous place they would rather not go to.

As the time to go gets nearer I pack and unpack my suitcase. Usually I never iron my clothes, but now I iron all my clothes and then I take them out of the suitcase and iron them all again. I am going home after twenty-four years.

Finally I am packed, and ready to go to the airport.

＊ ＊ ＊

After a long, tiring flight the plane lands and Mum and Dad meet me at the airport. I put my feet down firmly on South African soil. After all these years, I am home. Mum and Dad show me the sights – the mountains, the beaches.

"Don't talk politics. Just be quiet and look," Dad says. "I'm starting the Look Party, everyone must just be quiet and look at the view."

Dad is so proud, it is as if he has built the mountains single-handed. These are his mountains, this is his country and he is a free man, able to walk about without banning orders or prisons to restrict him. Mum and Dad don't have to worry about exceeding a two-mile radius of their house. They are free to go where they like – in Cape Town, anywhere in South Africa.

＊ ＊ ＊

The beauty of the landscape overwhelms me. As a child I took all this beauty for granted. That night, my first night home, I sleep like a baby. When I wake up in the morning I hear the birds singing. The blue sky and the sounds of laughing doves welcome me, tell me I am back home. But still, despite the familiar sights and sounds of my childhood, I can't quite connect to being back in South Africa. The dream doesn't feel real. I thought the landscape would be what would make me feel at home, but I feel like I am stuck in a bubble in a white suburb.

Where is Africa? I imagined it as a place of rich earth colours – ochre, reds and browns – the colours of my drawings and paintings that kept me connected all the years I was away. I had pictured a place of woven baskets, wooden carvings and gourds, music and dancing and laughing people, but here in suburban Plumstead, the streets are deserted and the houses are painted in pastel shades. All I see are suburban bungalows with immaculate gardens, blocks of flats and supermarkets.

After a week of being back home, I bend down to pick something up and hurt my back. I lie on the floor, immobilised.

If I keep still enough the pain is bearable, but I have to rely on Mum and Dad to attend to all my needs – to bring me food and water and to dress me. As I lie still the tick of the clock and the sound of breathing in the quiet house bring back memories of a time before I had words to shape my memories.

My helplessness takes me back to when I was a baby. I listen to Mum and Dad breathing in and out. The sound unsettles me, it disturbs me. I am thrown back into an uncomfortable place, one I barely remember. As I listen to them breathing, I start to imagine what it was like as a small child.

All my senses are alert. I have the sharpness of a dog's hearing, its sense of smell. I imagine Mum clapping her hands sharply, frantically, trying to distract me, to distract me from myself.

I am a baby, crying, and Mum cannot bear to hear me cry. I cry loudly as Mum claps louder and more frantically, she clicks her fingers and jiggles me up and down.

Mum is talking loudly now, hoping to pacify me. Mum is singing. My baby crying disturbs Mum, my crying is not allowed. I must stop. My imagined babyhood is intense as I lie there, feeling vulnerable.

※ ※ ※

The ANC has organised a huge rally with Nelson Mandela at Athlone Stadium. I stand with both feet planted firmly on home soil, singing 'Nkosi Sikeleli', my arm raised in the familiar clenched fist salute. The stadium is full of people. We are all singing and the singing touches me in a way that the spectacular landscape has not been able to. *This* is my country. *These* are my people. I hold in my tears and rejoice in the sweet ache in my chest. The singing touches me and opens my heart. I can look at the beautiful mountain as my mountain now, not as a stranger. I am home.

When I was in England I left an essential part of myself behind in South Africa. Now, as the missing piece of me finally fits into place, I feel a profound sense of wholeness. The history of this country is part of the texture of my life and when I connect to it something settles inside me.

※ ※ ※

There are two things nostalgic exiles do when they return home. They visit their old house and they visit their old prison. Dad stops the car in front of Mount Pleasant, the palatial mansion where we once lived. Granny is no longer alive and strangers have bought the house. I can't believe that I once lived in such a big grand house.

Mum refuses to get out of the car – the memories are too painful. Dad and I walk up the stairs, past the two palm trees that have grown taller over the past twenty-four years. A big dog greets us as I knock on the door but nobody is in.

Our family celebrate being back home together by eating a sumptuous meal in Franschhoek, a valley surrounded by mountains. As we drive through the spectacular landscape we see a sign post pointing to Bien Donné.

"Isn't that your old prison, Mum?" I ask. "Let's go and have a look at it." We drive down a road in a tranquil rural setting until we get to a picturesque white building, with green shutters.

"That's the prison," Mum tells us.

I don't remember the prison being so pretty when we used to visit Mum. We get out of the car and walk up the stairs to the heavy wooden doors. We pose for a photo at the door. A warden comes out and greets us. Mum tells him she was here in the sixties. He smiles broadly. "I was here as a prisoner during the Emergency," Mum tells him. His smile changes to a frown and he chases us away.

"You can't take photos here," he says.

* * *

I stand at the station in the early morning ,waiting for a train. I am not sure what carriage to get into. There is a first-class compartment and a third-class compartment, but no second, nothing in between. In England I can't afford to travel first class, but here people tell me third class is dangerous. All the black people are getting into third class and all the white people are getting into first. In London people are all thrown together on the train, but here I must reconsider my identity. Am I rich or poor, black or white? The first-class carriage is virtually empty and it doesn't feel safe. I feel safer in third class where there are more people, even if it makes me feel self-conscious about my colour. On the train people are singing and praying, clapping and drumming on their bibles, voices harmonising with such beauty it takes my breath away.

It contrasts with the years I spent travelling underground through dark airless tunnels in London. Sitting in trains where people averted their eyes and avoided eye contact, and avoided smiling as they hid behind newspapers, books and magazines. A smile was taken as a threat – a sign of insanity.

* * *

Mum and Dad spoil me, they treat me like a princess. They take me out and wine me and dine me. There is an air of excitement and parties are held to welcome exiles and released prisoners home. At a party I meet my new best friend, Zaahidah, and we exchange phone numbers. I phone her up and invite her for supper. I feel insecure as I pick up the phone. Does she like me, does she want to be my friend? Yes, she says, she will come to supper, but can she bring a friend? My circle of friends in Cape Town is increasing. I was scared that I would get to Cape Town and not know anyone and feel like a stranger. But now, every morning, Lisa, a friend I have known since she was a baby, fetches me and takes me for walks up the mountain or by the sea – all the places I went to as a child.

* * *

My three months in Cape Town have come to an end. The time has gone very fast. Soon it will be time to go back to London. I sit on a rock at St. James and watch the waves breaking. I want to stay in Cape Town, but how do I disentangle myself from my life in England? My children are in London, I don't want to leave them. But Mum and Dad are here and they are getting old. I need to be with them. My sons are growing up and soon they will be going their own ways, they are too old to uproot. I am torn down the middle, pulled in two directions, how can all of me ever be all in one place at one time? It is not fair that I have to uproot myself twice, once from South Africa and now from England. I let the sea wash away my tears.

When it is time for me to go back to London, Mum and Dad take me to the airport and wave goodbye as I disappear behind passport control. They look elderly and frail.

52
Summer love

After a long overnight flight, I arrive in Heathrow, feeling unbalanced. I never manage to sleep on a long flight. I am unwashed, tired and grubby after being shut up in the cramped aeroplane. My heart sinks as I see the grey London skies. I don't want to be here. I struggle with my luggage down to the tube station and do battle with the ticket machine. The machine eats my money and doesn't give me a ticket. I wait in the long queue to buy my ticket at the ticket office.

In the space of an overnight flight, the seasons have changed from the warmth of summer to the middle of winter. I look at the landscape and I want to yawn. I feel like a stranger, yet everything is so familiar. I feel a profound sense of boredom.

Noah is still living with his Dad. He comes to visit me and sits at the kitchen table in Stapleton Hall Road. "Is it all right if I come and stay for a few weeks?" he asks. We spend the weeks together in London slowly starting to mend what was broken.

In the summer, we leave the muggy city and go down to Totnes to stay for the summer.

I feel free, that summer in Totnes, liberated, strong and independent. Pam lives around the corner from our house in Parkers Close. I have known her for many years. She calls for me on her motor bike and we go for long walks together by the sea or over the moors. She is the perfect walking companion as she has the ability to be fully focused and present with nature and does not need to chatter endlessly. She knows how to be still as we walk along a stretch of beach with rocks and rock pools. She is like a child, clambering over the rocks and discovering sea anemones and stones with interesting shapes.

Pam puts her finger in the warm water of the rock pool and a small fish swims up and nibbles her finger. She laughs as he tickles her. We watch the birds sitting on the rocks, strutting on the shore. Pam knows all their names and habits and why the young gulls have feathers of a different colour and which gulls were hatched last year.

She is tall and strong and works on a farm driving a tractor. She wears a bandana around her forehead to keep her beautiful long brown hair from falling into her face while she works. She works outdoors in all weathers, washing leeks, sorting potatoes, cutting broccoli and cauliflowers, loading heavy bags of vegetables on to the truck. In the morning she wakes before dawn. In winter the sky is dark and the weather is icy cold when Pam starts up her motor bike. It is so cold that icicles hang off her nose.

Pam has lived in Totnes all her life, a small town, where everybody knows everybody, but it can be stifling and suffocating and at times she cannot easily be herself. She is shy, like a wild animal and needs to be approached carefully and slowly to win her trust. One sudden or unexpected move startles her, sends her running away. She is easy in the company of animals and knows how to converse with them, calling the cows and imitating birdsong and waiting for the birds to reply. But she finds it more difficult to communicate with people and breaks out in a cold sweat in a group of strangers.

Pam is secretly in love with me, but she is much too shy to tell me. Eventually she plucks up the courage to ask me if I would like to see the film *Salmonberries* with her.

On our first date we shyly and tentatively dare to reach for each other's hand. We hardly pay attention to the movie. The cinema is about to burst into flames or explode with the sparks flying off our bodies. Surely everyone in the cinema is looking at us and marvelling at the current that crackles between us as we hold hands.

Pam is my swan, I am her one and only. We get lost in each other's eyes and become dizzy from making love all day. Pam learns my body with a quiet focused intensity. When I go back to London to work we phone each other every night and have long conversations. At weekends we visit each other.

I juggle my time between home and work and being in a long distance relationship.

Noah is back at home and I am working as a nursery nurse to earn money and doing my art work at the same time.

※ ※ ※

In London, on the 10 April 1993, I am listening to the radio when I hear the news. Chris Hani has been assassinated. The anger and heartbreak people feel in South Africa threatens to spill over into violence and chaos. I worry about Mum and Dad and feel powerless so far away. A date is hastily set for the first democratic elections in South Africa. Free and fair elections – the point that we have all been travelling towards. I book my ticket for Cape Town, I don't want to miss the elections for anything in the world. Pam is coming with me.

53
Elections

I feel welcome in Cape Town. People are open and friendly. In Woodstock the friend's house where we stay is always busy and full of people.

Pam hides in the bedroom, overwhelmed.

"What's the matter?" I ask.

Her arms are tightly folded over her chest.

She shuts me out like a brick wall. I am at home here in Cape Town but she is a stranger here. I feel impatient and I don't want to understand her feelings of being lonely and far away from home. She wants me to herself but there are always other people around. She is upset but she does not communicate her feelings easily.

At night, Pam is restless. She wanders around by herself in the middle of the night, through the neighbourhood, walking the city streets. But the streets are not safe here, you can get robbed and raped, stabbed and shot. This is not small sleepy Totnes. I lie in bed, my nerves on edge as I wait for Pam to come back.

❈ ❈ ❈

27 April, 1994. The day we have all been waiting for and working towards has arrived. I wake up early, bursting with excitement like a child waking up on Christmas morning. This is the most exhilarating day of my life. I am going to vote in the first democratic elections. People are in and out of the house all day in a general state of euphoria. Outside the air is filled with elation, accompanied by a profound sense of peace.

Friends and neighbours in Woodstock are allowed to vote for the first time. We go together to stand in line to vote. The queue is very long and it is raining. I don't want the queue to move fast – I treasure every moment of standing in this line. Some members of my family have never been allowed to vote in their adult lives before. Lynn is voting in New York but comes to join us after a few days to join in with the celebrations.

A few days later, the results are announced. The ANC has won and Nelson Mandela is president. At ten o'clock that night we jump into the car and join a cavalcade of cars hooting and cheering with flags waving. All along the road people dance and cheer. When we get to the centre of town strangers hug and kiss us. Tears stream down people's faces. Comrades! We did it, we did it!

White people are scared, they have stocked up with cans of baked beans and candles and people want to sell up and leave the country. House prices plummet. I go house hunting. The pennies I planted in my garden have grown into a sizeable amount. I bought my Totnes house at a discount and sold it and now I have money to buy a home in Cape Town. I buy a flat in Wynberg with a view of the mountain. It is close to Mum and Dad and near the train station. It's my foot on the ground in Cape Town, a promise to myself that I will be back.

But now it is time to go back to England, my sons still need me. Mum and Dad drive Pam and me to the airport.

❋ ❋ ❋

It is spring time when we get back to England. Pam goes back to Totnes and I settle back into the house in London with Noah and start planning my next trip to South Africa.

Daniel says he will come with me to Cape Town for my next visit, but I cannot persuade Noah to join us. I will be able to show Daniel where I grew up. I find it hard to believe that I will be in Cape Town with my son. I look at photos of Cape Town to make it feel real.

When it is time to leave I do a huge amount of shopping for the month for Noah while I am away. I sit on the plane worrying that I didn't buy enough vegetables for him to eat. He is eighteen years old and I am anxious about leaving him to fend for himself.

Mum and Dad are waiting for us at the airport. They take us for breakfast at Kirstenbosch and we drink champagne and look at the mountain. I feel like I am in Paradise, sitting here with Mum and Dad and Daniel in such a beautiful setting.

Daniel and I go to my flat in Wynberg. I'm staying here for the very first time. I put down the beautiful rug Pam has given me and hang my pictures on the wall. Mum gives me cushions and a table and the flat starts to look like home. We sit in the flat listening to music and looking at the mountains. I am in my own home with my son in Cape Town feeling exceptionally content and happy to be here. I wish Noah could be here too, that is my only sadness. That, and missing Pam.

The next morning, it rains. I phone Pam and she says she is missing me and doesn't know how she can stand another two weeks without me. I take fright at the neediness in her voice. I don't like being in a relationship with someone who is so dependent on me. I phone Noah in London, I miss him so much.

The next morning, Daniel and I get up early and catch the train to the beach. We sit at the Brass Bell in Kalk Bay and have a meal and watch the waves crashing against the rocks. Our time together is a precious gift. Daniel tells me what has been happening in his life over the past few years, things I have only guessed at from a distance. We have time to connect without pressure, without the conflicting loyalties pulling us away from each other.

When we get home, I am very sleepy. Daniel is flying back to London tomorrow, I am going to miss him. We take Daniel to the airport and I stand and wave and wave as he disappears. Depressed and tired, I look at photos of Daniel and Noah and I wish they could live in South Africa with me.

I am divided. I need to go back to London, but I want to cancel my flight. Before I leave there is too much to do – I must shop, I must pack, and I must sort out the flat. I want to relax, but I have to rush. Time is going too fast. I am tired of coming and going, I want to stay. It feels painful to keep saying goodbye. I am cut off from my feelings, blank, but underneath the surface is a well of tears. I lie in bed and long for Pam. I wish I could snuggle up to her and feel safe and warm. My bed feels empty.

The past is present in every action. I feel the pain of leaving in 1967. I am disorganised – I have left everything to the last minute. I have two hours to pack the entire contents of the flat before I rent it out. I pack furiously. I finish at the last minute and rush to the airport. I wave goodbye to Mum and Dad then I board my plane.

54
London: Push me pull you

Unusually, I manage to sleep on the flight so it doesn't seem so horribly long and tedious. At Finsbury Park station I get a taxi home. Noah greets me at the door with a hug and a kiss. He looks well. The house is full of young people and activity. I make a pot of soup and light a fire, it is good to be back home. I fall asleep by the fire and wake up feeling well rested. I settle down to do some drawing.

✳ ✳ ✳

I have my name down with an agency for work as a nursery nurse. The agency phones me and asks if I can look after a baby at night in her own home. The baby is sick and her mother is sick. I am nervous about going to a strange house late at night in an unknown neighbourhood, it could be dodgy. When the baby's mother opens the door I am relieved that she looks trustworthy and decent. She shows me to the baby's room and shows me where the bottles and the nappies are kept before she goes to bed.

In the middle of the night, the baby wakes up.

"Hello," I say and she smiles her five-month-old toothless smile. Instantly I fall in love with her as if she is my own baby. I pick her up and give her a bottle, she sucks hungrily on the teat. I put her on my shoulder to wind her and gently rub her back. She vomits up her milk all over me and I am drenched. Every night I go and look after her and during the day I have time to draw and paint.

The mother is very ill and the doctors say she might die. What will happen to the child? They want to take the baby away and put her in a children's home. Horrified at the thought of the baby being taken into care, I say I will look after her, but they tell me she is sick and that she won't live long. I am angry I don't want to hear this, she won't die – she is a strong baby.

Her mother is angry, she sits on the chair crying. "I am not dead yet," she shouts at her husband. "Don't push me out of the way, don't try and organise my life for me as though I am not here already." She is angry with the doctors too. "You are not God," she tells them. "You cannot tell me when I am going to die or when my child is going to die."

The child is in hospital, she is thin as a rake and light as a feather, she shivers but her body is burning up with fever. She is afraid and in pain. I wake in the middle of the night "Please, God," I pray, "take care of this child, don't let her die."

She is put on medication, she looks well and grows bigger every day. On her birthday she looks beautiful in her party dress with her hair braided with beads. The table is laden with delicious food. She laughs as she sits on her mother's lap and blows out her candles.

She has grown into a strong healthy girl. She is cheating this cruel, creeping virus which has taken so many people.

❋ ❋ ❋

It is Daniel's birthday, and I go to buy him a gift. It is raining heavily as I stand at the bus stop waiting for what seems like hours for a bus that doesn't come. Eventually the bus arrives and I get home cold and wet. I cook Daniel his favourite meal for supper. After supper I talk to my sons about moving to Cape Town. My children are twenty and eighteen. Legally I am no longer responsible for them, they can sign on for the dole or work and support themselves financially. They are very close to their dad and he will be there for them. But I hate the idea of leaving them on their own in England. I wish they would tell me that they want to come back to South Africa with me, but I know they can't do this. I am asking them to leave their home so that I can go back to mine.

Mum and Dad decide to sell their house in London. They have been renting it out. I go to tidy it up so I can put it on the market. Pam comes to London to help me. The house is certainly not what it used to be when they lived in it. We clean the house from top to bottom and Pam tidies up the garden. In the evening I can hardly move from tiredness. Pam has to go back to Totnes and I panic at the thought of being alone at night in the house.

My chest is tight and my teeth are clenched. I make food and watch television and draw a picture and have a bath but I feel unsettled as I look around the room and realise how empty the house is without Mum and Dad here. It reminds me of being a child again, left on my own.

Selling the house is like closing a chapter. I have a sleepless night, I hate sleeping by myself – I am too aware of Mum and Dad's absence.

My chest is heavy. My family is scattered all over the world again. What does it mean to my sons, to have a fragmented family?

❋ ❋ ❋

Pam wants to live with me. I talk to Noah about this.

"If Pam moves in, I will move out," he tells me. "I won't have anything more to do with you. Why can't you just spend time with me? You say you are going back to South Africa, but then you don't go. Why can't you be clear about what you are doing?"

Pam and Noah don't talk to each other, they don't greet each other. When one of them walks into the room, the other one walks out.

"I must do things the right way," I tell Pam. "I don't want there to be a rift between my son and me."

I tell Pam it won't work if we live together. She says this will mean the end of our relationship – she can't come and stay with me again. It is too difficult for her. I am pulled in two directions and I am going to break in the middle. In bed that night Pam is distant and cold. I lie next to her and cannot sleep. I am falling apart. I just want to hold onto my teddy bear and suck my thumb.

Who is right, who is wrong?

I fall into a black hole and it feels like it is the end of the world. It is almost impossible to disentangle from our mutual confusion.

As long as there are only the two of us in our magic circle everything is fine, but when I step outside, Pam's punishing silences begin.

I am pulled backwards and forwards as places and people demand my loyalty. Guilt fuels my confusion. I have convinced myself my children are old enough for me to leave them, but I am leaving them stranded and I don't fully notice the effect it has on them. My mind is on other things, on leaving England and going 'Home'. Home for me is a country, a place, a memory. It is not contained within four walls. But my sons need a home with four walls and a mother.

I leave my sons before they are ready for me to leave. Noah looks unhappy and withdrawn – he feels neglected and abandoned. He doesn't want to eat and sleeps all day and is up all night. He looks pale and heavy-eyed.

※ ※ ※

It is not easy to disentangle and uproot myself from my life in England. For a few years I bounce backwards and forward between two homes. Each time I am back in South Africa my roots go deeper and I feel more settled.

Pam and I resolve our differences and decide to set up home together in Cape Town. We pack our bags and belongings and get ready to leave England fully. When the day arrives my sons stand in the hallway and wish me well as we hug and kiss each other goodbye. All our belongings, including all my art work, are in containers ready to be shipped over to Cape Town.

When we arrive in South Africa, we buy a car and go on a road trip visiting friends and family on the way. We leave from Mpumalanga and travel through the Kruger National Park and Swaziland. We drive to KwaZulu and the Eastern Cape and finally to Cape Town. When we get to Cape Town we move into a sparsely furnished flat and wait for our belongings to arrive.

55
The Island

On the first day of spring, the day after Princess Diana dies in a car accident, I stand in line at Jetty One at the Waterfront waiting to take the first boat to Robben Island. At seven thirty on this early spring morning the weather is cold and I feel apprehensive about going to stay on Robben Island by myself. I have been invited to stay on the Island as an Artist in Residence. I don't know what to expect, I am scared to sleep alone in a strange house and am relieved when I am told I will be sharing a house with another woman artist. Recently there has been a rape on the Island and I have heard many stories of ghosts on the Island. The security guard writes my name down on a board before he lets me through onto the boat. I travel on the Susan Kruger, the old boat that was used to transport the prisoners to the Island.

The sea stretches endlessly before me and Cape Town recedes into the distance. As I sit and watch the sea all around me, the boat ride takes on a dreamlike mythical quality. I watch the shimmering patterns on the water and the sea birds diving to catch fish. We are lucky that the weather is good today and the sea is calm. The boat rolls over the waves like a stately old lady and after three quarters of an hour we arrive at Murray's Bay Harbour. I get a lift in a bakkie and drive under an arch with the words "We Serve With Pride" written on top. We pass the bleak prison before I am dropped off at the ex-warder's house where I am going to stay. Zoulfa, my fellow artist greets me warmly and makes me a cup of tea.

I sit and drink my tea on the back door step and watch the yellow weaver birds fly in and out of the yard. I listen to the quietness all around me with only the sound of the waves and the sea in the distance. It is so quiet I can hear the wings of birds flapping as they fly overhead. I have a profound sense that I have finally arrived at the place where I am meant to be as I sit on the doorstep drinking my tea.

On the Island, I have uninterrupted time and space to draw and paint, think and dream. My mind happily expands into the space. I push beyond my limitations, exploring colours and shapes and textures. Undoing and re-doing, pushing the boundaries beyond the safe images I usually draw and paint. One image flows into another. Surprising images appear – faces, plants, snakes and people dancing pour out onto the page and I produce drawing after drawing. My energy is intense and focused as I dance on the page, the colours vibrant and glowing.

For the first two weeks I don't visit the prison, instead I go for long walks and explore the Island. I am tired of prisons and oppression and suffering.

The Island is carpeted in spring flowers, arum lilies and daisies. Everywhere I look, rabbits hop and play by the side of the road. I see fallow deer, spring-bok, eland, bontebok and small klipspringers. Tortoises cross my path and I see birds I have never seen before. The beauty of the Island is breath-taking. In the morning I wake up early so I can watch the sunrise and in the evening I watch the clouds catch fire as the red ball of the sun disappears into the sea. I feel safe here.

Pam comes to stay, and at night I sit around the fire in the back yard under the stars with my fellow artists, Zena, Anele, Yabo and Zoulfa, eating vegetables cooked on the fire, talking and singing late into the night.

※ ※ ※

This is an Island of many layered memories. By day the men who were im-prisoned on the Island tell their stories, over and over again to coachloads of tourists, at night they sit and drink away their memories. Their stories are what bring in the money to the Island.

All day long, the tourists come and go, waving from the buses, but when it is stormy there are no boats and the Island shuts down and becomes even quieter than usual. On no-boat days the bar stays open all day and the shop runs out of food. I make salad out of sour grass and sea weed. On nights when the Island is shrouded in mist you cannot see across to the mainland and the foghorn blows low and mournfully all night long.

For many years the Island has been a place of suffering, a hell hole, a prison, a place of banishment, a place where lunatics and lepers were dumped along with unruly slaves and political prisoners. But now the prison has closed down and the Island has become a museum. In 1997 there is a feeling of openness on the Island, of reclaiming the space and history.

※ ※ ※

After I have been on the Island for two weeks, I join the tourists for an official tour. We are taken into the prison cells. It is cold inside, the sunlight does not penetrate the thick prison walls. I think of the black prisoners who were issued with only shorts and sandals to wear during the long, cold winter months. The tour guide, an ex-political prisoner, tells us of the cruelty and the torture of political prisoners, he tells us of family visits that were few and far between. He was a young man when he arrived at Robben Island and was only released thirty years later, after his youth was gone. He tells us of the letters he received from his family and how they were severely censored, sometimes whole pages of family news had been cut out. I think back to all the friends I knew as a child who disappeared on to Robben Island.

We go to see Mandela's cell and I go inside the cell. The rest of the tour continues into the court yard but I stay behind, my heart heavy as I kneel down on the cold stone floor and feel the rough prison issue blanket rolled up in the corner. I think of all the years my dad spent locked up inside a tiny cell. I stay in the cell until my emotions have calmed down and my tears have stopped. I go back outside, into the sunlight.

❋ ❋ ❋

A concert has been planned for the Island. A new public holiday has been declared – Heritage Day – and Mandela will be coming to the Island. The musicians are staying with us, in the artists' houses. Our job is to feed them while they are busy rehearsing for the concert. I am woken up in the night by sounds of drumming coming from next door. Half asleep and half dressed in my nightie I go next door to see what is happening. My feet can't keep still and I dance the whole night long. The next day I sit in the prison hall and listen to the musicians practise. They blow through trumpets made out of sea weed as children run up and down the prison hall, playing and laughing. The doors of the prison have been flung wide open.

The Island needs to be cleansed of its long and painful history. One hundred sangomas come over on the boat to cleanse the Island of the pain and suffering of centuries and to lift the heavy energy that lies trapped here. The sangomas come dressed in traditional clothes – beads and skins. They bring sheep and goats and chickens to slaughter. From Friday night until Sunday afternoon the sangomas dance and drum and sing and pray without sleeping. The cleansing ritual continues for two nights and two days without stopping.

After three months on the Island, my time as an Artist in Residence draws to a close. My time on the Island has been a golden time, a gift. I am sad to leave but I am determined to be back soon.

❋ ❋ ❋

Noah phones me and tells me there are problems in the house at Stapleton Hall Road. Can I come back and sort them out? I fly back to London to see what I can do. As I enter the front door I see that the floor has not been washed since I left. Boxes of books are piled high on every surface and there is hardly room to move. Noah has just woken up. He hugs me. "Mum it's good to see you." He has lost weight and the fridge is empty.

There are problems with the other people in the communal house. Our once friendly household becomes a place of danger, intrigue and mistrust, letter writing and accusations. Our home has deteriorated into a battle-ground. The police are called and eviction notices are served. The housing co-operative want us out. I stand firm, defending our territory and Noah's home but I am feeling mad and insecure. I am ashamed of myself, this war has brought out the worst in me. It is time to let go, to move on, but I hold on for dear life, stubbornly, worried that Noah will be left homeless.

Finally I move out, but Noah hangs on obsessively. The house represents home and family to him, but it is an empty shell that weighs heavily on his shoulders. He rattles around by himself in this huge house, ghosts in every room. Junk clutters up every room, endless amounts of stuff left by people who have moved out.

I go back to Cape Town, back to the Island, this time to do a Post Graduate Course. But after the first semester I have to go back to London again to try and sort out the problems in the house.

❋ ❋ ❋

While I am in London, I go and see the doctor. The muscles in my womb have knotted and grown into lumps. The doctor diagnoses fibroids and suggests a hysterectomy. I am terrified of hospitals – I don't want to be cut open. I will put mind over matter, I think. I am in control of my own body. I imagine healing light flowing into my body. But the lumps grow bigger and I look like I am six months pregnant. My organs are all squashed up and I can't avoid going into hospital.

After the operation, I lie in the hospital bed with tubes attached to me, a catheter comes out of a hole in my stomach and there is a morphine drip in my arm. Tubes come out of my nose and a saline drip is attached to my arm. It hurts if I move. The morphine makes me feel nauseous.

Pam sits on one side of the bed and Noah sits on the other side. They say hello to each other and go outside together to smoke. This is a variation of my fantasy that they would at last talk to each other on my death bed.

The surgeon has cut me down the middle and I look like Frankenstein with my long bloody scar fastened together with metal staples. My divided self has manifested itself into this scar. For months I can hardly walk and Pam looks after me, but as soon as I am well enough we go back to Cape Town.

✵ ✵ ✵

I am determined I will get back to the Island. I apply for any job that is advertised on the Island and also for jobs that aren't advertised. Every week I phone to ask if there is a job for me. Eventually I receive a phone call, they need me at the crèche for the last week of 1999. We are approaching the end of an era, the end of the century, the turning point of a thousand years. The Island is busy with the build-up to huge celebrations for New Year's Eve. It will be televised and broadcast around the world.

The children on the Island stand in the shape of the map of Africa holding candles, the image is broadcast around the world. In the new year I am called in regularly to work at the crèche when they need me.

56
Endings and beginnings

Something is wrong – Dad is not himself. When I say something to him he doesn't respond. Dad has a migraine, his vision is blurred and his speech slurs and when he picks up a glass of wine it slips through his fingers. Dad goes for tests, he has a very large brain tumour. They tell us Dad has two months to live.

At home, Dad needs care, twenty-four hours a day. Mum and I take it in turns to stay up at night. Mum is struggling. Time is precious and Mum wants to do everything for Dad herself. When he falls she struggles to lift him up. Dad becomes weaker and weaker and Mum does not have the strength to do everything for him. Eventually Mum agrees to getting in a carer from an agency. Pam takes Dad to hospital for treatment every day. She is a rock, solid and dependable.

Lynn flies in from London and John comes as often as he can, driving through the night from Mpumalanga with his family to see Dad. Time is running out and we all want to spend as much time as possible with him. In the evenings I make up the fire and Mum and Dad sit together, holding hands. We sit and drink whiskey by the fire. Mum buys only the best single-malt whiskey for Dad. I stop going in to work. We only have weeks and days and hours left. We hold on to each moment, trying to make it special. Dad gets weaker and weaker, he is slipping away.

Noah, and Simon, Lynn's son, help to look after Dad. I make Dad's favourite food, but he is too weak to chew or swallow. We sit around the dining room table and make each meal a banquet, a special occasion. Dad likes to sit in the sun, he tells me that Jesus wants him for a sunbeam. I am not sure if he is joking or being serious – Dad has always been an atheist.

When Dad dies I imagine him as a sunbeam shining down on me.

When Dad dies there is no space for me to grieve. Mum doesn't like tears and sentimentality. The sorrow and seriousness of death runs too deep, on the surface I remain calm and unruffled. Besides, I think, Dad has just popped out to buy the paper. And he'll walk back in through the front door any moment now.

Simon and Nomvula, (John's mother-in-law) come and stay with Mum so she won't be alone and I go back to work on the Island. The children in the crèche ground me with their energy. Their demands are based in the present. They are not interested in my sorrow.

Every morning, I get up at five to catch the 7.30 boat to the Island. After many exhausting months I am given a house to live in on the Island and Pam and I move in with Susan, a teacher at the pre-school, and her children. Wherever I turn I can see the sea. My house on the Island is my million-dollar mansion.

Fallow deer come into the garden to eat the food I put out for them, rabbits and tortoises live in the garden, yellow weaver birds nest in the trees. Life should be perfect. I should be able to paint and draw and breathe in the fresh healing air. But it is not easy for Pam to have been uprooted and I am neither patient nor sympathetic to her moods as she struggles with her emotions.

"I don't want to live with you any more," I tell her. I don't want to be torn apart by the frustrations that are dividing us.

I end the relationship and walk away from the love and closeness we have shared for twelve years. On the eleventh of September Pam flies back to England, the same day that the Twin Towers collapse in New York.

In my house on the Island, I sit on my own in a dark room. In the corner a lone candle flickers. Outside the wind blows fiercely. The pigeons that live in the roof are restless, I hear their footsteps on the ceiling and the branches of the trees tapping on the window making the house sound haunted. I am not afraid – I feel safe in my house.

I am contained by water, held by water and rocked to sleep by the sea. I am soothed by the constant sound of the waves. In the morning when I wake up the first thing I see is the sea, bathed in soft early morning colours.

At work, I am Aunty Ruth. I greet the children as they bounce through the door and my day begins with the sound of children playing and laughing.

After work, I have time and energy to draw and write and listen to music and dance. At the weekends, I travel over to the mainland and stay with Mum. I settle into a comfortable, self-contained space where I am content. I have finally found a safe space, a piece of solid ground where my days are predictable. I have found a space I can dream in and call my home.

The Island has its own sense of time and space, the activities there are influenced almost entirely by the weather and the moods of the sea.

On nights when it is windy, I stand outside, and feel the wind on my body.

One night there is an eclipse of the moon. There is no wind and the night is unusually still. I put my mattress, a pillow and some blankets outside. I lie under the stars and watch as earth's shadow falls on the full moon. I am warm under my blankets. I doze off, slipping in and out of sleep. When I wake up I look up at the moon and the stars and feel a great sense of peace.

At night, I lie in bed and all I hear are the waves and the sea. I fall asleep and when I wake up I catch the tail end of a dream as it vanishes into thin air. I inhabit a whole other world while I am asleep. I sometimes catch just a glimpse of it when I wake up, but most of the time I am totally unaware of this other world. It lies just below the surface, a potent, powerful force that shapes me and pulls on me. In the darkness between sleeping and waking I journey back to myself through my memories, trying to pull the fragments together to make a picture that is coherent and whole. I look back at myself and explore half-remembered events as I try to reach out and touch the parts of myself I have forgotten. Important events in my life appear hazy and distant while small insignificant details suddenly jump into sharp focus. The quietness and stillness in the middle of the night is uninterrupted by any of the usual daily demands.

※ ※ ※

There has been another rape on the Island. I visit the woman who was raped to see if I can help in any way. She lies on her bed in a foetal position, eyes tightly shut. One or two tears trickle down her cheeks – she is silent and in pain. Her son sits, anxious and bored, watching a horror movie on TV. No one is paying him any attention.

The man who has raped her must leave the Island with his family. People stand around and watch with a sinking heart as the alleged rapist, his wife, his child and all their belongings are loaded on the back of a truck and taken to the harbour. In this small community of a hundred and fifty people where everyone knows everyone else, people are talking. They are divided, some people blame the woman who has been raped, saying she should not have laid charges. What will happen to his wife and child if he is sent to prison?

The women on the Island are scared and traumatised after the rape. I double lock my previously unlocked door. The safe space of the Island has been violated.

I suffer from insomnia and wake up frequently in the middle of the night. I lie in bed covered in sweat. Out of the blue, the intensity of my feelings winds me, like a sharp punch to my stomach that leaves me unable to breathe. The pain surprises me. The rawness of old memories feeds my longing for closeness and intimacy. It also strengthens my fear of loss. Childhood memories come flooding back to me – the smell and taste of my anxiety has caught up with me, nearly fifty years later. I remember Mum and Dad disappearing and being left alone. Anxiety constricts my breathing, leaving me emotionally unprotected.

I lie in the dark and I don't know what time it is. I am wide awake, my mind clear and uncensored as I toss and turn and long for sleep. I want to be done with this habit of sleeplessness. I need to shift my mood and replace the energy of the ghosts that swirl and dance and have given meaning to an identity I hold onto. I am my history. I know I always will be. But I am also more. I must shake off the past and shift my life into a different direction.

❈ ❈ ❈

On Heritage Day, 24 September, a jazz concert is held on the Island with an impressive line-up of musicians. My friend and her baby are staying with me. At the concert, we bump into an old friend of hers who introduces us to his friend. The friend of the friend sits behind me. He leans over and says he wouldn't mind kissing me.

"Okay, why not?" I dare him. But we barely know each other, we have only just met. His unexpected kisses are surprisingly sweet and I melt into them. We remain glued together all evening. I see my fellow Islanders watching me and worry that my reputation as a chaste middle-aged aunt is ruined. The stranger sings love songs to me and tells me his name – Ricardo. I tell him he must go home, I chase him away. He is sure to be trouble and I don't want him to complicate my life. But when I get home I wonder how I could have given up on such sweet kisses so easily. I have not been attracted to a man or slept next to a man for more than twelve years. Men have been outside my frame of reference. The part of me that wanted intimacy with a man has been shut down and out of action for years.

❈ ❈ ❈

Rico and I become friends and slowly get to know each other. He visits me on the Island. We make a fire outside and cook food on the fire, we drink red wine and go for long walks and look at the stars. Rico sleeps over and snores next to me. I envy his ability to sleep soundly all night. I lie awake in the shadows with demons chasing me, but in the quiet darkness Rico's warm body reassures me as he reaches over and curls his body into mine.

I dream I am in the sea and Rico is holding me. I am scared we will be swept away and float too far out to sea. I want to get back to the land. I ask

Rico to put his feet on the ground but strong currents sweep us further and further out to sea, away from the shore. It is getting dark and I am afraid that we will be drowned and never reach land again.

✳ ✳ ✳

The Island is changing, the rot has set in. People have hidden agendas. I have a new boss. She sits in my office in front of my computer. She calls me into the office – the room smells of cheap perfume and stale cigarette smoke. Outside the sun shines brightly, but inside the office the heater is on and the windows are shut. She lies, she steals, she cheats. She accuses me of insubordination. She wants to break my spirit.

This is a dirty fight and I cannot win. I am not always good at fighting, my lack of emotional defences leaves me wide open and crumbling. I decide to resign from work and to walk away while I am still intact, but this means I will have to leave the Island. I thought I would always live here, contained and safe. I can't imagine living anywhere else. The mainland seems dangerous and alien to me after living on the Island.

The Cat Killer is here, he has come to shoot all the cats on the Island. They say the cats are eating the sea birds. When all the cats are gone, the rats eat the bird's eggs and their chicks.

A contract has been awarded to a company to clear the Island of all the alien vegetation. Bushes and trees are hacked and chopped down and the Island becomes a dust bowl. There is nothing for the animals to eat, no place for the birds to nest. Without the cats keeping the rabbits under control the rabbits eat everything in sight, in the spring time they eat the small green shoots growing through the dry ground. The starved rabbits even climb up trees to eat the leaves. The buck are not as resilient and are slowly starving to death. Their skeletons litter the fields and the few remaining live buck have ribs sticking out of their pelts.

Rico and I save our feral cats. We take them to the mainland. The cats are used to being wild and hunting in the bushes and we are taking them to Muizenberg, to a suburban house and garden by the sea. We have to – if we don't they will be shot. We pack our belongings and get ready to leave the Island, my home, where I have lived and worked for ten years.

✳ ✳ ✳

Before I leave, I walk around the whole Island saying goodbye to all the places that have become a part of me.

I walk through the empty female lunatic asylum which lies derelict as much of the Island does. In photographs of the former inmates the women wear long skirts and bonnets. Many of the women never left the Island – they were trapped here, cast out and exiled from the mainland.

I sit by myself in the derelict asylum and remember going to the edge and falling in, going to the edge and flying.

Dad is arrested

PRISON LETTERS

Letters to my father 1968–1971

I wrote to my father while he was in prison. The letters were stamped and read by the prison authorities before he was allowed to read them. Each word had to be counted and we were only allowed to talk about personal things – nothing political. Often chunks of the letters were cut out and censored.

Dear Daddy,

I have been thinking about you a lot and am very proud of you. How is your cough? My sore thoat is cured completely, Mommy woudnt let me go out on Saturday or Sunday night because of it. Rynnette sends her love. She is at Cape Town High and is doing French, Latin, Maths, Science, English, Afrikaans. And Social Studies. I am still enjoying school although at times I get fed up with it and at the moment I am looking forward to the holidays when I shall be going to Baines Kloof. Habanim is holding a seminar there. I was there fairly recently at a C.LL. camp. I had a lovely time ~~there~~, we went on hikes etc. etc. (I cant remember the other things we did) It was sort of summer and we had good weather, but it was <u>cold.</u> It will be even colder when I go there in winter. The subjects I most like at school are Maths and English and the eating part of Dom. Sc. I have been getting the highest marks for poetry reading in our class. I got 18/20 the next highest is 16 ½. I have been having quite a few chats with Mr Taylor. I find him very intelegent and like him. He admires you tremendeosly.

It went in for the Eistedford and got one merit. Karlie is having his Barmitsva this month.

I m going out with the most Fabulous boy at the moment. He has blonde, blonde hair and blue eyes and his name is Sidney.

At the moment Im reading sweet Thursday Its terrific.

I put "At the moment" twice which is bad. Last Saturday night I went to go and see Teuya and his daughters. What do you think of short dresses?

Ive shortened one of my dresses quite a lot. While on the escalator I over heard some Ladies passing not very complimentry remarks about it.

Lot of love And lots of more love
I, me, myself.
(Ruth)

✳ ✳ ✳

... I write a letter to my father. It is the first time I have written to him in six months. I write it out over and over. I change words and sentences. I don't want him to know that I am sad, that I want to die, I don't know how to live. I can't say anything that might upset him, he has enough worries and enough to make him sad. But I do want to write to him, so I change my letter over and over again until it feels right and I can send it to him. "Dear Mouldybaldy," I say...

1968

13th January, 1968

Dear Mouldybaldy

Happy 21st birthday. Christmas with Macgregors, food, wine plentiful. Present – quantity plus quality, people much quality. Snow thick on ground, trees, powdery white iceingsuger., tastless and cold (indigestable) Television, saw part of November show, interesting, good. Bolshoi ballet, beautifull and exciting. Extracts from various ballets. Loved the Stone flower.

Just finnished reading "Gone with the Wind." Not know whether to love or hate Rhett (hero) thought he'd like me better then Scarlett.

School – I approve, no uniform, call teachers by first names. Subjects – English, Spanish, Biology, Physics, art, history, geography. Much better then Westerford. Lynn and I have mutual crushes – Mike, John, Don Hawthorn and sexy headmaster. John- crushes on Naidoo girls. John happy at school, likes it in ordinary way, grumbles Lynn doesn't like school.

Lynn taking us (birthday treat) Royal Shakespeare Company twice (Macbeth, Ghosts) Exibitions; Picasso sculpturs, Cubist art and others. Roland says Ive got artistic talent.

Holidays – France, Lynn and I alone in car – ha ha. Incredeble lorry cafes – loud mouthed French and good food.

Spain – hot long white sanded beaches. Village-towncrier, goats, pigs, well for water. Villa –veiw. Pyranees, own vineyard, plenty wine. Moorish charming Othello like host, teaches in Saudi Arabia. Friendly, good Catalonian villagers.

We siested plus fiested in great style. (Three day festival) First – church. Much rehearsed out of tune male choir. Tipsy padre, one cup communion wine per person during service.

Villadge square decorated. Began with national dance – Saldana – then danced with plenty handsome gallant braves. Bow and handshake . Traditional graceful manners, special perfect brave Giambe.

Beautiful drive through mountains to white washed little port and beaches (Cadaques) home of Salvidor Dali, ex home Picasso. Full of female starletts, Lynn and I didn't like them. Ate to hearts content – all sea-foods, oysters, prawns, squibs, delicious paella. As usual.

Trip back – no money, taught Charles to nick grapes. Charles extremely nice, typical Scottish rooineck scared of sun. Good brother-in-law.

Travelled comfortably, 1st class, filled our belly's with bread, margerine, pate and left over liquor from Spain.

Thrilled by your merry Christmas and overall results. ~~G~~ Congratulations – your results. Making arrangements for your money. Happy about Anne, writing congratulations. Send you a bit of snow if you'll send us a bit of ~~so~~ sun

Lynn and Charles, Quaker wedding (no religeon but cederiny) Reception Esme's Chinese food, March 23rd.

Mom making enquiries about Tommy.

Miniskirts cause frozen knees in winter but maxiskirts in. Mom fashionable.

~~Mom~~ England very beautiful country. We go to cottage in lovely, soft, hilly surroundings near Wales. Seen Black Mts, beautifull. Climbed windy hills. Accents misunderstandable. Cockney accents birthright. English sense of humour different but funny.

Been lent Mews Flat (ex-stable) with – it modern, centrally heated. Moving into new house end February

✳ ✳ ✳

1970

In future only Three Photos per months will be allowed, ...

16th. October.

Dear Daddy,

America's a strange place. I lived in afluence there. I liked Tom's family, his sister is an amazingly strong person, never touches alcohol and is the only person who doesn't touch drugs in her whole school. Far more people in america take destructive drugs then in England, the Mafia make a lot of money and don't get touched, they're moving into England now. Advertisments on television were horrific, realy playing with peoples feelings, so many adverts, every 2nd one about bad breath. worse ads then England has. newspapers and television didn't report what wasn't hapning to America, very cut off. People i met were totally fed up with violence. I was very sad to leave Tom, don't know if i'll see him again. Working in a new place, have shorter hours and no domestic work, its in a school, i like it. The nursery class is good, but schools destroy children. On one of the walls there's a picture of fruit and other produce like Kellogs, Craft cheese etc. and a heading saying Thank you God for food Just what the adverts want Thank god for Kellogs. Worked in convent for a month 1 to 6/6.30, 1 day off every 10 days, scrubbed Floors all day, food terrible, nuns terrible. Children weren't fet fed properly, were hit a lot, hygiene wasn't good, 1 ½ yr. old child gets hit for wetting herself. Children cried a lot, threw temper tantrums, very agressive. Were hit for crying no one bothering to find out why they were crying, toys were kept in a cuboard because the nun said the children would brake them. Attitude of one of the girls was that the children were spoilt, i was expected to hit a 13 month old girl for knocking over a cup. The children had nothing. A lot of them were there because their parents couldn't get housing. I found myself hitting the children, a thing I never usually do, my friend found the same thing hapning to her. We got dysentry, nothing was done to prevent it spreading. I miss the children very much, more then other children i've looked after. very intense looking after them two children who's parents where studying for exams. Very nice family. Very easy, enjoyable work, bit boring, couldn't look after just 2 children for long.

The children had everything, what a contrast contrast. I was out of any city for 3 months which I liked, when I came home I got tonsilitis, lay in bed thinking I would leave London imediatly, changed my mind when I went to work. Will be good deciding what to do when finnished training. Autumn in America is beautiful, trees are bright yellow, red, orange, purple. Don't draw abstract pictures any more, was a dead end, got caught up in meaningless things like the importance of circles. Draw a lot of Faces now. Will make a collage out of comics for and Lynn can show you, so you can get an idea about them.
Love Ruth.

※ ※ ※

1971

Dear Daddy,   10 January
Fantastic hearing about you from Lynn, brings you closer. Todays a typical Sunday, very lazy up late. Mommys gone for a walk in the woods. Read Lord of the Rings yet?
Went to comic exhibition last night all dressed up, similar to Superwoman, stars in my hair, on my forehead. Had a toy gun. In the tube and street said to people Zip Zap POW. Great fun. Exibition not fantastic the place gives me the creeps, culture vulture place. Save 10/- film there for free. Three films, Jimmy Hendrix – good, two other music films, music films, music good, films not. Jimi Hendrix dre dead. –dry drugs Janis Joplin dead – drugs.
Back at college now after the holidays, horrible exams etc, are Rubbish. Four people were suspended from college for publishing 'there will be an orgy in the common room at 3' o'clock. This was for the last day of term. The union might call for a strike. Electricity go slows etc. are realy nice, when the lights don't work its like beeing in the country.
Christmas celebrations were fun, Christmas eve met an old friend who i hadn't seen for

ages and went to a pub where there was a man dressed up as a woman singing Christmas carols in a very sexy voice, everyone was joining in. Big lunch with Charles's parents, very genteel, respectable. Watched the queen on television, seriously someone said seriously 'lets turn the queen on' (one way of saying taking drugs) John said 'put L.S.D in her tea.' Completely the wrong place to say such a thing. Afterwards went to Camilla, there there was loud music, boosing, Camilla falling down the stairs, children everywhere, the diference was incredible.

Remember long ago I told you that i had a bust up with a boy friend and was very upset, ive met up with him again recently.

Read some of Herman Hesse's books, impressed me a lot at the time. He speaks about their being an intelectual, spiretual elite, don't agree with him.

Can't realy remember what ive been doing lately, mucking about mostly. Went up with some friends to Hampstead (snotty place) one night. Went to a pub, then to see a film, made fun at some people in a great big car, a man came up to us and said in a very snobby voice 'your behaviour is beneath contempt'. That was hilerious. Hundrends of realy beautiful little episodes kept hapning that night. Ma Talking to some people in front of us in the cinema in a friendly way, then bumped into one of them at Camilla's on Christmas and spent ½ hour. Figering out where we had seen each other before. They had also a Fantastic night that night, people kept giving them things. Often I find people not in the same place, maybe they don't know each other will be having the same things happn to them at the same time, like that night. Someone I know said 'we all live each others lives but we can't let other people live our lives for us. I liked your last poem very much, every now and them I make up a verbal poem. Not all that long before I see you, all my friends ask when are you coming out.

Love Ruth

❋ ❋ ❋

1971

12 March

Wrote mocks yesterday – load of rubbish, if I was in my write mind, I wouldnt have, there are better things to do. You say my approach to college is wrong but how would you like to learn cooking and sewing all afternoon just because you're a girl and your place is supposed to be in the home and cooking teacher tells me too take that grin off my face etc. And our child education teacher (who is kind and sweet) expects you to have her ideas, otherwise no marks in the exams, although she will tell you a different story. I don't think much of a lot of her ideas although she is a very kind and genuine person. She was away ill and we had someone to take her place for 3 weeks who I did learn from, ~~and~~ she got right down to the root of things. Also things which I realy beleived in she supported, which is nice because in ther nurseries and schools I've found often that the attitudes towards the children are often wrong ~~(not totaly)~~ but I've compromised, not always stuck to what I think, felt confused, hypocritical. She had thought things out in a very clear, logical way. She runs a very good nursery. Some good things happen in college, the people there are nice. Last week we visited a Maternity holpital and special care unit, premature babies etc. The babies are gorgeous. It was very interesting, some babies are only born weighing 1 1/2 ilbs and they live.

You've got it ~~all wrong~~ about music, not completely, a lot of it is commercialized, rubbish.

The fault of record companies. Some music brilliant. Now a days ~~its n~~ there isn't idol worshipping, not in the same way as there was.

Wanted to blow my top when I heard all you said about pop musicians.

George Allen and Unwin Ltd. Have published a paperback edition of 'Lord of the Rings' for 30 shilling – R3.00

England has changed to new money, its like toy money, doesn't make sense, good way for people to get diddled. You see something priced 3 pennies, ~~a~~ think that's cheap but realy costs about 7 pennies.

John's at Jenny's, mummy is watching television in the lounge. I'm in my room. Its fairly large, I'm sitting at a long type trestle table by the window, curtains are sort of orange and grey striped. My beds unmade, it's a low bed, my low dressing table's at the foot of my bed, both along one wall. It has a photo of you, Tom (in America) mom, granny & family when mom was 4yrs old. A picture of a woman by me, pattern by child called Debbie, round circle filled with coloured and gold stars, tiny poem in the stars that was accidental) I love stars and made the circle, i love circles. Poem is ~~s~~ by my friend Ed

i love ~~ladies~~
ladies
who
have to
walk
on walls
laugh
at men
and
hold
flowers
to sad

ness
they sometimes
walk
in my
sleep
By the window, either side of ~~my~~ me picture by John of 2 faces in one and other side abstract
by me, sort of sun rays and star. Wall behind me has big poem- red and black on silver, a
butterfly kite. Stacked under table lots of pictures
    Cuboards built in. Books on mantleshelf above which is another picture of face by John
and a painting by Robert.

Lots of love
Ruth.

✳ ✳ ✳

1971

Dear Daddy,

I had lunch with Charles' mother today, then went to Ethnographical Exhibition with her. It
was fantastic, masks, beadwork, turquoise things from South America. Lovly easter, sunny.
Sunday went to festival of life, music, poetry, lots of people, children happy atmosphere. I'm
on holiday. Being doing lots of collages, cutting out eyes, lips and sticking them on the wrong
faces. Lyn and Charles are in France stayed with them the other night, stayed up all night
doing a collage, I got so involved in it, found a lot of the pictures in the wastepaper basket. ~~Wal~~
    Walked part way back home through Parliment Hill, Hampstead Heath, Highgate woods,
beautiful places. Might be going to Liverpool next weekend, a schools being opened there, ~~in a~~
children round about ~~having~~ being playing traunt from their skools to go to this school. They'll
be taking children and teachers who've been kicked out of other schools. Its realy unfair my
friend whose gone to art school for 2 years and will be going for another 3 yrs, won't be able to
teach art in schools because she doesn't have o'levels which have nothing to do with art. Would
it be possible when i write to you to stick small pictures on the letter? I'm sitting here drawing
pictures between sentances, I'de like to draw them on this paper. What a drag, i have to go to the
Laundrette to night and wash up. What films you being ~~sin~~ seeing lately. I've been going to late
night double feature horror movies with a friend of mine, but she's gone to Turkey on holiday.
Everyone laughs through the scary films so its not easy to get scared. Saw Performance with Mick
Jagger (Rolling Stones) I was totaly confused. Saw the middle of anther film befrore that, which

213

i thought was performance, so i kept trying to connect the 2 films up ~~with~~ and they were totaly different.

We had a passach supper, prayers and everything. Reading Tom Woolfes 'electric koolaid acid test' very funny, about some of the first people who took L.S.D and they travalled around in a brightly covered bus and called themselves the merry pranksters. When different people and policemen wanted to make trouble with them they would leap out of the bus and start filming them, the people realising they were being filmed started behaving very differently.

I hate the Tate. They never let me in ~~two~~ time in a row they said i couldn't come in because i didn't have enough money. Went to Russian Art Exhibition, wasn't very good, didn't show very much. I like Russian artists like Kandinsky and Chagal. At one time there was an art school train traveling all over , brightly painted, stopping at the villeges so the villagers could share the art. Some friends of mine are going climbing up Welsh mountains with their baby in a pram, they go practising up Hampstead Heath. Don't know what what i'll do in the summer, might stay in London, havn't realy done that yet, and go somehwere when its horrible and cold.

Love Ruth

✳ ✳ ✳

1971

Grass Valley Cottage,
Grass Valley, Treswithian Downs,
Cambourne.

Dear Daddy,

Sitting writing in sunny Cornwall, lovely fields all around me. This morning I walked along the beach barefoot feeling nice and warm. I've just managed to find a place to stay in Foulmouth. Double room, nice and big. Not ideal, price is £4. 10 p.w. which is avarage London price for grotty room. Idealy like isolated cottage, but I'm very happy, incedibly happy to find the place. We've been staying in a freezing cold caravan with no heating. Insecure not having a place to stay. When we first ~~stayed~~ got here, stayed at a place that advertises as crash pad. Atmosphere was terrible. There was a guy called Golly there who is about the nastiest person i've met, staying there, he was very unfriendly, saying things like "have you found a place to stay" "no" Its pouring with rain outside so he says "where you going tonight then" He's at only been staying there a week and he's trying to take place over. We moved to grass valley were the people are friendly. Couple who stay down here (its their caravan) have known Golly for years also hate him, told us nasty tales about how he'll rob you and how all over Corwall there people who won't let him in their houses.

Eds gone to London for a few days to get somethings, its terrible being without him, I nearly went up to London this morning, he nearly came down here this morning, it wouldn't have been funny if we had missed each other. We both worked in the same pta factory for awhile, he cleaning the floors, me wrapping bread puddings. Work was alright, people friendly, didn't work their long enough to get sick of it. You could eat yourself silly in there. Lovely warm children/ mushroom pies, cakes etc.

A herd of cows was just about to come in the field were i am but Dilly the dog chased them away, i'm glag glad cause i'm never sure when cows are bulls. Dogs round here are realy nutty and friendly.

Applied for job as auxiliary helper for handicapped children, part time job with as much pay as i'd get doing full time work.

You and mommy must come and live in Cornwall. So far I haven't been in a place down here as isolated as the ptas were i was in wales, like to go back there in the summer, hope youre good at walking, there's some nice places in England. Had my wisdom teeth out. It was terrible, aneasthetic was horrible, mouth ached for weeks.

Ed writers realy incredible poems, can't remember any only bits and pieces

in a world so big with a heart so small how can anyone love any one at all

Well i used to be a woman you know driving everybody wild till my friends stole all my make up and discoved i was a child.

lots of love
Ruth.

·

Acknowledgements

This book would never have seen the light of day without the wonderful support and encouragement I have received from the many people who were part of my journey.

Special thanks to:

Anne Schuster who gave me the tools to re-cover my memories and shape them into a story and who, together with my fellow writers, shared writing, inspired me, and gave me valuable feedback and belief in the creative process of free writing,

Rosamund Haden who got excited when she first saw an early draft of my book and helped me deal with unruly chapters,

Maire Fisher who did an extraordinary job of editing my book, with great insight and sensitivity,

Rebekah Ball who listened to my secrets with love and understanding,

My family, who I love dearly, and who keep me connected and grounded,

My Mum, who is the most courageous woman I know, and my Dad, who took on the inhumane system of apartheid and helped change history,

Rico who has never abandoned me, and our dogs Django and Sheba, Mama cat and Paws and Mr. Fish, who teach me how to live in the present,

Robben Island – the landscape and the community, where I found home and a safe space to write,

Cover2Cover who had enough faith in my book to make it possible for me to share my story. Rosamund Haden and Dorothy Dyer who were wonderful to work with and made a potentially nerve-wracking process easy,

All the many people, both in and out of my book, whom I have known and loved and who have helped shape my life.

I would also like to thank all my readers. Please read my book with an open heart. I do not lay claim to writing the only truth, but have crafted my memories into a story. I have tried to be as true as possible to what I remember without offending too many people, including my older and slightly wiser self.